THE AHMANSON FOUNDATION

has endowed this imprint

to honor the memory of

FRANKLIN D. MURPHY

who for half a century

served arts and letters,

beauty and learning, in

equal measure by shaping

with a brilliant devotion

those institutions upon

which they rely.

The publisher gratefully acknowledges the generous contribution

toward the publication of this book provided by

The Graham Foundation for Advanced Studies in the Fine Arts

and by

The Art Book Endowment Fund of the Associates of the University of California Press,

which is supported by a major gift from the Ahmanson Foundation.

FRANK LLOYD WRIGHT

FRANK LLOYD WRIGHT

EUROPE AND BEYOND

Edited by Anthony Alofsin

UNIVERSITY OF CALIFORNIA PRESS   BERKELEY   LOS ANGELES   LONDON

University of California Press
Berkeley and Los Angeles, California

University of California Press, Ltd.
London, England

© 1999 by The Regents of the University of California

Chapter 1 © 1999 by Anthony Alofsin

Library of Congress Cataloging-in-Publication Data

Frank Lloyd Wright : Europe and beyond / edited by
    Anthony Alofsin.
        p.   cm.
    "Ahmanson Murphy fine arts imprint."
    Includes bibliographical references and index.
    ISBN 0-520-21116-2 (alk. paper)
    1. Wright, Frank Lloyd, 1867–1959—Influence.   2.
Architecture, Modern—20th century.   I. Alofsin, Anthony.
NA737.W7F6785   1999
720'.92—dc21   99-10128
                                    CIP

Printed in Singapore
9   8   7   6   5   4   3   2   1

The paper used in this publication meets the minimum requirements of American National Standards for Information
Sciences—Permanence of Paper for Printed Library Materials, ANSI Z39.48-1984.

To Bruno Zevi, lifelong protagonist for an architecture of democracy

CONTENTS

The preparation of this book was made possible in part by a grant from the Graham Foundation for the Visual Arts.

My thanks to the Museum of Modern Art, New York, and the Society of Architectural Historians for sponsoring the symposium in April 1994 that led to this publication, and to the participants in the symposium. Numerous individuals were helpful in diverse ways during the preparation of the book. I would like to thank Dr. Christiane Crasemann Collins, Dr. Herman van Bergeijk, and Bart Lootsma. At the University of California Press, Deborah Kirshman, fine arts editor and director of development, Rose Vekony, senior editor, and Steve Renick, art director, helped realize this book. Bruce Brooks Pfeiffer, Margo Stipe, Oscar Muñoz, and Indira Berndtson of the Frank Lloyd Wright Archives, Elizabeth Dawsari of the Taliesin Associated Architects Archive, and other members of the Frank Lloyd Wright Foundation were particularly generous in their assistance. Angela Giral, Avery Librarian of Columbia University, and Micheline Nielsen of the University of Pennsylvania Fine Arts Library provided much-appreciated help. Thanks are also due to David Dibble, Anne Dibble, C. Jos Biviano, Mary Beth Mader, and Marcia Maria Workman.

Kathryn E. Holliday, Research Intern in the Graduate School, University of Texas at Austin, deserves special appreciation: this was the first book she helped publish, which meant learning not only the challenges of editing, but also what is involved in bringing ideas into reality. A fellowship from the Graduate School of the University of Texas at Austin provided the financial support that allowed her to contribute so significantly to this project.

Finally, the authors of these essays deserve the most thanks for their protracted efforts and literary labors.

ONE: WRIGHT, INFLUENCE, AND THE WORLD AT LARGE

Anthony Alofsin

Frank Lloyd Wright and his work are icons of modern American architecture. Few Americans have not heard of the Guggenheim Museum or Fallingwater. Wright's portrait has appeared on a U.S. postage stamp; his personal life reads like a novel and has been made into an opera. But despite his fame and his status as America's most celebrated architect, we are only beginning to understand how his ideas were dispersed and the impact his architecture made throughout an active practice that spanned from 1896 to 1959.

Although the culturally adept may know of the revolution in domestic architecture associated with Wright's early work around Chicago and Oak Park in his Prairie period, they often overlook the use of Wright's design ideas in the housing boom and the expansion of the American suburb after World War II, to cite just one example of our incomplete grasp of his impact. During the most productive period of his architectural practice, beginning in the mid-1940s, Wright's organic architecture infiltrated the ranch style house; his idiom informed the split-level houses of the 1950s and 1960s; and his ideas intertwined with those of other American architects who tried to define modern life through architecture.

The popular press contributed to the powerful impact of Wright's architecture in the 1950s. Articles on Wright in *Time* and *Life* magazines and in the mass-market home design magazines, such as *House Beautiful* and *House and Garden,* disseminated Wright's ideas to the very heart of the American public, far beyond the limits of the architectural press that had often featured his work.[1] As a child in the 1950s I saw my parents studying Wright's latest work in *House Beautiful,* and I remember their search in our hometown of Memphis for the architects most sympathetic to Wright's ideas. His work seemed to me as natural and appropriate as the Eames furniture in our house seemed normal; the pioneering roles of these masters of modern design escaped me until my college years. After Wright's death in 1959 his reputation took one of its cyclical dips, but by the mid 1980s, as postmodernism in architecture waned, Wright became a subject of interest again, as evident not only in the scholarly reconsideration of his life and work but also in the virtual industry of picture books and artifacts ranging from key rings to calendars. His furniture, art glass windows, and some four hundred buildings that remain have steadily increased in commercial value despite market fluctuations.[2] This revival returns us to the problematic question of Wright's impact on American culture. Does the legacy of his work represent a new source of merchandising or a call back to the basic issues of architecture and democracy? If he was such a towering genius, why did he not make an even greater mark on American architecture?

The penetration of Wright's ideas into American architecture constitutes what we casually consider to be his influence. Influence, however, normally entails three basic processes: imitation, transformation, and parallelism. Imitation implies some attempt to copy, usually relying on the external appearances of objects. Transformation suggests an effort to move beyond making copies to altering either appearance or the meanings underlying forms. Parallelism occurs when objects that appear similar have independent origins. Although the processes of influence can be conscious, most often they are unconscious and open to misinterpretation.

These three modes of influence played out through Wright's work not only in his homeland but also around the globe. In some ways his work is so well known in the United States that familiarity blinds us to a deeper insight into his impact on American life; the effects are so broad that they have simply been ignored. Wright's role in American architecture is so large that decades of study may be required to fully grasp its complexity. Moreover, the impact of his apprentices and students who went on to set up their own practices remains incompletely explored.

This collection of essays looks not at the United States—the context usually associated with Wright—but around the globe, from Japan to Great Britain and from France to Chile, as well as to Mexico, Russia, and the Middle East. Interwoven in these essays are stories of champions and critics, of books and exhibitions, and of the transmission and transformation of ideas through which Wright's work came to the world.

Historians and critics have traditionally pointed to Wright's impact in Germany around 1910 as a key factor in the evolution of the Modern Movement. The canonical view used to be that Wright's famous publications of 1910–1911, printed in Berlin by the Wasmuth Verlag, had an immediate and dramatic influence on German architects and the rest of the European avant-garde. Every standard architectural history credits these publications—the *Ausgeführte Bauten und Entwürfe von Frank Lloyd Wright,* a two-folio monograph of Wright's buildings and designs; and the similarly titled *Frank Lloyd Wright: Ausgeführte Bauten,* a small picture book

Figure 1.1
Cover of *Frank Lloyd Wright: Ausgeführte Bauten*
(Berlin: Ernst Wasmuth, 1911), published for American
distribution.

Figure 1.2
Cover of *Frank Lloyd Wright, Chicago: 8. Sonderheft
der Architektur des XX. Jahrhunderts* [8th special
edition of architecture of the twentieth century]
(Berlin: Ernst Wasmuth, 1911), published exclusively
for European distribution.

of executed work—with this seminal role, particularly vis-à-vis Walter Gropius
and Ludwig Mies van der Rohe.[3] Kuno Francke, a professor at Harvard, is said to
have been the impetus for these publications, and their impact was supposedly
reinforced by an exhibition of Wright's work held in Berlin.

These standard views nicely demonstrate the complexities of influence. Our
notion of Wright's influence in Germany came about by one historian repeating
the accounts of another without bothering to check if they had any factual basis. Indeed, archival and documentary research has shown them to be a series of
myths.[4] The widespread impact of the Wasmuth publications, particularly the folios, is dubious in light of their limited distribution in Europe; they were a vanity printing, paid for by Wright, with only 100 copies of the folios and 3,900
copies of an inferior edition of the picture book (or *Sonderheft,* as Wright called
it then) reserved for a European audience, while Wright retained another 900
and 5,100 copies respectively for his American audience (Figs. 1.1 and 1.2). More-

Figure 1.3
Studio of Frank Lloyd Wright,
Oak Park, Illinois, 1898. From
Volné Směry 4 (1900): 178.

over, Kuno Francke was not the key player in the Wasmuth affair; Wright's connection appears to have been Bruno Möhring, the eminent architect, city planner, and Wasmuth editor who had visited Wright's office in 1904 but missed Wright. Nor is there any evidence of an exhibition open to the general public; Möhring simply lectured on Wright's work and showed a small selection of drawings one evening in February 1910 to an architectural club in Berlin. Decades later Mies and Gropius would recall an "exhibition," but this lecture is the only documented showing of Wright's work in Germany at that time.

The realities of the Wasmuth affair do not contradict the view that Wright's work began to be disseminated in Europe after 1910. Otto Wagner showed a copy of the folio monograph to his students in Vienna in 1911 and proclaimed Wright a paragon worthy of study. Although Le Corbusier would deny that he knew of Wright at the time, he had obtained a copy of the *Sonderheft* for his mentor Auguste Perret during World War I. Others who saw the publications, including the young Austrians Rudolph Schindler and Richard Neutra, would work for Wright in the late 1910s and 1920s. To understand the influence of the publications on these and other figures, however, we need to look more closely at how the images were transmitted, assimilated, and finally interpreted (or misinterpreted) in terms of both intellectual response and built works. Rather than looking closely, many historians have tended to rely on simple visual analogies that reduce the phenomenon of making architecture to a crude transitivity: if A looks like B, then B has influenced A.

Figure 1.4
Detail of stork relief and floor plan,
studio of Frank Lloyd Wright, Oak Park,
Illinois, 1898. From *Volné Směry* 4
(1900): 177.

Europeans learned about Wright by other means as well, and these also set the stage for his influence. One unexpected source is the avant-garde Czech journal *Volné Směry,* published in Prague, whose editors included Jan Kotěra, a former student of Wagner's and a young leader of the Czech modern movement. In 1900, the journal featured an article on architecture in America by a member of the avant-garde Mánes Group who had traveled in the United States; he reported that Louis Sullivan was the emerging modernist, and although he did not mention Wright, the article included two images of his studio in Oak Park (Figs. 1.3 and 1.4).[5] Reproduced from the *Architectural Review* (Boston), these may be the first images of Wright's work to appear anywhere in Europe. In 1904 the noted Viennese critic Max Dvořák referred to *Volné Směry's* illustrations of Wright's work, also pointing out that American architecture had been exhibited at the Prague Modern Gallery.[6]

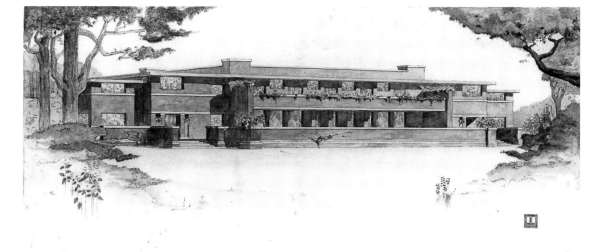

Far more significant than this early reference was the dissemination of Wright's ideas through Dutch architects in the 1910s. Hendrik Petrus Berlage was Wright's first and most important early champion. A major pioneer of the Dutch modern movement, Berlage visited America in 1911 and saw several of Wright's buildings but missed meeting the architect. Returning to Europe, he gave three lectures in Zurich on American architecture in which Wright's Larkin Company Administration Building and the Darwin Martin House, both in Buffalo, figured prominently. The lectures, which immediately appeared in Dutch and in German-language Swiss publications, stimulated the interest of young Europeans, establishing a critically important "Dutch Connection" between Wright and Holland and sensitizing Swiss architects and engineers to Wright's ideas.[7] Several young Dutch architects even studied Berlage's copy of Wright's Wasmuth folios; chief among them was Jan Wils, who learned presentation techniques by copying the folio's rendered trees and perspectives (Fig. 1.5).[8]

While the Dutch initiated the critical discourse about Wright in the 1910s, his work and ideas were ignored in Germany until the 1920s, when they would play an important role in German debates about modernism. In the years leading up to these debates a series of young European architects sought Wright out, and

Figure 1.5 *(opposite)*
Design for a pavilion in the municipal
park, Groningen, 1917. Jan Wils,
architect. (NAI 012212)

Figure 1.6
Kameki Tsuchiura *(left)*, Richard Neutra
(center), and Wright at Taliesin, 1924.
From Heinrich de Fries, *Frank Lloyd
Wright: Aus dem Lebenswerke eines
Architekten* (Berlin: Ernst Pollak, 1926).

several came to work with him at Taliesin, in Wisconsin. The European invasion of Wright's office began with the arrival of the Czech Antonin Raymond, who went to work for Wright in 1916. He had studied at the Technical College of Prague, where Kotěra held a position similar to that of Otto Wagner in Vienna, training a generation of modern architects. Although Kotěra had seen buildings by Wright in 1904, when he came to America for the St. Louis World's Fair, Raymond appears to have learned of Wright's work only after arriving in the United States. In 1919 he went with Wright to work on the Imperial Hotel in Tokyo and then remained in Japan to establish his own office in 1920.[9]

The Austrian Rudolph Schindler worked for Wright from 1918 through 1921.[10] In December 1919, while in Japan, Wright sent Schindler to California to oversee his practice there and to work on the Barnsdall House. After Schindler's departure from Wright's domestic office, his Austrian friend Richard Neutra arrived. Neutra had met Schindler in 1912 and knew of Wright's work through the Wasmuth folios, which he saw in Vienna (Fig. 1.6). In 1923 Werner M. Moser, a member of a famous family of Swiss architects, came to work for Wright at Taliesin; upon his return to Switzerland five years later he became a founding member of the Congrès Internationaux d'Architecture Moderne (CIAM).

At times Wright's Wisconsin atelier took on the air of an extended family of international architects and their spouses: in July 1924 Wright entertained Richard and Dione Neutra, Werner and Sylva Moser, and Kameki Tsuchiura and his wife, Nobu, from Japan.[11] This soirée preceded the Neutras' move to Taliesin that October and the subsequent arrival of Erich Mendelsohn, for whom Neutra had worked in 1921–22.[12]

Despite the prior arrival of all these young Europeans, Wright welcomed Mendelsohn as "the first European to come and seek him out and truly find him." Indeed, Mendelsohn, who had learned of Wright from Neutra, was the first famous German architect to meet the master.[13] Mendelsohn had recently completed his Einstein Tower in Potsdam (1917–21), and his office was one of the most successful in Berlin.

Mendelsohn became Wright's most distinguished architectural connection to Europe in the mid-1920s. Their meeting reawakened interest about Wright in Germany and made Wright more aware of European developments. Mendelsohn published an early appraisal of Wright in which he described the intimate angularity and abstraction of Wright's work as a synthesis of expressionist tendencies.[14] Subsequent articles stimulated a new round of publications and drew additional visitors.[15] In another reawakening of German interest in Wright, Wasmuth reissued a reduced edition of Wright's folio monograph in 1924, apparently without his permission. The original Wasmuth folios of 1910–11 were out of date and out of print. Meanwhile, two books in preparation, one by the Dutch architect and editor Hendricus Theodorus Wijdeveld and the other by the German architect and writer Heinrich de Fries, promised a more current treatment.

Wright played the authors against each other as a means of disseminating his work, and he used their interest in his architecture to get his designs published in Europe, often long before they appeared in the United States. (Indeed, several were never published there in his lifetime.) As a result, European modernists saw a new version of Wright's modernism, while Americans relied on memories from the Prairie period, if anything. Wijdeveld's major Dutch publication came out in 1925 as *The Life-Work of the American Architect Frank Lloyd Wright*. It consisted of most of the articles that had appeared in seven consecutive special issues of the journal *Wendingen,* which Wijdeveld edited. The book, which became known by the journal's title, marked a high point of interest in Wright; he later said it was his favorite publication of his work (Fig. 1.7).[16]

Wright admired *Wendingen* despite the mildly critical contribution to the volume by J. J. P. Oud, a leading exponent of the New Objectivity—the hyperrational wing of the Modern Movement—who saw Wright's influence in Europe as "a less happy one." For all its "exotic peculiarities," Oud wrote, the simplicity of motifs, expression of structure, and integration with its site made Wright's work immediately convincing—to the extent that it had become too influential on the modern developments in Europe. Architects seduced by Wright's work were emulating form—in this case Wright's—over function. Wright's influence was consequently weakening the role of Cubism, which had developed parallel with his work but in complete independence of him.[17] Oud had defined the central problem of Wright's influence on Europe: images of his architecture commingled with distinct European developments, blurring the differences between them. Wright ignored this assessment, as did historians who subsequently replicated the myth of Wright's influence in Europe without alluding to its problematic nature.

Oud also identified another problem: Wright had never absolutely rejected the past, as the most ardent European modernists did. Speaking of both Wright and the Italian futurist Sant'Elia he noted, "In architecture the old form element was never annihilated, and the emerging products of modern design were always a change of image and an abstraction rather than the creation of shapes."[18] Oud was entirely correct in perceiving Wright's obsession with abstraction, which Wright termed "conventionalization," with the "old form element" emanating from nature and the primary forms of architecture, particularly those still to be found in the non-Western cultures of Japan and the Maya. He saw no need to invent new shapes when nature and "pure" cultures uncontaminated by European values contained the raw material for an infinite variety of expressions.

By the mid-1920s the Dutch painter Theo van Doesburg, a protagonist of neoplasticism, identified Wright exclusively with modern developments in the United States. His opinions summarized those of many critics. On the one hand he consistently appreciated Wright's innovations from the turn of the century, noting that among leading European architects Wright provided a "constructive conscience," that he helped create a new architecture based on contemporary materials, and that he was one of the first to use reinforced concrete appropriately.[19] On the other hand, his influence on German architects resulted in an "imitation of the outer effect" that was fatal to innovation. Furthermore, summing up Wright's recent work, van Doesburg saw Wright as completely ignorant of new developments in the plastic arts in central Europe and as having returned to "rustic, decorative building."[20] He observed that by 1927 Wright's influence, so unmistakable ten years earlier, had not been seen for a long time; its complete absence at the Werkbund housing exhibition in Stuttgart was strong proof of its eclipse.[21] But in fact Wright may have wanted to show the Germans his approach to low-cost housing on their own soil. That same year he designed five flat concrete roofs, presumably for houses to be built in Frankfurt am Main; we know little else about the project.[22] Nevertheless, by 1929, when familiarity with Wright's work of the 1910s and 1920s had grown in Europe, van Doesburg caustically stated that Wright "has fallen into the most barbaric decorativism (Midway Restaurant, Chicago; Maison Millard, Pasadena, California etc. etc.) and archaism, with no significance whatsoever for the elementaristic architecture of our time."[23]

Van Doesburg had pinioned Wright's weakness from the European perspective, condemning the persistent use of ornament. Ironically, the "archaism" that

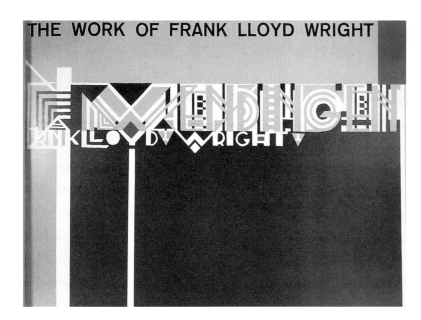

had fostered Wright's "barbaric decorativism" was stimulated by Wright's travels to Europe in 1909–10, when he encountered the primitivist forms of the late Secession in Vienna.[24] This contact confirmed his interest in archetypal forms and launched new explorations in his ornament. While Wright continued to integrate ornament into his experiments in construction, the major currents of the Modern Movement in Europe saw ornament as absolute decadence; the castigations heaped on Wright had long been leveled at the Viennese, as if ornament and construction were antithetical.

In Germany, meanwhile, Heinrich de Fries's *Frank Lloyd Wright: Aus dem Lebenswerke eines Architekten* (From the life work of an architect; Fig. 1.8) came out in 1926, the first new German book on Wright in sixteen years. In it de Fries attempted to show that Wright's opening of interior spaces made him modern. He also assessed Wright's recent work, seeing in a speculative development for Lake Tahoe a "unity of landscape and water, of solid and moveable building, of air, earth, sun, plants, people and flowers" brought to poetic heights. He defended this design and the grandiose project for Doheny Ranch, in Los Angeles, against accusations that they were fantasies, asserting that visionary schemes were a proper domain of all artists.[25]

At the same time de Fries pointed out what many critics considered a limitation of Wright's work: his designs were essentially for an elite class, to which Wright himself apparently belonged. This observation reflects the intense social consciousness that was part of the European debate on modernism. Ultimately, however, de Fries judged Wright to be not only a socially conscious architect, who, like the European modernists, was concerned with problems of minimum human requirements, but also an architect of nature, whose preoccupation with space, plants, and water led to a higher spiritual goal. One of the reviews of de Fries's *Aus dem Lebenswerke* highlighted some of these issues. Another review appeared in the *Frankfurter Zeitung* in December 1926, proof that the debate about Wright had expanded from the architectural press to the daily newspapers. Wright kept a copy of that review in one of his scrapbooks; whether he was aware of its content is not known. Written by Grete Dexel, the wife of the art critic Walter Dexel, it reflected the social consciousness of European modernists. Dexel declared that Wright's open letter in *Wendingen,* "To My European Co-Workers," said little, that de Fries was overenthusiastic, that the Tahoe and Doheny projects catered to the wealthy elite, and that Wright was aligned with class interests that made his work strongly antisocial. "We all know that Frank Lloyd Wright has decisively influenced the European building of today. Some of his country houses (villas) and ground plans are found in every book on new architecture and shown to us in slides in every pertinent lecture. Nevertheless, Wright's work is also not by a long shot understood yet by the better informed."[26]

It is not surprising that Europeans questioned Wright's commitment to a social program during the 1920s. When they saw illustrations of his project for the hotel and resort San Marcos-in-the-Desert, they assumed Wright was designing exclusively for a leisure class. Their critiques demonstrate how European modernists understood and misunderstood Wright's architecture. Misunderstood were Wright's continuing efforts—even in projects for the wealthy elite, like the Barnsdall House and Doheny Ranch—to find solutions to economical middle-class housing. De Fries published examples of the Textile Block houses, including the Barnsdall House, but overlooked the system's potential uses in mass housing. He also failed to grasp the extent to which Wright, an artist arguing for democratic principles in society, was a misfit in the middle-class mainstream of America. Finally, it was difficult for Europeans to realize that the provision of delight in architecture was in fact part of Wright's social program. On the other hand, they could well understand Wright's vision of social transformation as not merely the expressed coordination of technology (the machine and the materials of construction) and society but as a spiritual transformation. Wright's ideas about the future recalled the manifestoes of the avant-garde and the Bauhaus before 1922 in particular; he called for a renovation of the soul, not merely of the building trades.

Another view of Wright came from Adolf Behne, a German art historian and commentator on the early Modern Movement. In a study written in 1923 and published in 1926 as *Der moderne Zweckbau,* Behne drew on Wright's essays and designs that appeared in the *Architectural Record* of 1908 and on contemporary perceptions of Wright. He noted that Wright had made two particularly important contributions: a free plan of balanced spaces emanating from functional considerations of comfort, quiet, and clarity; and an emphasis on horizontality, which made houses appear a part of the streets on which they were situated. Beyond Berlage, Otto Wagner, and also Alfred Messel (whom Behne cited with reservation), Wright provided the first real breakthrough toward a *sachlich,* or objective, plan. Behne

also noted the architects whom he perceived as influenced by Wright: in Germany, Peter Behrens, Gropius, Mendelsohn, and Mies van der Rohe; in Holland, Oud, Wils, Robert van 't Hoff, and W. Greve; and in Switzerland, Le Corbusier. The influences affected the designs of elevations more than the floor plans, Behne remarked, because Wright's floor plans had only recently become understood.[27]

At the same time, like most commentators, Behne saw in Wright what he wanted to see: flat roofs and no ornament. But Wright mixed the use of flat roofs and pitched roofs, and ornament remained essential to all his designs. Behne also read into Wright's plans, with their asymmetrical organization, a fluidity of lifestyle not borne out by the actual fixity of Wright's interiors, particularly in regard to his built-in furniture.[28] Perhaps most telling was Behne's inclusion of the skyscraper design for the *San Francisco Call*, redrawn from Wright's original. A trilingual French, German, and English caption gives the project a date of 1920 and identifies it in French as a project for a house in the form of a tower but in German as a design for a skyscraper. In fact the project for the newspaper's building dates from 1913 and was one of Wright's most Secessionist designs, belonging to the early experimental phase of his work following his return from Europe.[29] Since the Secessionist idiom would have been anathema to Behne, he re-visioned the project as more objective and of a later date.

Figure 1.10

Exhibition installation, "Frank Lloyd Wright, Architect," State Historical Library, Madison, Wisconsin, October 1930. Model for Richard Lloyd Jones House *(center)*, relief detail for the Imperial Hotel *(upper left)*, perspective drawings for the Doheny Ranch project *(left)*, and perspective for the A. D. German Warehouse *(right)*. (FLWA 3000.0002)

The critical debates about Wright in Germany and Holland moved into a broad European forum in 1931 with the first major retrospective of his work. Whereas the purported exhibition of Wright's work in Germany in 1910 was actually a rather small event lasting only an evening, the 1931 show provided an important reference point for his German audience and for architects and critics in other countries, although it had originated in the United States. The exhibition opened in 1930 at the Wisconsin State Historical Library in Madison, only a few miles from Wright's home at Taliesin (Figs. 1.9 and 1.10). There it demonstrated Wright's accomplishments to his fellow citizens, many of whom had disapproved of the unorthodox architect. The exhibition then went to New York, Milwaukee, and Eugene, Oregon, before traveling to Europe, where it appeared in several countries and under variations of the title "Frank Lloyd Wright, Architect," from May to October 1931.

The first European venue of Wright's 1931 international exhibition was the Stedelijk Museum in Amsterdam. Wijdeveld, the publisher of Wright's works in the journal *Wendingen* and collator of his *Life-Work* monograph, organized the exhibition, arranging all the details, from designing a striking poster to installing his daughter, Ruscha, as the ticket taker (Fig. 1.11). This devotion arose from the immense bond Wijdeveld felt with Wright, whom he saw as a kindred spirit ca-

pable of bringing a new social consciousness to the world through architecture. Wijdeveld documented the critical reactions to the exhibition, in Holland and subsequent European venues, by making a beautiful scrapbook for Wright.[30]

After Amsterdam the exhibition headed for the Prussian Academy of Fine Arts in Berlin (Fig. 1.12). In contrast to Wright's first visit to Berlin in the fall of 1909, when he arrived virtually unknown in Germany, the exhibition marked a triumphant return, with Wright's architecture receiving both public recognition and critical notice. In January 1932 the Prussian Academy of Arts honored Wright in absentia by naming him an Outstanding Member.[31] The critical reactions placed Wright more squarely in the discourse about modernism in Germany than at any other time in his career. The big debates centered on whether Wright was too much of a romantic and an individualist to allow him a central role in a modernism that privileged rationality and collective action. Ornament, long identified by the avant-garde as decadent, was still considered a sign of reactionary architecture. Yet it was the soul of Wright's architecture, embodying his design concepts at every level of detail, from a floor tile to the plans, sections, and elevations of his buildings. Struggling with where to fit Wright into the Modern Movement, some writers saw his work as expressionist. One journalist called him "the American Poelzig," comparing him to the leading expressionist architect in Ger-

many, Hans Poelzig.[32] While attacked by modernist critics, Wright was also defended by his proponents, including Erich Mendelsohn.

The exhibition moved on to Frankfurt, Stuttgart, Antwerp, and Brussels before returning to the United States. From this point forward Wright's work occupied an international stage, but his problematic role vis-à-vis European modernists was only underscored by the reluctant inclusion of his work in "Modern Architecture: International Exhibition," the Museum of Modern Art's famous introduction to America of the International Style.[33] Nevertheless, architects from around the world continued to seek out Wright. The German Ernst Neufert made the journey to Taliesin in 1936, followed by Mies van der Rohe in 1937; Wright felt a special empathy for the latter's work until late in their relationship.[34] Walter Gropius was less fortunate; though he admired Wright's early work, Wright received him rudely after he moved to America.[35]

Postwar Germany saw Wright's work suspended between two positions, one increasingly propping up rationalistic ideals, the other embracing an organic aesthetic. Both positions were part of a complex situation and often in conflict with each other. Apart from the pioneering work of Heidi Kief-Niederwöhrmeier, who considers Wright's influence in Germany up to the early 1980s within the context of architectural pluralism, postwar study of Wright's work has been limited.[36] As Nina Nedeljkov, one of the few Wright scholars in Germany, has pointed out, Wright's ideas were often not part of any critical dialogue, and his writings and books in translation were generally unavailable.[37] Consequently, German scholars still apply the perceptual framework of the 1920s and 1930s, with little updating or revision, in their views of Wright.

Other German-speaking countries have their own histories in regard to Wright. Wright's impact in Switzerland presents a situation almost as complex as the one in Germany. The obvious starting point is Berlage's introduction of Wright to the Swiss in 1912. However, it was Werner Moser, a graduate of the Eidgenössische Technische Hochschule (ETH) in Zurich and assistant to Wright in the mid-1920s, who most actively propagated Wright's ideas in that country from 1926, when he returned to Switzerland, through the 1960s. Moser's own architecture displays Wright's idiom, as seen in his competition entry for a primary school with gymnasium and parish house in Rapperswil-Jona (1954), whose plan consists of a pair of pinwheels of squares (Fig. 1.13). Kief-Niederwöhrmeier has suggested that images of Wright's work found their way into the work of other Swiss architects, including Otto R. Salvisberg, Alfred Roth, Tita Carloni, Franco Ponti, Ernest E. Ansderegg, Peppo Brivio, André M. Studer, Peter Steiger, and Justus Dahinden.[38] But other developments in the evolution of the Modern Movement often overshadowed Wright's architecture. Detailed study will be needed to sort out his influence—whether imitation, transformation, or parallel development—in the work of Swiss architects and to determine the vehicles by which it was transmitted.

In Austria and the successor states of the former Austro-Hungarian Empire Wright's influence is more limited. Schindler and Neutra remained in the United States after their contact with Wright and did not return to live in Austria. Wright did meet Josef Hoffmann, cofounder of the Wiener Werkstätte and a leading figure in the Vienna Secession, when Wright returned from his trip to Russia in 1937.[39] And Wright's work emerged, if obliquely, in the studio of the German Peter Behrens, who, in the lineage of Otto Wagner's successors, taught the master class at the Academy of Fine Arts in Vienna. Wright's Wasmuth folios appear to have been required reading in the Behrens class in the mid-1920s for future modernists like Ernst Plischke; these folios may well have been the same ones Wagner had shown to his students some fifteen years earlier.[40]

Wright's work apparently made an impact on the emerging generation of Czech modernists working in the early 1920s. In discussing Wright's impact, Adolf Behne cited, in addition to other European architects, almost the whole range of *sachlich* modernists among Czech architects: Vít Obrtel, Jaromír Krejcar, Oldřich Tyl, František Černy, Jan Víšek, Jaroslav Fragner, and Bedřich Feuerstein.[41] Precisely how they were influenced by Wright requires more careful scrutiny than Behne provided. So many currents intersected their work that such assertions require

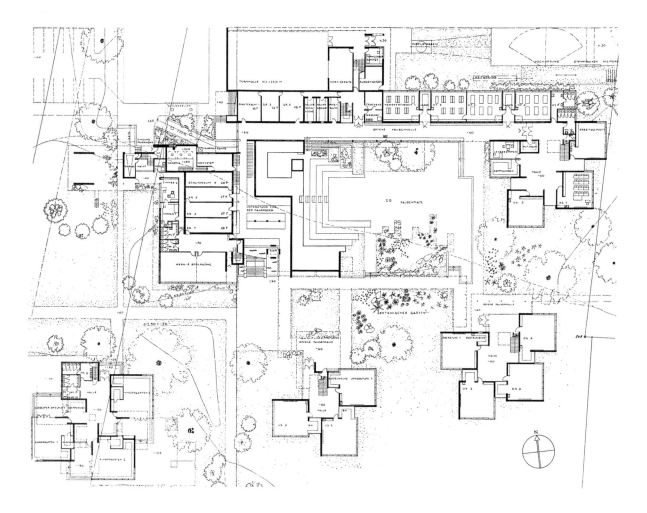

Figure 1.13
Competition entry, plan for a primary
school with gymnasium and parish
house, Rapperswil-Jona, Switzerland,
1954. Werner Moser, architect.
(*Schweizerische Bauzeitung*,
5 March 1959, 141)

caution. Nevertheless, the quick appearance in 1931 of a translation of Wright's
lecture "The City of the Future," which had been part of his Princeton series on
modern architecture that same year, attests to Czech interest in Wright's work.[42]
On the whole, however, after the dissolution of the Empire, Austria, Hungary,
Czechoslovakia, and the countries that would become Yugoslavia were engaged
in an immense struggle for both survival and identity. In the midst of this polit-

ical and economic turmoil, the Modern Movement was undergoing dramatic changes. Our historical understanding of these developments, and Wright's role in them, if any, has barely begun.

Wright's influence in Europe and around the globe ebbs and flows in cycles. The end of World War II marked not only the beginning of his most productive period, in terms of numbers of commissions and projects, but also the emergence of his ideas in several countries where he had had little impact earlier.

Exhibitions continued to play a significant role in bringing his work to large audiences. "Sixty Years of Living Architecture," which opened at Gimbel's Department Store in Philadelphia in April 1951, was the last great international exhibition during Wright's lifetime and the largest exhibition of his career; it disseminated his ideas widely, as we will see in these collected essays.[43] The chief organizer for the event was Oskar Stonorov, a German-born architect committed to a socially responsible architecture who lived in Philadelphia.[44] The exhibition then began a long international odyssey, heading first to the Palazzo Strozzi in Florence. When it next traveled to Zurich, the natural contact person was Werner Moser, who not only mounted the exhibition but also produced a German-English catalog.[45] Subsequently the exhibition traveled to Paris, Munich, and Rotterdam (Fig. 1.14). In 1953 it returned to the United States, where it opened in New York City on the proposed site of the Guggenheim Museum, and then continued to Mexico City. In 1954 it was shown in the Barnsdall House in Los Angeles, and returned finally to Taliesin. The exhibition was reprised on a smaller scale in 1956 in Chicago in conjunction with the city's proclamation of 16 October as Frank Lloyd Wright Day. Combined with his last comments on organic architecture and his final book, *A Testament,* this global demonstration of a lifetime devoted to architecture provides the background for seeing how the themes of Wright's modernism played out.[46]

Exhibitions in the United States and around the world after Wright's death in 1959 bring the question of Wright's impact up to the present. Although often informative, for the most part these exhibitions have focused on a certain time period or location, a narrow group of projects, or specific genres like decorative arts or facsimiles of original materials. The lone exception, remotely analogous to "Sixty Years of Living Architecture," was "Frank Lloyd Wright, Architect," held at the Museum of Modern Art in New York from February through May 1994. The exhibition did not travel, and it is too early to assess its impact, alongside the current resurgence of interest in Wright, on the production of architecture around the globe.[47] Many of the essays that follow were originally given as lectures by an international group of scholars in a symposium held at the museum in conjunction with that exhibition and cosponsored by the Society of Architectural Historians. These have been revised for this volume, which also includes new contributions. Together the essays represent a first look at the impact

Figure 1.14
Wright *(third from the right)* with exhibition-goers viewing the Broadacre City model at "Sixty Years of Living Architecture" in Paris, April 1952. (FLWA 6808.0035)

of Wright's ideas abroad, some from the perspective of natives of the countries under discussion and others from that of an informed outsider.

Margo Stipe brings the latter perspective to bear on her analysis of the relation between Wright and Japan. The Japanese influence on Wright has been a subject of considerable debate since 1910. Stipe not only summarizes the traditional view of how Wright set out to absorb Japanese aesthetics and transform them in his own work, but she also reverses the issue by exploring the differences between Wright's concepts and those that underlie Japanese architecture and by discussing the reception of his ideas in Japan up to the present.

Bruno Zevi was a major participant in bringing Wright's ideas to Italy. After studying at Harvard in the early 1940s, he returned to Italy to help launch the movement for organic architecture. Wright's philosophy of a democratic architecture, expressed in a fresh language of form, acquired political significance in postwar Italy. Zevi tells us how Wright's ideas took hold and relates his personal experience accompanying Wright during his 1951 visit to Italy.

In her essay Maristella Casciato amplifies the story of Wright's impact in Italy, revealing the role he and others—including the magazine *Metron* and the Association for Organic Architecture, in which Bruno Zevi was actively involved—played in the evolution of the Modern Movement. She also provides an account of Wright's critical reception in Italy and discusses the impact he had on Italian architects after World War II.

As we become more familiar with the important role of Dutch architects in disseminating Wright's ideas, we appreciate even more the efforts of H. Th. Wijdeveld. In 1931 Wright invited Wijdeveld to come to the United States and direct the School of Art that Wright and his wife were planning at the former Hillside Home School. Wijdeveld was delighted; in his view the new school paralleled his own ongoing efforts to create an International Guild that would promote goodwill through the arts. Willing to uproot himself and his family and to invest his modest financial resources, he announced his acceptance in a charming and emotional letter loaded with utopian idealism.[48] Alas, this noble gesture did not succeed. Wijdeveld arrived at Taliesin in October 1931 but returned to Holland in early 1932.

Mariëtte van Stralen further scrutinizes the Dutch Connection, examining the reception of Wright's ideas among the architects and artists of the various Dutch schools of modernism: De Stijl, the Amsterdam School, and the Hague School. She then concentrates on the vital relationship between Wijdeveld and Wright, revealing the spiritual connection between the two artists that made Wijdeveld one of Wright's greatest proponents.

The enthusiasm that Wright's ideas and work found in Holland was not universal, as these essays also demonstrate. France had powerful traditions and its own champions, and Wright's work was either at odds with French developments or critiqued as if it were. Jean-Louis Cohen's study of the late consideration of Wright's ideas in France, Wright's reception in Russia, and Wright's perceptions of Soviet architecture shows how both countries used Wright for their own purposes, taking turns portraying him as an opponent of capitalism, an innovator in the use of concrete, and a traditionalist—interpretations that prevented a deeper understanding of his architecture. The context for these vacillating presentations of Wright, as Cohen emphasizes, was the notion of Americanism, a powerful force of attraction and repulsion throughout Europe.

Another contextual factor in the perception of Wright was his position in relationship to Le Corbusier. Although an issue in France, this relationship was also a recurrent theme on the international front. Grappling with the modernist equivalent of the old question of "in what style should we build?," architects in many countries often looked to one or the other of the great masters for inspiration. Thus, the battle was launched between two visions of modernity: Wright's based on the individual, Le Corbusier's on the establishment of a collective identity found in an international style. The reasons for one's momentary success over the other require a more extensive study than is intended here, taking into account the personality and charisma of each architect, as well as the effectiveness of their rhetoric, particularly as published in their various manifestoes and theories.[49]

Great Britain presents another case of conflicting views on roles of architecture and a sluggish resistance to Wright's ideas. Andrew Saint charts the mutual overlaps and misunderstandings between Wright and British architects and critics. Charles Robert Ashbee, a preeminent arts and crafts ideologue and Wright's first British promoter and friend, advocated that architecture represent the collective, while Wright argued for the individual. Their differences strained their friendship even in 1910, when Wright, virtually unknown in Great Britain, briefly visited that country for the first time. By the time of his next visit, in 1939, he was a distinguished figure, and his Prairie period designs, at least, had become common currency. Yet by the early 1940s Le Corbusier would win over the modernist avant-garde. Saint describes with wit and charm the sometimes heated and sometimes cool reception to Wright's widely attended public lectures. The figurative brickbats tossed between Wright and his critics in the debates that followed clearly show that both had limited understanding of the other's values and positions.

Even South America bears traces of the opposition between Wright and Le Corbusier. Le Corbusier had been asked to propose a city plan for Rio de Janeiro in 1929; Wright was invited to Brazil as a judge representing North America in the design competition for a Christopher Columbus Memorial Lighthouse in 1931.[50] Wright gained further recognition in Latin America in 1940, when Uruguay awarded him a diploma and a silver medal at the fifth Congreso Panamericano de Arquitectos.

In this collection the architect Alberto Sartori offers a personal and impassioned view of how Wright's ideas took root in South America, particularly in Chile after 1940. Like Zevi, Sartori discovered Wright's ideas while still a student. In the 1950s an entire generation of young Chilean architecture students was inspired by Wright's ideas, and their impact has endured for decades. Discussing some of the buildings he and his fellow architects conceived, Sartori reminds us of the cultural and geographical diversity of a continent we too often forget. He concludes by showing how a professional life devoted to Wright's organic principles can interweave with the rich and varied cultures of Latin America.

Farther north, Wright's efforts were recognized in 1943 when the Sociedad de Arquitectos Mexicanos named him an honorary member, an indication that Wright's ideas were part of the evolving Mexican discourse on modernism. Although here too, as Keith Eggener points out in his essay, Le Corbusier became the major figure of emulation, Wright had an important influence on architects and painters like Juan O'Gorman, Max Cetto, Diego Rivera, and Luis Barragán. Architects elsewhere often copied Wright's forms; in Mexico, however, Wright's ideas had more impact than his formal language.

Wright's formal language did have broad adaptability in his own hands, as his little-known impact in the Middle East attests. In 1957, Wright and other Western architects were each invited to design one building for the modern capital of Iraq. Although commissioned for an opera house, after traveling to Baghdad Wright apparently secured permission to proceed with the design of an entire cultural center, which would include the opera house and a civic auditorium, as well as a new post office. He then added designs for an art gallery, a museum of archeological antiquities, and a campus for Baghdad University. The immense scope and the exoticism of these projects appealed to Wright, who quickly pro-

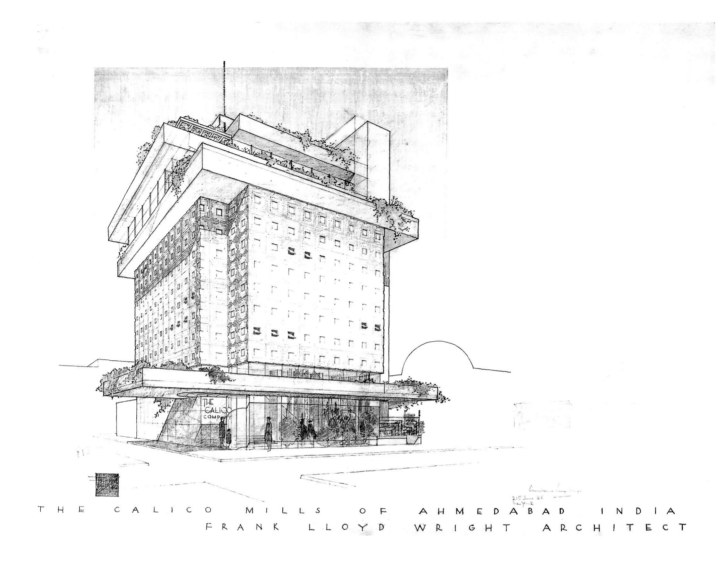

THE CALICO MILLS OF AHMEDABAD INDIA

FRANK LLOYD WRIGHT ARCHITECT

Figure 1.15
Perspective view of the Sarabhai Calico
Mills Store, project, Ahmedabad, India,
1945. FLW, designer. (FLWA 4508.001)

duced numerous designs. None were realized; the royal clients, King Faisal II and Crown Prince Abdul Ilah, were assassinated in July 1958.

Mina Marefat shows, for the first time, that after the Guggenheim, the Baghdad projects were Wright's principal focus in his last decade. In them he brought together concepts from many projects, including, for example, Broadacre City and Crystal Heights. Marefat also considers the project as Wright's tribute to the Orient. Excited to be working in the cradle of civilization, between the Tigris and Euphrates Rivers, and stimulated by the long-remembered tales of the *Arabian Nights,* Wright created a grand entertainment, a sort of Disneyland for adults. But instead of indulging in a simple kitsch fantasy, Wright was far ahead of his time in imagining the city's historic center as a tourist attraction, using many of the techniques that would make theme parks a global phenomenon. As Marefat persuasively shows, had his scheme been built, it would have been the crowning project of his career. In addition to the Baghdad project, Marefat discusses Wright's connections to Iran, where he designed a house for a friend and where Taliesin Associated Architects, his successor firm, continued to participate in projects after Wright's death.

The topics covered in these essays are not exhaustive—we offer only an introduction to Wright's impact around the globe, searching out the little known instead of reexamining the well established. Our look is open-ended, subject to further refinement and revision, with a variety of topics yet to be explored. Future studies may consider what impact Wright had on the Scandinavian modern movement, or how his ideas were used in Spain and Africa. The repercussion of Wright's designs for India is a potentially rich topic. Among the several young Indians who came to study with Wright after World War II were Gira and Gautam Sarabhai, a sister and brother for whose family Wright designed the Sarabhai Calico Mills Store in 1945 (Fig. 1.15). Intended for the city of Ahmedabad, the design required construction technology beyond the grasp of Indian engineers and builders of the day, and the project was abandoned.[51] These unexplored histories only hint at the further relationships that await unraveling.

I hope the reader derives as much pleasure as I do from realizing that the most American of architects was also one of the most international. The dispersal of Wright's vision of organic architecture around the globe, however it was understood, provided alternatives to a solitary modernism, ones that we are only now beginning to appreciate and critique.

TWO: WRIGHT AND JAPAN

Margo Stipe

Frank Lloyd Wright's interest in and appreciation of Japanese art and culture are both well known and well documented. He was a major collector of Japanese art, especially woodblock prints, an admirer of traditional Japanese architecture, and the architect of the second Imperial Hotel in Tokyo (demolished in 1968). He made eight trips to Japan beginning in 1905, spending nearly three full years there between 1916 and his final departure in 1922. Such involvement with another country by one of the century's most brilliant architects leads inevitably to the question of possible influence, both that of Japanese aesthetics and philosophy on Wright's work and of Wright's work and philosophy on the development of twentieth-century Japanese architecture.

Wright outspokenly admired Japan and acknowledged its inspiration but denied its overt influence. Just when and how this admiration began, however, are matters of speculation. Although there are arguments for an earlier date, the latest date generally accepted for Wright's introduction to Japan is 1893, the year the World's Columbian Exposition opened in Chicago.[1] The Japanese buildings there were widely published, and it is unlikely that Wright, at that time the chief draftsman in the office of Louis Sullivan, who designed the fair's Transportation Building, would not have seen them.[2] Photographs of the interior of Wright's Oak Park home show that he had begun to acquire, if not actively collect, oriental scrolls and Japanese woodblock prints by at least 1895. By 1905, Wright's interest in Japan and its art was so keen that he decided to make his first trip abroad (Fig. 2.1).[3] Given his tendency in early writings to mention authors or ideas that captured his attention or influenced his thought, it is curious that he did not mention Japan in any of his existing manuscripts or lectures before this 1905 journey. From 1906 forward, however, Japan was mentioned in some context in virtually everything he wrote for the rest of his life.[4]

In 1905, Japan was still undergoing critical political, economic, and social change, the result of contact with an aggressive West in the 1850s after 250 years of almost total isolation. The demise of the shogunal government, the restoration of imperial authority, and the landmark shift of the capital from Kyoto to Edo (later Tokyo) in the late 1860s marked the beginning of Japan's modern era.[5]

Modernization meant westernization. Westerners pointedly inferred that the Japanese were culturally, technologically, and materially inferior. The Japanese apparently accepted this verdict, and from the beginning of the Meiji period they sought and welcomed Western expertise and systems of thought while they dismissed and dismantled their own. Imperial commissions were sent to Europe to study, and Western scholars, architects, engineers, and business professionals were invited to teach and work in Japan.[6] Wright seemed to be one of the few, among foreigners and Japanese, to realize the devastating toll modernization was taking on Japan. He was dismayed by the modern culture that he saw in 1905 and later, especially as it was expressed in architecture, noting the prevalence of "bad copies, in bad technique, of bad originals."[7]

Despite the West's presumption of their cultural inferiority, the Japanese proved to be a remarkable international presence. After claiming victories over both China in 1895 and Russia by 1905, the country had emerged as a formidable world military power, by far the strongest in Asia. Arriving early in 1905, even before the Russo-Japanese peace treaty was signed, Wright chose largely to ignore the "mod-

Figure 2.1
Sutra Library, Chion-In, Kyoto. Photograph taken by Wright on his 1905 trip to Japan. (FLWA 7121.0007)

ern" state of Japan. Like many travelers today, Wright was enamored of the charms of old Japan as seen through the views captured in woodblock prints: he looked for old Edo, not new Tokyo. In his autobiography he issues this invitation: "Come with me on a journey within this journey in search of the print. Let us see Yedo as the prints saw it and as Yedo saw the prints."[8]

Wright had come to Japan in March 1905 to buy prints and to pursue the romantic legacy prints represented. By the time he returned to the United States two months later, he had been seduced and conquered by the traditional arts of this oriental civilization. He would remain their champion for the rest of his life.

In 1906, almost as a protest against the toll extracted by Japan's modernization, Wright staged the world's first exhibition of prints by the landscape artist Ando Hiroshige. Held at the Art Institute of Chicago, the exhibition proposed that

> properly considered [the work displayed] is the art not of a Hiroshige merely but of a people. The appeal that it makes is a spiritual one unlikely to be heard by Western materialism with more than amused tolerance. It is too restrained, too chaste, for our immediate comprehension. . . . It is no longer the sequestered art of an isolated people but one of the most valuable contributions ever made to the art of the world.[9]

Two years later, in 1908, Wright lectured at the Art Institute and joined other collectors in producing a larger and more widely representative exhibition. In 1912 he published *The Japanese Print: An Interpretation,* a book on Japanese aesthetics and the woodblock print.[10] In 1913, almost accidentally, he became a print dealer as well as a collector when he agreed to purchase prints for William and John Spaulding, important Boston art collectors, during his second trip to Japan,[11] undertaken to secure the commission for the new Imperial Hotel in Tokyo.[12] Wright was successful in both ventures: effectively promised the commission during this visit, he was officially awarded the contract for the hotel in 1916,[13] and while in Japan he continued actively to collect and sell woodblock prints until his final return in 1922. His collection still contained more than six thousand prints at the time of his death in 1959.[14]

Wright admitted quite freely the role that the Japanese print played in his work, and he also openly admired traditional Japanese architecture.[15] In *An Autobiography* he writes that he found the "native home in Japan a supreme study in [the] elimination . . . of the insignificant" and "a perfect example of the modern standardizing" that he had been developing.[16] He added that the search for a modern architecture seemed to have more affinity with Japanese architecture in principle than with any other because of the great honesty of its traditional structure.[17]

The question of Japan's influence on Frank Lloyd Wright's work was posed early. In his introduction to the 1911 German monograph *Frank Lloyd Wright: Ausgeführte Bauten,* the English architect Charles Robert Ashbee wrote: "We can often trace the influence of Japan, or the effort to adapt Japanese forms to American conditions, though I know the artist himself disavows this; doubtless the touch of the East is an unconscious one, but I notice it most in his architectural drawings."[18] Although admitting "their debt to Japanese ideals, [which] these renderings themselves sufficiently acknowledge," Wright responded strongly to what he considered the unjustness of Ashbee's statement: "Do not say that I deny that my love for Japanese art has influenced me—I admit that it has but claim to have digested it—Do not accuse me of trying to 'adapt Japanese forms' however, that is a false accusation and against my very religion."[19]

Later, though, perhaps tired of scholars' attempts to discover influences in his work, Wright insisted:

> To cut ambiguity short: there never was exterior influence upon my work either foreign or native, other than that of Lieber Meister, Dankmar Adler and John Roebling, Whitman and Emerson, and the great poets worldwide. My work is original not only in fact but in spiritual fiber. No practice by any European architect to this day has influenced mine in the least. As for the Incas, the Mayans, even the Japanese—all were to me but splendid confirmation.[20]

Confirmation implied Wright's belief in order in the universe that could be discerned in its purest artistic and architectural expressions.[21] An astute and perceptive observer, he no doubt recognized the time-honored principle of order, with its resulting tranquillity and beauty, and appreciated the visible characteristics of simplicity, use of natural materials, and structural honesty that all underlie traditional Japanese architecture.[22] Furthermore, he was particularly struck by the inherent spiritual quality in Japanese life and art, a spirituality of everyday life that would have been in keeping with Wright's romantic ideals.

It is easy to recognize in Wright's architecture, especially that of the early 1900s, elements derived from the vocabulary of traditional Japanese architecture: the hipped roofs, overall proportional relationships, strong horizontals, and masterful manipulation of light and shadow. This visual congruence is perfectly exemplified in the seventeenth-century imperial villa of Katsura and Wright's 1902 residence for Ward Willits (Figs. 2.2 and 2.3). Nevertheless, one would hardly mistake a Wright home for a Japanese one. While they may display similar architectural principles and characteristics, Katsura and Wright's house are quite distinctively different, not only visually, but in intent. Japanese residential architecture, of which Katsura is often considered the quintessential example, represents the strictly hierarchical society that created it, both in design and in decorative programs. Wright's architecture was diametrically opposed: it was an attempt to create an architecture that would reform society and create for the American citizen a democratic environment largely devoid of social distinctions.[23]

This outward resemblance of Wright's early domestic architecture to Japanese prototypes only scratches the surface of the connection Wright forged with Japa-

Figure 2.2
Katsura Rikyu Imperial Residence,
Kyoto, seventeenth century.
(Photograph by author)

Figure 2.3 *(opposite)*
Ward W. Willits House, Highland
Park, Illinois, 1902. FLW, architect.
(FLWA 0208.0001)

nese culture and aesthetics. His repeated visits to Japan and the large number of
projects he designed for the country created a complex and intense relationship.
Of the eleven projects he designed for Japan, the Imperial Hotel was, without
question, his greatest Japanese project and, many would argue, one of his greatest buildings (Fig. 2.4).[24] It is probably as legendary today, despite its demolition
in 1968, as it was controversial at the time of its construction in the early 1920s.
The hotel provides a key to understanding Wright's admiration for Japanese aesthetics as well as his interpretation of the Japanese sense of space.

The eleven-million-dollar dismantling, move and reconstruction of the entrance hall and reflecting pool of the Imperial Hotel at Meiji Mura, a huge outdoor architectural museum north of Nagoya, can only hint at what must have
been, regardless of criticism, a glorious structure whose demolition was a great
cultural loss.[25] Japan's first modern hotel, it was a national symbol and the social
center of the capital city. Wright himself described the hotel as a "social clear-
ing house" for East and West for a country "making the transition from wood to
masonry and her knees to her feet."[26]

The captivating visual and social mystique of the building was matched by
its engineering technology, which was revolutionary by Japanese standards, even
if later questioned by Western engineers. In an effort to create an earthquake-
resistant structure, Wright floated the foundations on concrete piles as flexible sections so that they could move and settle back in place without breaking up in a
quake. Wright also kept the building's center of gravity low by focusing its mass

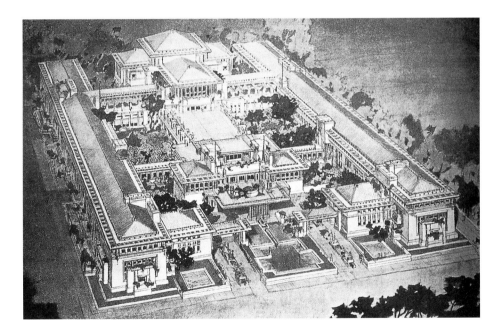

Figure 2.4
Perspective view of Imperial Hotel,
Tokyo, 1909–22. FLW, architect.
From *Wendingen,* 106.

near the ground: the walls were two brick shells with a concrete center, tapering as they rose, and lighter copper replaced the traditional heavy roof tiles. Ornament was not attached to the building but was made integral by the carving of structural elements, made from native *oya* stone. To help "fireproof" the structure, pools were created throughout the gardens to provide immediately available water sources. Skepticism about this new design was silenced upon the news that the building had survived, almost unscathed, the worst earthquake in Japan's recorded history, the great Kanto quake of 1 September 1923.[27] Its survival alone earned the new Imperial Hotel a place in architectural history almost before its own history had begun.

Upon its completion, Western and Japanese scholars and critics expressed a variety of opinions about the Imperial Hotel. The *Japan Advertiser* declared shortly after its partial opening in July 1922: "There will be none who will deny the originality of the design, the boldness of the conception, artistic unity and beauty of the whole." But the article also correctly predicted that the design of the hotel would "give rise to much criticism and cause many controversies because the building is a bold challenge to old habit of thought. The new always lacks authority."[28] At about the same time, the *Christian Science Monitor* reported:

> One would be safe in saying that there is not another structure in the world that could be compared to the new hotel, for the architect has worked both ancient and modern types of expression into the great mass of brick, stone and steel. . . . Mr. Wright has tried to create a building that would typify the Far East, yet would be conveniently and practically modern. He has worked Western, Japanese and even a bit of old Egyptian architecture in one mass, and the surprise of all is its uncommon unity.[29]

Wright himself claimed that the hotel was not intended to be a specifically Japanese building, but one that paid tribute to Japanese traditions.[30]

There were also negative reviews. American architect Louis Christian Mullgardt immediately despised the hotel, calling it a "freak" and a monument of disgrace to American architecture, "fantastic and prehistoric."[31] In its defense, Louis Sullivan wrote in 1923: "In this structure is not to be found a single form distinctly Japanese; nor that of any country; yet in its own individual form, its mass, and subsidiaries, its evolution of plan and development of thesis; in its sedulous care for niceties of administration and for the human sense of joy, it has expressed, in inspiring form as an epic poem, addressed to the Japanese people, their inmost thought."[32] Despite this eloquent rejoinder, Wright's onetime assistant on the hotel, Czech architect Antonin Raymond, one of the few foreign architects to establish a practice in Japan, later reflected that the "design had nothing in common with Japan, its climate, its traditions, its people or its culture."[33]

The American manager of the hotel during the postwar Occupation also found the building to be challenging:

It splatters out from the focal point of the lobby in all directions. The corridor system is so winding and complicated that when you try to retrace a path you have followed, the patterns seem to have changed while your back was turned. The ceiling of the entrance lobby is so low that a normal-sized person instinctively ducks his head as he enters . . . but after walking up the six steps to the main lobby a person suddenly finds that the ceiling is three stories high and he is standing in the middle of a huge space.

He admitted, however, that at the end of his tenure, despite the building's many practical difficulties, it still intrigued and pleased him.[34]

From the Japanese perspective the building was always a bit fantastic. The rich ornamentation traditionally present in Japanese architecture, though familiar to Wright, provided no precedent for the elaborate schemes he executed at the Imperial Hotel.[35] Some have called the building Wright's "first faintly Mayan" structure,[36] an impression that has led to a fairly popular but erroneous assertion among the Japanese that the building was originally designed for a site in Mexico. Although the building's geometric grammar was indeed reminiscent of Maya architecture, the forms employed were, in fact, universal.[37] Anthony Alofsin has suggested that in his search for an archetypal American architecture, Wright, through the use of these universal forms, was "honoring Japan with a gift of what he perceived as the noblest forms of the architecture of the Americas."[38]

Despite these peculiarities, the hotel was not totally alien to Japan. In plan and character it emulated the symmetry, structural detailing, and integration of the buildings and gardens of ancient Japanese governmental, residential, and religious compounds. From the seventh century on, Japanese architecture drew heavily on Chinese precedent. Although organic materials soon replaced the stone and tile in residential buildings, the floor plans and symmetry were often retained in both public and private Japanese buildings. Most compounds, therefore, had a central hall, oriented to the south, connected to subsidiary halls by a series of corridors and galleries. The main facade was fronted by a courtyard (in the case of temples and government buildings) or a pond-garden (in the mansions of the aristocracy). Courtyard gardens filled open spaces throughout, and long corridors ran forward on either side terminating in pavilions. The overall symmetry of a plan arranged around a central court, as seen in the Kyoto imperial residence, depended on Chinese models, and is also reflected in the plan Wright developed for the Imperial Hotel (Figs. 2.4 and 2.5). In basic plan, the hotel, although oriented to the west, followed this standard. Furthermore, the canted walls of the hotel are suggestive of castle walls, and the interior structural supports, especially in the dining room, recall the bracketing system of the twelfth-century Todai-ji temple in Nara.

The Imperial Hotel reflected Wright's new sense of space, something he had developed in the first decade of the century. Through simplification of form, line, and color, lessons he claimed were learned from the study of the Japanese print,

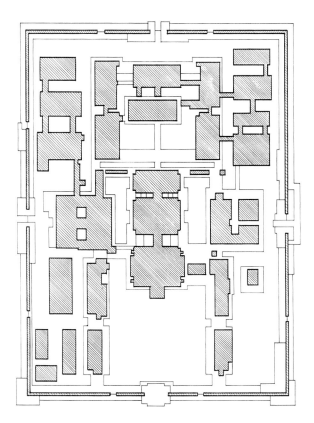

Figure 2.5
Plan, Imperial Palace, Kyoto, 1855.

Wright created plastic, fluent, and coherent spaces that complemented the changing physical and spiritual life of modern Japan. Wright explained his concept of space through a paraphrase of the words of Lao-tzu illustrating the metaphor of the vacuum: "The reality of the building does not consist in the roof and walls, but in the space within, to be lived in."[39] For Wright, these words suggested that his spaces were spiritual, not material; in this way he aligned his ideas with oriental philosophy in general.

But in fact, Wright misunderstood the concept of the oriental void. Wright's spaces are not voids; they are zoned, functionally defined areas, and, open and flexible though they might be, once created they exist in and of themselves, regardless of the use to which they are put. Japanese space, at least traditionally, was not so formalized. Although proper spatial relationships were critical to the maintenance of a harmonious balance within the social group—between the human and natural worlds, between inside and outside—the word "space" in the Western sense (*kukan*) did not even exist in Japanese until the twentieth century. The key to understanding the Japanese concept of space, rather, is the word *ma,* which might be translated as "place," "pause," "interval," or "void." It always implies relationship—as in the "distance" between two columns in a building, the "interval" between two notes in a musical composition, the "space" between two rocks in a garden or between two people in a room—and it is highly subjective. The Japanese notion of having "too much" or "too little *ma*" (overdone or weak, out of balance) or "good *ma*" (skillful, well done) clearly demonstrates the qualitative, emotional nature of this word. *Ma* underlies all feelings of order, harmony, and beauty.[40]

Japanese "space" was a void in which all things were inherent; it had no identity until required for some use. Japanese architectural space, then, was one of total flexibility. The ceiling, columns, and floor were the only fixed structural members of a building; furniture was easily movable. Except for the kitchen, rooms could be completely changed by the addition or removal of screens and doors and the temporary placement of appropriate objects as the occasion demanded. The same room might easily fulfill the functions of reception, dining, and sleeping by a simple change of furnishings. Architect Fumihiko Maki summarized this condition thus: "Space gains its quality depending on the things, events, or phenomena that it helps define, among which it establishes relationships and, in turn, by which it is also evoked."[41]

In an essay on Wrightian space, architect Arata Isozaki further clarified the Japanese perceptions of space and time: they begin, he said, "the instant at which a human being enters and perceives a space in relation to himself." Isozaki noted that although Wright was "impressed" by his encounter with Japan and Japanese art, he manipulated his understanding of the experience in a very personal way, to create "solid space, textured with stone and brick, that could by no means be identified as 'Oriental.'" But if Wright's space was not oriental, it was also not particularly Western. Wright, in fact, created an entirely new sense of space, according to Isozaki: "a space to which no civilization can lay claim."[42]

The Imperial Hotel's objective of creating a "transition building" for East and West, a place where Japan could easily make an entrance into the modern world, illustrates this transcultural quality of Wright's architecture. While relying on "Western style," Wright tried to incorporate elements and create spaces that would make the oriental hosts as comfortable as the visiting foreigners they were hoping to attract. And although the hotel incorporated a vast complex of rooms, corridors, and balconies, the human proportions to which the building was scaled created an intimacy more common to residential than public spaces, inviting restful occupancy. The use of *oya* stone, brick, and terra cotta, the low ceilings, and the placement of narrow windows in many areas created an interior of shadowy spaces, enhancing this feeling of shelter and repose. The winding corridors led the guests through constantly varying visual and spatial experiences, not unlike the gardens for which the Japanese were famous.

Wrightian space, therefore, shares with traditional Japanese architecture the idea of creating spaces of movement and change, of repose and activity. But in a Wrightian space, these effects come as much from the shifting lines, planes, and textures of fixed architectural elements as from the changing human activity that those el-

ements frame. Thus, although the elaborately designed Peacock Room (banquet hall) of the Imperial Hotel might be arranged to serve a variety of functions, the fundamental character of the room did not change (Fig. 2.6). In such a space, the "stage set" created by the room remains intrinsically the same whether anything happens or not; in Japanese space, by contrast, there is no stage set until some human event calls it into being.

While scholars have extensively addressed the question of Japan's influence on Wright, they have less frequently discussed Wright's role in the development of architecture in Japan. Twentieth-century Japanese architects have been very much concerned with incorporating a modern, Western-style sense of space into their designs. They also admit that Wright, as one of the giants of twentieth-century architecture, is a potent figure for anyone involved in architecture, and they acknowledge familiarity with, and often admiration for, Wright's work. But Japanese architects and architectural historians alike suggest that Wright's direct influence in Japan has been minimal at best.[43] Kenzo Tange, perhaps the best known of the Japanese modernists, was outspoken in his assertion that Wright's stylistic individuality was irrational and that "from an objective viewpoint" his designs were too arbitrary to be influential,[44] and some Western scholars have come to a similar conclusion, stating that Wright's impact was brief and limited.[45] These views are not unanimous, however. Dennis Sharp, for example, has observed that "notwithstanding the accumulation of interest in the work of Le Corbusier in Japan in the period after World War II and also in the growing regard for Louis Kahn's buildings, the legacy of Frank Lloyd Wright has remained clear. . . . His work was received as a way to a new architecture and as a means of architectural expression."[46]

But the lessons that Wright hoped to demonstrate of an "organic" architecture—an architecture appropriate to time, place, and humankind—went largely unheeded as Japan struggled toward modernization in the 1920s and 1930s. Drawn by the International Style, progressive Japanese architects turned not to the United States but to Europe for inspiration. A number of young Japanese designers, including Kunio Maekawa and Junzo Sakakura, studied with the European champions, Le Corbusier and Walter Gropius, in the 1930s; unfortunately, their efforts would have little impact until after World War II, when modernism finally began to move forward with considerable momentum. Even today, Japanese architects usually cite Le Corbusier as their inspiration. Only a few architects, such as Arata Endo, Wright's assistant on the Imperial Hotel, persevered in the "cause of organic architecture."[47] His Koshien Hotel in Kobe (1930), commissioned by former Imperial Hotel manager Aisaku Hayashi, exhibits a striking resemblance to Wright's Midway Gardens (1913–14),[48] and his auditorium building at the Jiyu Gakuen in Tokyo (1921) reflects the influence of Taliesin itself (Figs. 2.7 and 2.8).

Perhaps Wright failed to have a major impact on twentieth-century Japanese architecture because his approach had so much in common with the building traditions the Japanese were largely rejecting in their efforts to modernize and industrialize, both in the early 1900s and following their devastating defeat in World War II. However, historical circumstances also need to be considered. The widespread destruction of Tokyo and Yokohama in the 1923 earthquake necessitated the immediate reconstruction of thousands of buildings. Such activity was familiar to the Japanese, whose cities were frequently destroyed by fires, earthquakes, typhoons, and civil wars. Shelter was the issue, meaning rapid reconstruction of the same kind of buildings that had stood previously on the same sites. Wright's advice that Tokyo be rebuilt on a more permanent and rational plan, with wires underground, widened and shaded streets, and the principal residence and business areas restricted to two or three stories, was simply ignored.[49] The 1930s, moreover, saw stepped-up militarization and the development of imperial aspirations in Asia. Competitions for major building projects during this period of rising nationalism stipulated "Japanese-style" designs, though this did not preclude the use of modern materials. Traditional facades now often concealed modern concrete and steel cores, as exemplified by Jin Watanabe's Imperial Museum in Tokyo (1937; Fig. 2.9), while neither Wright-like designs nor those inspired by Le Corbusier's internationalism found favor.[50]

World War II and the resulting physical and spiritual devastation of the country again made shelter a critically important issue. Entire cities had to be rebuilt. This time arguments for creative urban and architectural design began to be heard,

Figure 2.7
Koshien Hotel, Kobe, 1930. Arata Endo,
architect. (Raku Endo, photographer)

but Wright's voice seems not to have been among them. The practical realities of postwar Japan made many of Wright's ideas unsuitable. Broadacre City, his forceful argument for American decentralization and the primacy of the individual, would have been incompatible with the traditional Japanese values of community and conformity, despite the country's conversion to democracy. But beyond the question of sovereignty of the individual, Wright's antiurban posture and arguments for decentralization could have little application in a country where over 60 percent (67 percent today) of the population lived in densely settled urban areas. The urbanist theories of modernists such as Le Corbusier and Walter Gropius, who believed strongly in the necessity of cities, had broader appeal in Japan.

In commercial and civic design, too, the allegedly rational International Style, with its easily grasped abstract forms, proved more suitable than Wright's architecture for fulfilling the industrial and functional requirements of postwar urban

Figure 2.8
Midway Gardens, Chicago, 1913–14.
FLW, architect. (FLWA 1401.0032)

Figure 2.9
Tokyo Imperial Museum, Tokyo,
1937. Jin Watanabe, architect.
(Photograph by author)

Figure 2.10
Kurashiki City Hall, Kurashiki, 1960
(now a museum). Kenzo Tange,
architect. (Photograph by author)

design. Le Corbusier's "machine for living" and Gropius's collaborative design approach, typified by Kenzo Tange's Kurashiki City Hall (1960, now home to a museum; Fig. 2.10), thus provided the architectural foundation for Japanese efforts to rejoin the world community after the war.

The pioneers of Japanese architecture in the Meiji period (1868–1912) left a legacy of Western emulation, which continued through the Taisho era (1912–26) and into the Showa period (1926–89). The third generation of architects (Sakakura, Maekawa, Tange) largely followed the dictates of the International Style, introduced in the 1930s and pursued again after World War II. While they did not abandon national traditions altogether (Tange's buildings, in particular, made specific historic references), the strong influence of Le Corbusier on their work was unmistakable. The next generation began a retreat, which continues today, from the cold objectivity of science to a more subjective approach: they chose to revisit the premise that human beings need more than merely shelter; they need environments that nourish the body and the spirit.

Kisho Kurokawa, a founder in 1960 of the Metabolist movement, explains that this movement sought to use Japanese cultural traditions to reconstitute the Western-derived rules for modern architecture and to replace the mechanical model of design with a biological one. The Metabolist philosophy had its roots in the Buddhist concept of "mutability"; their model, consequently, was one "in which the parts, like living cells, could [quite literally] come to life, develop and die out while the whole body—the building, the city or the entire built environment—went on living . . . where all the elements are interchangeable."[51] This was a different kind of "organic architecture" from Wright's, based as it was on technology but given a biological analogy. In attempting to achieve this symbiosis, one of past and future, of East and West, the Metabolists were also seeking to reaffirm the value of history and the vernacular. While acknowledging the significance of modernism and modern architecture, and the validity of their underlying rationalism and functionalism, the Metabolists wanted some "allowances for vagueness [which] the functionalists cast away."[52]

Contemporary designers are increasingly reincorporating traditional qualities into their work—in principle at least, if not necessarily in form. For example, Tadao Ando's inward-turning, polished concrete spaces have been observed to be connected by a common thread to traditional teahouse architecture, though not by any particular resemblance in style or form.[53] Although both are enclosed and focused, simple in appearance, calm, and quiet, Ando's buildings are a stunning combination of solid Western technology and the more intangible presence of nature.

This shift toward traditional aesthetics has been accompanied by renewed attention to architects like Frank Lloyd Wright and Alvar Aalto. Indeed, Kurokawa asserts that today these architects have "far more supporters in Japan than Le Corbusier," saying the reason can be traced back to the tradition of "living in symbiosis with nature."[54] He also states that the pattern of Western-oriented thinking long prevalent in Japanese architecture is at an end and that younger designers "have begun to explore the Japanese tradition and the many different cultures in the world."[55] Whether this return to traditional principles can be attributed to Wright's lingering influence or to the inevitable rejection of rigid functionalist manifestos underlying the International Style may be impossible to determine.

However far-reaching the influence of the International Style may have been on Japanese architecture, Shozo Uchii, a contemporary champion of Wright, believes that the lessons of Wright's Imperial Hotel were important to Japanese architects. Despite losing sight of their own roots in the outward search for a model of modernization, he says, the Japanese were able to understand Wright's architecture, recognizing in it "oriental ideas and views of nature." Uchii personally appreciated Wright's work because it "was tied to the earth," and he believes Wright was the only architect to construct an alternative to a modernism that espoused technological progress first and foremost. The integration of all parts into the whole, the use of local materials, and emphasis on the integrity of materials might eventually, Uchii argues, exert a great influence on the direction architecture takes in Japan.[56]

Uchii's own work reflects a respect for materials and an awareness of textures and patterns reminiscent of Wright's work. In the Shimamura residence in Omiya (1985; Figs. 2.11 and 2.13), the low, hipped roof rising from the broad overhanging eaves (narrow by traditional Japanese standards), strong horizontal orientation, and discrete treatment of lower and upper stories on the exterior recall Wright's Winslow House in River Forest (1893; Fig. 2.12). The use of plaster and the interior wooden beams are suggestive of the Prairie Style, in general, and of the Thomas House in Oak Park (1901) and the Tomek House in Riverside (1906; Fig. 2.14) in particular.[57]

Figure 2.11
Shimamura residence, Omiya,
1985. Shozo Uchii, architect.
(Koji Horiuchi, photographer)

Figure 2.12
W. H. Winslow House, River Forest,
Illinois, 1893. FLW, architect. (FLWA
9305.0039)

Figure 2.13
Dining room, Shimamura residence,
Omiya, 1985. Shozo Uchii, architect.
(Koji Horiuchi, photographer)

Figure 2.14
Dining room (without original furnishing),
Tomek House, Riverside, Illinois, 1907.
FLW, architect. (FLWA 0711.0036)

The Setagaya Museum of Art in Tokyo (1985; Fig. 2.15) evokes in spirit, if less distinctively in form, Wrightian ideas of public place as human space. Here Uchii has attempted to bring the scale of a traditionally monumental building type to a more human level by lowering overall heights and emphasizing strong horizontal lines. He has also skillfully integrated the building into the surrounding park by softening the exterior wall surfaces, allowing them to absorb rather than reflect light, and by covering the building with a green copper roof, which blends in with the surrounding greenery; a front pergola, hung with plants, creates a smooth transitional space between park and building.[58] The Setagaya Museum does not hold its visitors at arm's length, but rather invites them to participate in the experience of many different art forms. It is a museum that is trying to bring art both back *into* life and back *to* life.

Despite Wright's clear influence on Kurokawa and Uchii's skillful homage to him, there is little evidence to suggest that Japan's premier architects embraced his philosophy. However, there is one major area where Wright's influence is openly implied, and that is the housing industry. In a country so densely populated that one's "home" is most often a small apartment providing cramped shelter with few amenities, builders are incorporating Wright's idea that the home can be a place to live in and enjoy into their marketing strategies. Often this may amount to little more than assigning the name of a Wright house to a design that

本物は美しい。

otherwise has nothing in common with the original (Mitsui Norin's "Heurtley" home, for example). A case in point is Mitsui Norin's "Frank Lloyd Wright Residential Style" homes.[59] A brochure for the "1200 Series," for instance, shows the homes to be large and well appointed, displaying a Wrightian character very much in keeping with traditional Japanese taste (Fig. 2.16). At one time homes like this would have been within reach only of the very wealthy, but the economic boom of the 1980s and early 1990s has changed all that. Although the tremendous growth of those years has been tempered by the recent recession, families still have sizable incomes. Sophisticated and well traveled, the Japanese are now acquainted with the larger homes and the more home-oriented way of life common in the United States. This is the new target market for the housing industry, one for which it hopes Frank Lloyd Wright will have special appeal.

The Japanese have always looked outward for fresh ideas and inspiration, but never before had they so completely disowned their own culture as they did in the attempt to modernize.[60] Architecture was no exception to this rejection.[61] Within the chaotic environment of our time, however, Wright's belief in architecture as "a great spirit" may still provide some inspiration for the Japanese.[62] His principles of an organic architecture, and the resulting simplicity and serenity that characterize his spaces and their surroundings, are again attracting attention and support. This renewed interest among Japanese in Wright's work may reflect the rediscovery of the timeless principles of order and simplicity at the core of their own traditions as well as the return of the human spirit into their architectural spaces. In a world largely propelled by accelerating technology, the loss of poetry and beauty in everyday life should be mourned. Many of Japan's contemporary architects are attempting to recapture these qualities, if not in the tradition of Wright, certainly in the same spirit.

THREE: KINDRED SPIRITS

HOLLAND, WRIGHT, AND WIJDEVELD

Mariëtte van Stralen

Frank Lloyd Wright had more impact on architecture in the Netherlands than in any other European country, and the relationship is well known and much discussed.[1] A logical point of departure for this reconsideration of Wright's influence in the Netherlands is Hendrik Petrus Berlage's 1911 trip to the United States and his subsequent reports of it, including the book *Amerikaansche reisherinneringen* (Reminiscences of an American journey, 1913). Berlage conformed to the general European view of America as a land with enormous industrial and economic potential, but one that owed its culture to Europe.[2] As for American architecture, he named three exemplary practitioners: Louis H. Sullivan, Henry Hobson Richardson, and Frank Lloyd Wright. He considered Wright's work in particular to be original and exceptionally attractive; he saw him as a "spirit freed from all tradition," a statement which suggests that Berlage embraced the present and had no need to copy precedent.[3] Thus he helped lay the foundations for what he described, in 1921, as Wright's "peaceful American penetration."[4]

Because of Berlage's extensive publications and numerous lectures, historians have taken too much for granted that he—as the "Nestor" of modern Dutch architecture—started the trend of interest in Wright by publishing articles acclaiming his work.[5] This accounting disregards the fact that Dutch magazines had already focused on American architecture before Berlage's trip, and that many Dutch architects had traveled to the United States before Berlage. For instance, J. A. van Straaten worked as an architect in America between 1883 and 1892; Jan Frederick Staal spent six months there from 1901 to 1902, when he certainly visited New York and Chicago; and J. L. M. Lauweriks made a trip to the United States in 1909. With such interest displayed by architects, it is reasonable to conclude that American architecture in the Netherlands was already a subject of discussion when Berlage embarked on his trip in 1911, and that other Dutch architects who visited America also played an important part in bringing Wright's work to public attention.[6]

From this initial interest, two different perceptions of Wright eventually emerged that mirrored the positions, respectively, of De Stijl and the Amsterdam School. While De Stijl championed an abstracted, industrial ideal, the Amsterdam School emphasized the creative spirit of the architect.[7] Though both groups shared the same goal, "the betterment of society through contact with its art" (a goal that Wright himself shared), the means to achieving this "betterment" differed.[8] On a large scale, the perception of Wright as an "industrial" architect by De Stijl and as a "romantic" by Berlage and the Amsterdam School rests squarely in the center of the debate between the Functionalists and the more romantic architects.[9]

The expressionist Amsterdam School, which counted Hendricus Theodorus Wijdeveld, Michel de Klerk, Jan Staal, and Piet Kramer as members, paralleled Wright in its idealistic, organic approach to design. Interest in the inherent expressive nature of materials and in vernacular forms of architecture, and a belief in the individual genius of the architect, earned the group their "romantic" label. Visual similarity between their work and Wright's can be seen in the horizontalism of Wright's Prairie houses and of the Amsterdam School's buildings, a look that in the latter case may have been intended as a foil to the popularity in Holland of the neo-Gothic with its vertical lines. While these connections alone do not imply influence, Wright certainly served as a catalyst for the debate in the Netherlands between romantics and Functionalists—a debate that the Functionalists finally won, thus imprinting the way Wright's influence on Dutch architecture has been charted.

Historians' emphasis on De Stijl's limited interpretation of Wright as an "industrial architect" has resulted in the exaggeration of his influence on members of the group, who championed a rationalist vision of art and architecture. De Stijl formed in 1917 as an aggressively "rational" aesthetic group of architects and painters; a few of its members had personal contact with Wright, and many of their works bear a striking resemblance to his. But the question of influence, both of Wright on De Stijl and of De Stijl on Wright, has been misrepresented. As a group, De Stijl identified with Wright's interest in the potential of the machine for society and art. They saw Wright as an architect who, early in his career, had great expectations for the role of the machine in society and who was therefore a precursor of the "neue Sachlichkeit," the new objectivity or rational aesthetic. Gerrit Thomas Rietveld's (1888–1964) copies of Wright's Avery Coonley House chairs, made for Robert van 't Hoff's Verloop Villa in Huis ter Heide just outside Utrecht (1914–15), for example, can be seen as an example of Wright's direct influence; they can also be seen as an early step toward Rietveld's development of furniture prototypes suited for industrial production, a move that was influenced by Pieter Jan Christopher Klaarhamer and others.[10]

By the same token, historians have exaggerated the influence exerted by De Stijl on Wright. Kenneth Frampton, for example, states that such an influence

Figure 3.1

J. N. Verloop summer house, Huis ter
Heide, 1914–15. Robert van 't Hoff,
architect. (NAI 014752)

first emerges rather hesitantly in the Mesa project of 1932 and then again in the
Malcolm House of 1932–34, the first of a long series of so-called Usonian houses
dating from 1934 to 1950. He further asserts that Wright adopted De Stijl's spatial concept, though not the typical De Stijl neoplastic palette of primary colors.[11]
However, nothing in this argument actually substantiates the influence of De Stijl
on Wright; moreover, no reference is made to source material.

A discussion of Wright's meaning to some of the individual members of De
Stijl will help clarify the varying degrees and mechanics of influence. Robert van
't Hoff (1887–1979), a founding member of the group, was the first De Stijl architect to be significantly influenced by direct contact with Wright, and as a result he and his work became important instruments in the dissemination of
Wright's work to other group members. After his father gave him a copy of the
Sonderheft in 1913, he became so enthusiastic about Wright that he traveled to
America to study his architecture in situ.[12] He visited Wright's Oak Park house
and the Unity Temple, Midway Gardens, and the Larkin Building; he was also the
first Dutch architect to meet Wright, and they apparently discussed the possibility of collaborating on a design for a house and adjoining museum.[13] Wright,
however, does not mention such a collaboration.

Prior to this time, English country-house architecture was a major stylistic
source for Dutch architecture, and for van 't Hoff, Wijdeveld, and Jan Wils in
particular. Wright's influence, however, moved van 't Hoff to turn from designs
inspired by the rural English model, with the characteristic central hall acting as
the connecting element between all the rooms, toward an abstract architecture
realized with the help of modern building techniques. This new style is seen immediately in van 't Hoff's villa for J. N. Verloop in Huis ter Heide (Fig. 3.1).

The villa, with its cruciform plan, dominant horizontal planes, and low over-hanging roof, has the standard features of Wright's Prairie Style houses. Van 't Hoff's new use of reinforced concrete as a building material also accorded with his political convictions: a member of the Communist Party, he anticipated that a rationalization of the building process would produce improved working conditions.[14]

The country villa van 't Hoff designed for A. B. Henny in Huis ter Heide (1919; Fig. 3.2) shows a refinement of the Verloop model. While similar in detail to the earlier villa, the overall effect is radically different and shows van 't Hoff's grad-ual move toward abstraction in his designs. The closed course of windows in the Verloop design is transformed into large areas of glass without mullions; sloping roofs become flat; unbroken wall surfaces form a counterbalance to the domi-nant horizontal planes. Despite these early examples, however, after 1919 Wright's influence is no longer apparent in van 't Hoff's designs: the American architect's stylistic impact was not permanent.[15]

When van 't Hoff joined in establishing De Stijl, he brought his first-hand ex-perience of Wright's work to the notice of other members of the group. Van 't Hoff showed his extensive visual documentation of Wright's architecture to J. J. P. Oud (1890–1963) during one of their first meetings, possibly the first occasion that Oud saw any of Wright's work.[16] In the case of Oud we have another ex-ample of influences that are more complex than has thus far been assumed. For instance, the generally accepted account of Oud and Wright exaggerates the im-portance of the personal relationship the two architects shared.[17] In fact, their con-

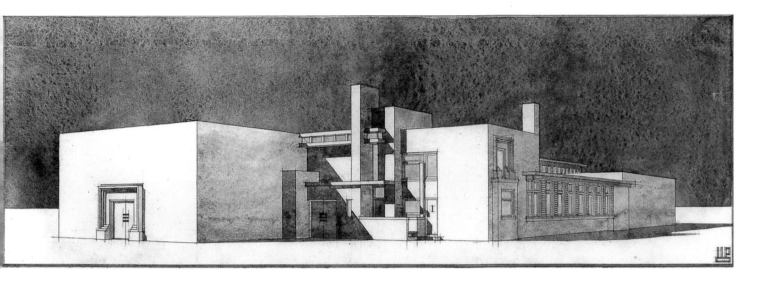

Figure 3.3
Factory design, Purmerend, 1919.
Jacobus Johannes Pieter Oud, architect.
(NAI 003277)

tact was slight: over the years they exchanged a few brief, formal letters, but met on only one occasion, in Paris in May 1952, probably in connection with the "Sixty Years of Living Architecture" exhibition, which Oud was coordinating; they immediately quarreled, however, bringing an end to their contact.[18] Moreover, Oud wrote considerably less about Wright than his list of publications might suggest, because his article on Wright's influence on European architecture was reprinted several times.[19]

Oud's design for a factory in Purmerend (1919; Fig. 3.3) is often cited as an example of Wright's influence. However, examination of the design shows a complex interaction of parts: the factory has a Berlagian left half and a Wrightian right half, while the recessed central section shows Oud's developing architectural sense of cubism and neoplasticism. Oud designed the factory while studying Wright's work closely; in 1918 he wrote about Wright's creation of a "new plasticity" in the Robie House in *De Stijl* magazine.[20] Oud expressed his sense of this "new plasticity" in the central section of the factory, with its asymmetrical arrangement of interpenetrating vertical and horizontal masses, but chose to combine the section with other elements that reflected other aesthetics.[21]

Although Wright's influence is clearly visible in the Purmerend factory design and Oud at one point declared that the road to Cubism in architecture had been paved by Wright,[22] he later emphatically denied Wright's influence. Instead he insisted: "I know something about these cubist 'dynamics' because the first attempts (from 1917: see *Wasmuth's Monatshefte*, volumes 1–2) were produced by me. Cubism in architecture goes back to Mondrian, not to Wright: I introduced

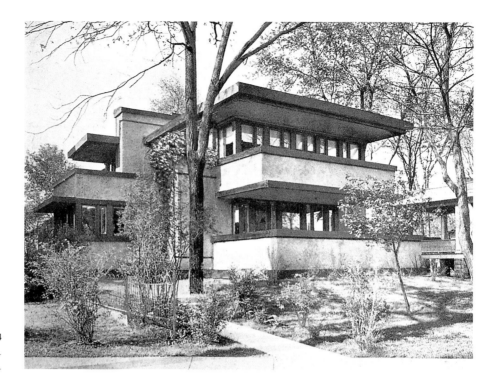

Mondrian's ideas into architecture."[23] With these protests, Oud sought to secure his own position in the international debate. The influence of Wright prompted a temporary swing in Oud's early work that, for opportunistic reasons, he later refused to acknowledge.[24]

Wright's impact on De Stijl architect Jan Wils (1891–1972) was, by contrast, considerable. Wils—who, like van 't Hoff, had previously modeled his interior spaces on English country-house architecture—first learned of Wright's work in 1914 when he began working in Berlage's office.[25] Wright's Prairie houses were, Wils believed, better geared to modern living because the rooms connected in an open manner, allowing free movement throughout the house.[26] Beginning in 1916, Wils combined Wrightian elements with local building types,[27] but eventually his explorations resulted in a full-fledged Wrightian design: the pavilion in the municipal park in Groningen (1917), which, strongly indebted to the Robie House (see Fig. 1.5), develops a Prairie Style composition quite literally.[28]

In late 1917 Wils joined the De Stijl group, and from 1918 on his work reflects the dilemma of whether to work in the style of Wright or De Stijl. Wils wrote that in Wright's work internal space is reflected in the exterior view and that, by using this concept, Wils could express a "closed" plasticity with volumes that advanced and receded on a purely constructional basis.[29] Despite his use of what he considered to be a Wrightian technique, Wils's designs were heavier and more austere than Wright's, of a somewhat monumental order. In comparison with

Figure 3.5
Café-restaurant-hotel De Dubbele
Sleutel, Woerden, 1919. Jan Wils,
architect. (NAI 012327)

Wright's relatively light and open Gale House (1909; Fig 3.4), for example, Wils's café-restaurant-hotel De Dubbele Sleutel (1919; Fig. 3.5) appears as an asymmetrical grouping of spaces that project themselves like monolithic masses into a cubist composition.

In 1919 Wils disassociated himself from De Stijl; from this point on he evolved an entirely individual and independent architectonic idiom.[30] His work is difficult to place, falling between functionalism and the Amsterdam School, reflecting at once an intellectual and an emotional approach to architecture.[31] Because of the De Stijl influence Wils appeared to be more "modern" than he actually was, a fact further supported by his close ties with the Hague School.

The term "Hague School" is used to denote a cubist building style typical of The Hague in the 1920s and 1930s and realized by architects, such as Wils, Johannes Duiker, and Bernard Bijvoet, who were influenced by Berlage, Wright, and De Stijl. This style made use of austere brick wall surfaces with expressive horizontal articulation provided by the addition of concrete bands in the facades, protruding canopies, wide window boxes, and projecting eaves. These details accentuated, as we have seen in Wils's work, often asymmetrical compositions of cubist building-masses with spatially interpenetrating volumes that recall Wright. The whole served to give organic expression to the more or less free organization of the designs based on a search for a compositional harmony between a "dynamically floating" horizontalism and a "monumental" verticalism.[32] The early

work of Duiker and Bijvoet in particular shows the influence of Wright: their design for the State Academy in Amsterdam (1917) consisted of a complex organized around a series of closed interior courtyards with a varied articulation of the interior building volumes expressed on the exterior, recalling Wright's design for Unity Temple.[33]

For each of these individuals, and for a broad range of other Dutch architects as well, Wright served as a starting point, an inspiration, and a catalyst. Willem Marinus Dudok (1884–1974), for example, who remained independent of the Hague School, the Amsterdam School, and De Stijl, saw himself, like Wright, as a "building poet." Although his work assumed an entirely individual position within Dutch architecture,[34] Dudok's interest in Wright appears to be typical of his colleagues: Wright's designs allowed a broad spectrum of aesthetic possibilities, from modernist to romantic, theatrical, and even utopian elements, allowing architects of divergent ideologies to project their own vision into his work or, conversely, to see their vision reflected in his work.

Wright's vision found no greater reflection than in the work and ideas of Hendricus Theodorus Wijdeveld (1885–1987; Fig. 3.6). As the editor-in-chief of *Wendingen,* the main outlet for expressionist architects in the Netherlands, Wijdeveld related closely to Wright's more "romantic" side. Discussions of Wright's influence in the Netherlands have focused little on Wijdeveld, a curious fact since he came into contact with Wright's work early, published seven special *Wendingen* issues on Wright in 1925, and, among Dutch architects, had the most long-lasting and intensive personal contact with the famous American.[35] Critic Lewis Mumford asserted that no other architect was as close to Wright:

I know no one else who stands closer to him in abundance of gifts,
in creative capacity, in imaginative ebullience, in range and vision, than

Figure 3.7
Beach cottage, Zandvoort, 1915
(now destroyed). Hendricus
Theodorus Wijdeveld, architect.
(Bernard F. Eilers, photographer;
Nederlands Fotoarchief 194)

you do. It is as if nature, having brought forth Wright, was a little anxious as to what might happen if some accident should stop him in mid career and so, almost a generation later, produced a second Wright, in another part of the world, blessed with the same store of gifts, but with all the many marks of individuality that place and time and temperament and experience produce. This often seems to happen in the world: Shakespeare and Marlowe, Goethe and Schiller! And there it happened once again.[36]

Wijdeveld and Wright shared more than stylistic similarities; they shared similar visions and dreams. Both architects likewise had dominant personalities, and although they had a high regard for each other, they also came into conflict. After one meeting, Wright commented that Wijdeveld was an even greater egotist than himself, which surprised him: "I thought I was the limit."[37]

During the 1910s, Wijdeveld used Wright's architecture as a means to distance himself from the classical formal language of his first building, the country house Endymion in Bloemendaal (1909–10), and to embrace a form of architecture that had representational significance. This early phase of influence resulted in designs that are almost copies of Wright's work. Typical examples are a design for a country house on the river Vecht (1914) and a small beach cottage in Zand-voort (1915; Fig. 3.7).[38] Wrightian influences in both include the horizontality of the composition, the course of identical windows, the colored facade tiles, the

stained-glass windows, the flowerpot terraces, and the roof structure. The most immediate counterpart for the latter is Wright's Avery Coonley House in Riverside, Illinois (1906–8); although much more elaborate than Wijdeveld's house, it also features a decorative exterior tile pattern and upper-floor living quarters, for instance.

Wright's presence in Wijdeveld's designs, however, extended beyond the exterior and into the interior. In many of his country-houses Wijdeveld, like Wright, designed specialized spaces to focus and define the attention of their inhabitants. Even in an early design like that for Endymion, each domestic function is allocated a separate, individually designed room, with the drawing room and the living room arranged around central hearths. The June 1919 issue of *Wendingen,* an issue dedicated to contemporary designs for interiors, displays Wijdeveld's interest in what can be called a "theatricalization of living." Wijdeveld included two studies for interior designs, "Study for an Actor's House" and "Study for a Musician's House." Both feature large open interiors with spaces defined by changing forms and heights in the ceilings and floors and separate, partly unenclosed corner spaces. The inclusion in the same issue of an article by Wils on Wright accompanied by two illustrations, an interior drawing of the Avery Coonley House (Fig. 3.8) and a photograph of the Susan Lawrence Dana House in Springfield, Illinois (1902–4), reinforces the generally Wrightian details of Wijdeveld's designs. But Wijdeveld takes his idea of spatial specialization a step further by vi-

sually inhabiting the space: in the musician's house, for example, Wijdeveld designed performance platforms, where he depicts a group of musicians playing,
with casual seating areas around the hearths for listeners (Fig. 3.9).

   Wijdeveld's interest in Wright never led to copying; instead their shared interests spanned Wijdeveld's career. For both architects, a close relationship to nature was essential. Wright's designs are rarely symmetrical; he sought, instead, to
suggest natural growth and evolution.[39] The transition from the building to the
landscape had to be as smooth as possible. Both architects used window boxes
and terraces to effect this transition physically, and the use of stained-glass windows and other decorations that found their inspiration in organic forms likewise
reaffirmed associations with nature.

   Following Ruskin, Wright tended to emphasize the weight of his buildings at
ground level, so as to reinforce visually the grip they had on the soil. The next
higher level opened up to allow in air and light.[40] Wijdeveld, too, used this basic
model. His country houses, for example, always show a clear distinction between
the base, the second floor, and the roof, all of which are nevertheless harmo-
niously integrated. Similarly, he frequently emphasized the way the building stood
rooted in the soil by cladding the first layer in brick.

   Despite such similarities, there are unmistakable differences in the way both
architects set their buildings in the landscape. Although he designed gardens,
Wright usually adapted to the landscape, achieving a synthesis between building

Figure 3.10
Plan for a residential tower, undated.
Hendricus Theodorus Wijdeveld,
architect. (NAI 011598)

Figure 3.11 *(below)*
Model for Broadacre City, 1934.
FLW, architect. (Skot Wiedemann,
photographer; FLWA 3402.0090)

Figure 3.12
National Park, Amsterdam (city),
Haarlem (nature), Zandvoort (sea),
1926. Hendricus Theodorus Wijdeveld,
architect. (NAI 006380)

and nature. Wijdeveld, in contrast, when given the opportunity by his clients, would select a site and create a staged relationship between house and garden, as illustrated by his houses Endymion, De Wachter in Amersfoort (1922–28), and De Bouw in Hilversum (1927–30). Indeed, until after World War II Wijdeveld continued to draw heavily on English turn-of-the-century country-house precedent as designed by architects such as C. F. A. Voysey and Sir Edwin Lutyens. Wright was more "modern" than Wijdeveld in his approach to the landscape.

On a larger scale, Wijdeveld's designs for residential tower-houses, which probably date to the early 1930s and possibly to after his initial visit with Wright in 1931, are visually similar to some of Wright's residential plans based on complex geometric forms, such as St. Mark's-in-the-Bouwerie (1929), which Wright planned for New York City but never built (Fig. 3.10; cf. Fig. 3.16). Both tower designs are based on plans with polygonal models and glass exteriors and cantilevered floors.

The two architects also shared an interest in urban planning designs directed at the creation of "ideal living communities" in more rural environments. Wright had already demonstrated his attraction to community planning in 1901 with his "Home in Prairie Town" and with his plan for Broadacre City (1934–35), in which he proposed a decentralized grid of communities separated by open spaces (Fig. 3.11). In a similar vein, in 1926–27 Wijdeveld had envisioned a national park, with Amsterdam representing the city, Haarlem representing nature, and Zandvoort representing the sea—a hypothetical zoned reorganization of the Netherlands into tower communities in which the historical cities would be preserved, with people moving from them into the towers (Fig. 3.12). Both designs center

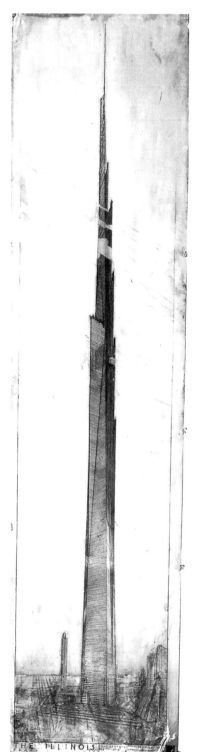

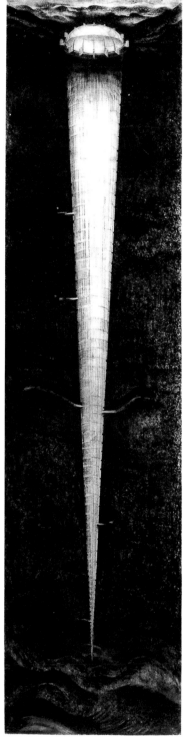

Figure 3.13 *(right)*
The "Illinois," or Mile High project,
Chicago, Illinois, 1956. FLW, architect.
(FLWA 5617.002)

Figure 3.14 *(far right)*
"Plan for the Impossible, 15 Miles into
the Earth," 1944. Hendricus Theodorus
Wijdeveld, designer. (NAI 011429)

around population nuclei that are connected by motorways and punctuated by skyscrapers set in the midst of woods and pastureland. While neither scheme is particularly practical, Wright's plans were a form of social criticism based in a complex vision of American society, whereas Wijdeveld's scheme is based in a metaphysical belief in the power of nature to improve society and humankind.

The two architects resembled each other also in the fact that they both generated fantastic designs. In Wright's case, this applies in particular to his later designs such as the Mile High in Chicago (1956; Fig. 3.13), his fantastic plan for an office tower of cantilevered floors that would reach one mile into the atmosphere. Although he could not realistically expect that it would ever be built, Wright nevertheless promoted the idea actively. An example of the same implausible idealism in Wijdeveld's work is his "Plan for the Impossible, 15 miles into the Earth" (1944; Fig. 3.14), a proposal for a research center dedicated to studying the earth's core that consisted of a fifteen-mile-deep hole in the earth roofed by an enormous glass dome. Surrounding the dome were skyscrapers designed to accommodate the researchers and students who would flock from all over the world to take part in the research. By comparison to this research center, a project idealistically intended to advance scientific knowledge and to promote international cooperation and harmony, Wright's Mile High seems merely an exercise in braggadocio.[41]

A second example of Wijdeveld's utopian bent is his design for a "Hall of Life" (1948; Fig. 3.15), one of a series of six drawings accompanying his self-published book *A Work in Progress*.[42] In this story a professor (Wijdeveld, in the guise of a professor at the University of North Carolina, a position he actually held) and his students go on a journey together seeking universal truths. They see the Wall of Life, a rock wall transformed into a representation of the history of the planet earth, and the Museums of Memory, a place for exhibiting excavated artifacts and the principles of the world's evolution. Finally, they arrive at the Hall of Life. Like Wright's Guggenheim Museum in New York (1943–59), Wijdeveld's Hall of Life has a concentric design oriented toward a dome. The Hall was intended to house a large auditorium in which two thousand people could view a holographically projected "film" about the creation of the world and its natural history. Inside the building a spiral walkway leads to the auditorium, where chairs are arranged in concentric rows from which the public gazes up at the dome. The Guggenheim has a similar concentric form that widens as it spirals upward into an open center, ensuring that one never loses contact with the dome. Wright also initially imagined that movies could be projected onto the domed ceiling and viewed from reclining seats on the museum's floor below. Despite these parallels, Wijdeveld's design was part of a wildly fictional work describing an idealized vision of the potential for the study of history and science to improve humankind.[43] In contrast with Wright's very real achievement in the Guggenheim, the Hall of Life is a fantastic utopian project, wrapped up in Wijdeveld's sense of a "new religion" and fascination with theater, light, sound, and movement.

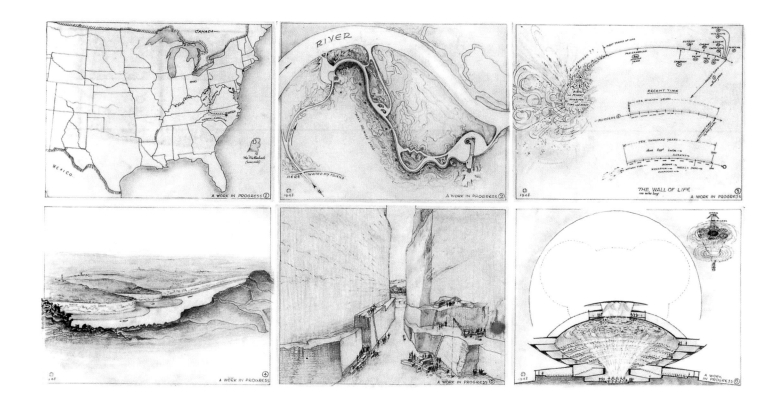

Figure 3.15

Illustration for *A Work in Progress*, with Hall of Life depicted at bottom right corner, 1948. Hendricus Theodorus Wijdeveld, designer. (NAI 011711)

For both architects, this utopian strain extended to an interest in education and in creating communal colleges for fellowship. Little known is the fact that Wijdeveld exerted a strong influence on Wright with regard to his college, the Taliesin Fellowship.[44] From 1927—thus earlier than Wright—Wijdeveld toyed with the idea of founding an international community on the shores of Holland's Loosdrechtse Plassen. He published these plans along with an introduction and program in the booklet "Naar een internationale werkgemeenschap" (1931), which appeared in English under the title "An International Guild," and sent copies all over the world.[45] Among the recipients was Wright, with whom he had corresponded since 1923.[46] Wright subsequently extended several invitations to Wijdeveld to come and work with him on just such a project.[47] On 12 July 1930, before the booklet's official publication, Wijdeveld sent a telegram saying how he longed to realize his fellowship plans but wavered between choosing Wisconsin, where Wright lived, or the Netherlands for the location.[48]

A great deal had to be done before the two architects could begin their joint venture and set up what was to become the Taliesin Fellowship: Wright's buildings in Hillside, Wisconsin, were in ruins and required drastic renovations. Wright warned Wijdeveld that they still had a daunting amount of work to do, that they

were in for many disappointments, and that he (Wright) was not used to working with other people but that the time now seemed ripe for him to do so. He
felt convinced that their similar outlook on life and attitude toward work would
make him and Wijdeveld "comrades in arms."[49] Brimming with enthusiasm, Wijdeveld planned to move into part of the Taliesin complex with his family once
renovation was completed. This physical proximity would enable the two architects to continue working on their plans for the fellowship, and Wijdeveld could
support himself by working in Wright's office.[50] In preparation for their collaboration, Wijdeveld stayed with Wright for several months beginning in October
1931. It was during this period that the brochure "The Taliesin Fellowship" (1933)
was compiled, based on Wijdeveld's publication "An International Guild." In a
letter from Taliesin Wijdeveld wrote to his wife, Ellen:

> Wright says he hadn't read the proposals in the yellow book because he
> thought it was in Dutch. I put them to him and read him the program
> out loud. A few hours later Wright's own proposals had been completely
> revised—shortened and amended to incorporate half of my own interna-
> tional guild plan. Here and there *word for word* even. It seems I've drawn
> up a plan that even Wright can go along with. We're now elaborating and
> revising this plan and intend to have it printed.[51]

In this brochure Wijdeveld is cited as the college principal and head of the architectural department, and his wife is listed as the "lady principal."[52] Later, Wright
would mention that Wijdeveld had influenced his plans, writing: "When he [Wij-
develd] came to America in 1929 [Wright noted the date incorrectly; it was actually 1931] I had in mind a quite different affair for Taliesin than the one I eventually worked out."[53]

In the end, however, the collaboration was stillborn. Wijdeveld returned to
Holland in January 1932, and in February Wright informed him that he had to
call off the plan for them to work together in America: bringing Wijdeveld's family to a foreign country was too big a responsibility for Wright to accept.[54] This
abrupt end to the architects' collaboration must have come as a huge disappointment to Wijdeveld, though no record remains of his response. That same year
Wright proceeded to launch the college on his own.

In the ensuing years Wright wrote to Wijdeveld on at least two occasions ask-
ing him to become the college principal.[55] Again, Wijdeveld's response to these
letters has not been preserved. After his initial disappointment, he was perhaps
no longer interested in the post. In the meantime, in any event, he, along with
the architect Erich Mendelsohn and the painter Amédée Ozenfant, set about establishing another college, the Académie Européenne Méditerranée, in Cavalière
in the south of France, though these plans, too, failed to materialize when the
first new college buildings were gutted by fire. But the idea of founding a fellowship continued to haunt him, and in 1938 he opened his international guild

Elckerlyc in Lage Vuursche, the Netherlands, which remained open until well after the onset of World War II.[56]

Wijdeveld and Wright reconsidered the possibility of a collaboration after the war, though again Wright wrote telling Wijdeveld that he felt too old to collaborate with anyone.[57] In the summer of 1948, however, Wijdeveld did spend a few weeks with Wright during which he gave "Sunday morning lectures" at the Taliesin Fellowship. Wright also arranged for Wijdeveld to act as a visiting professor in the College of Architecture at the University of Southern California in Los Angeles in 1948–49, where he lectured in aesthetics in architecture,[58] a subject for which Wijdeveld, according to Wright, was well suited. Indeed, Wright regarded his Dutch colleague above all as an aesthetician: "a tireless worker; an enthusiast beyond compare with an artistic sensitivity certainly beyond Mendelsohn, Gropius and others: a true aesthetician I should say."[59] Lewis Mumford was so struck by the similarities between Wright and Wijdeveld that he suggested in 1959, when Wright died, that the Taliesin Fellowship should be taken over by Wijdeveld. He was convinced that no one was better qualified than Wijdeveld to continue the college in the spirit of Wright.[60]

To what extent was Wright's Taliesin Fellowship comparable to Wijdeveld's Elckerlyc? Both were at once architectural firms and residential colleges: not only did the students work together, but they also led a communal and strictly regimented life of learning and recreation. Both colleges paid ample attention to the arts in general, rather than being confined to architecture and town planning; the curricula included musical appreciation as well as, at the Taliesin Fellowship, film screenings and, at Elckerlyc, visits to the theater.

One notable difference between the two colleges lay in the importance attached to craft and practical work, which occupied a prominent place at Wright's college. Students at Taliesin served kitchen duty and farmed. While Wijdeveld clearly valued practical training in the course work and stressed the self-reliant character of his guild, he did not always put these ideas into practice. For instance, nothing came of the projected vegetable garden at Elckerlyc, nor did the students turn out real merchandise, as they did at the Bauhaus. There were no machines at Elckerlyc, only drawing boards and an extensive library. Wijdeveld's Elckerlyc was also much smaller (it trained a total of twenty students) and operated for a much shorter period than Wright's Taliesin Fellowship, though they do have in common that neither put forth any famous architects. The cult of personality that characterized both colleges may indeed have hampered students' development.

Even as the two architects communicated in 1930–31 about the possibility of collaborating on the Taliesin Fellowship, Wijdeveld made another significant contribution to the dissemination of Wright's work by arranging for a major exhibition to be mounted at Amsterdam's Stedelijk Museum in May 1931 (Figs. 3.16 and 3.17).[61] The exhibition, "Frank Lloyd Wright, Architect," had previously been on tour in the United States, and Wright asked Wijdeveld to arrange for it to be shown in the Netherlands. Wijdeveld agreed: not only did he admire Wright's work, but he had already organized and designed a number of exhibitions on previous occasions. Although no money was available to publish an accompanying catalog, a special issue of the Dutch architectural weekly the *Bouwkundig weekblad* devoted to Wright's work marked the occasion, reproducing several texts by Wright and an introduction by Wijdeveld.[62] In this introduction, Wijdeveld rather oddly pointed out the unconventional character of Wright's architecture and urged that Wright's work should not be condemned for its seeming unorthodoxy. He was very likely responding to the growing criticism by Dutch functionalist architects, who dominated the architectural debate in the Netherlands in the 1920s and 1930s.[63]

In the years that followed, criticism of Wright's work continued to mount. Fallingwater (1934–37), for example, was described in 1938 as a "strange" house.[64] In another instance, Wright's design for the Price Tower, an office building in Bartlesville, Oklahoma (1952–56), was called a "peculiar" building because of its unusual construction: the building weighed only a seventh of other similar-sized buildings.[65] And of the Desert House (1950), which he built for his son David, it was said that the "unusual" design made for "a house that looks like a monster or rattlesnake from some angles."[66] These comments were typical during this less accepting period.

Despite this criticism, Wright's work continued to receive popular attention. Notable in particular is the visit of the "Sixty Years of Living Architecture" exhibition mounted in the Ahoy Building in Rotterdam in 1952. The exhibition had previously toured several other venues, and Wright asked Oud—rather than Wijdeveld, who was professionally isolated[67]—to supervise it in the Netherlands. To contextualize the exhibited works, Oud suggested featuring a number of objects, such as a fountain that evoked the Fallingwater House, flowers, cactuses, boulders, animal skins, exotic rugs, and, last but not least, two living parrots. In a letter to Wright Oud wrote: "No, don't be afraid; it does not at all look like 'kitsch' but gives the whole show a bit of the atmosphere that your houses must have in reality."[68] But Oud was mistaken: the appointments were carried out in poor taste and looked overdone. Wright's work was reduced to a caricature of itself.

Despite its kitschy appearance, the exhibition was a popular success: no fewer than ten thousand people visited.[69] It was widely covered by the daily and trade press, where it was warmly received. Reviews tended to focus on the utopian aspects and exuberance of Wright's work, and one writer drew a parallel between Wright and Wijdeveld, pointing to the utopian element in the work of both architects.[70] Although this might be construed as a positive response to Wright's work, this was not in fact the case. At that time people were afraid that Wright might exercise a negative influence on young architects; some claimed his architecture was so exuberant that it was a dangerous example for those who lacked his talent. Implicit in these complaints was the objection that Wright was not sufficiently dogmatic.[71]

From the end of the war until shortly after Wright's death in 1959 articles on his work appeared occasionally in Dutch magazines. Many of these took stock of the impact he had had on Dutch architecture in the 1910s and 1920s: in short, they acknowledged Wright's influence on Dutch architecture in the past. They also tended to focus on the unusual structure of his buildings, describing them in an objective style, as shown by this report on a design for a mile-high skyscraper (probably the Mile High Illinois; see Fig. 3.12): "He has envisaged his latest cosmos-scraper as a steel colossus sheathed in a golden aluminium skin. This he has chosen to site along one of the lakes near Chicago [*sic*] where, glistening in the sunshine, it stands eye in eye with the flabbergasted sun. Construction costs are put at 330 million [florins]."[72] Another article depicted Wright's Research Laboratory Tower in Racine, Wisconsin (1943–50), alongside a concrete diving tower in Miami, Florida, by the obscure architect Igor Polevitsky.[73] This spurious comparison suggests that Wright had by then lost the special significance he once had in the Netherlands.[74]

This preoccupation with the unusual structural aspects of Wright's work and the contradictory judgment that his architecture was overexuberant, even strange, may have a simple explanation, one that rests in the fact that functionalism had temporarily won the architectural debate in Holland. The following comment from 1957 captures the consensus on his work:

> Once a pioneer of new architecture, Frank Lloyd Wright has now lost his way and, in his eagerness to please, has neglected function for form. This is the view taken by most contemporary architectural experts and Functionalists. . . . Wright claims that Sullivan's famous statement ["Form follows function"] was misinterpreted in the Netherlands. We have taken it to mean functionalism in the literal sense, whereas it was apparently meant to point to the need for an organic architecture. Organic architecture was indeed introduced by Frank Lloyd Wright. But then he went wrong: his architecture was not organic but romantic. The battle began.[75]

Even the independent architect Dudok, who had enthusiastically acclaimed Wright's architecture in 1926, thought Wright had taken the utopian character of some of his designs—the Guggenheim Museum and the Mile High Illinois, for example—far too far.[76] Wijdeveld alone rejected this new attitude toward Wright. As we have seen, the Guggenheim actually served as a source of inspiration in Wijdeveld's own work. It is therefore not surprising that Wijdeveld's work in this period, like Wright's, is dismissed as overly utopian.

After a long period of relative unpopularity, Wright's work is currently enjoying a reappraisal. A number of other contemporary architects have discovered a fascination for Wright's work, including Rem Koolhaas of OMA, who finds particular significance in Broadacre City.[77] Among younger architects, Ben van Berkel, Kees Christiaanse, and Wiel Arets cite as especially important the enormous overhangs Wright used in his country houses, the link he established between his houses and the surrounding countryside, and his skillful use of new technology, as shown by his Research Laboratory Tower in Racine.[78] And yet these three architects produce work that is very different from Wright's. It is as if we were back at the beginning of this century when architects working independently and steered by a totally different vision saw their own ideas projected in Wright's work, though now, of course, architects have an added advantage: access to a broader critical and historical grasp of Wright's long relationship to the Netherlands.

FOUR: WRIGHT AND ITALY

A RECOLLECTION

Bruno Zevi

Just before the American Academy in Rome decided that you could no longer keep it here, in the United States (I speak of course of the Italian Renaissance), and that it should be sent back to where it came from, we experienced in the peninsula a short, splendid season of true architectural culture.

That moment was dominated by Frank Lloyd Wright, the genius of the twenty-first century. And when in 1951 he came to Italy to receive honorary citizenship in Palazzo Vecchio, Florence, and the degree *honoris causa* in the Palazzo Ducale of Venice, it seemed like the acme of a sublime itinerary in space. We were buoyed with joy and delight, and could never suspect what was to come with the return of a fake Renaissance filtered through French and American Beaux Arts and the subsequent explosion of a most foolish eclecticism under the title of Postmodern.

My story starts on 21 January 1935 in Turin. Edoardo Persico, a great architectural critic still quite unknown in the United States, delivered a lecture called "Architectural Prophecy." Fascism was then at its peak, and Persico was an uncompromising antifascist for whom architecture served as a barometer of a country's civilization. He spoke of Wright's vision as being the very root of the modern movement and the unique embodiment of a desperate quest for freedom, individuality, and the right to diversity in contemporary society. So the Taliesin master became a rallying point for the fight against dictatorship, not only in Italy, but also, for instance, at Harvard University's Graduate School of Design, where in 1941 a group of students, mainly foreign, published a pamphlet celebrating Wright's stature against the skeptical teaching of Walter Gropius.

In fact, Persico inspired in fascist Italy three masterpieces of antifascist architecture: the Casa del Fascio at Como, by Giuseppe Terragni; the magnificent Florence Railway Station, by Giovanni Michelucci and his group; and Sabaudia, the

Figure 4.1

The first Italian edition of *Towards an Organic Architecture,* by Bruno Zevi (Turin: Einaudi, 1945), featuring Fallingwater on its cover.

democratic city on a human scale planned by Luigi Piccinato and his partners. I do not mean that these works were directly stimulated by Wright. No, but they could be built because there was in Italy a revolutionary atmosphere, instigated by Persico and by Giuseppe Pagano, editor of the magazine *Casabella,* who died in a Nazi camp.

We leap to 1945. The first architectural book to appear after the war was my *Towards an Organic Architecture.* Because of a shortage of glossy paper, it contained only one photo, and that was on the cover: Fallingwater at Bear Run (Fig. 4.1). Italian architects lived on this image for months; it alone was enough to inject them with vitality.

In 1945 the Association for an Organic Architecture (APAO) was founded in Rome, and it soon had outposts in Turin, Genoa, Venice, Bologna, Florence, Naples, and Palermo. A Milan group was also federated with the association but had no formal chapter.

Three designs reflect the animus of the time immediately following the war: the Fosse Ardeatine Memorial on the outskirts of Rome, in memory of victims

Figure 4.2
Fosse Ardeatine Memorial, Rome,
1944–47. Nello Aprile, Gino Calcaprina,
Aldo Cardelli, Mario Fiorentino,
and Giuseppe Perugini, architects;
sculptures by Mirko Basaldella
and Francesco Coccia.

Figure 4.3
Rome Railway Station, 1950. Leo Calini,
engineer; Eugenio Montuori, Annibale
Vitellozzi, M. Castellazzi, V. Fadigati,
and A. Pintonello, architects.

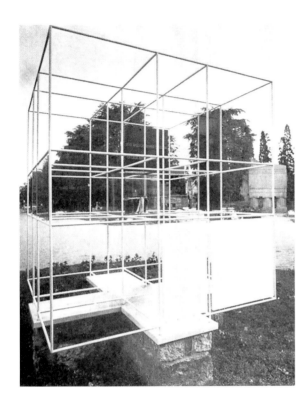

Figure 4.4
Monument to the Dead in the
Concentration Camps in Germany,
Cimitero Monumentale, Milan, 1946.
BBPR, designers.

of Nazi criminality, perhaps the best monument of its kind in the world (Fig.
4.2); a correct modern solution to the front of the Rome Railway Station, which
was about to be completed with a most awful fascist-style colonnaded portico
(Fig. 4.3); and a small, almost transparent monument in the cemetery of Milan,
dedicated to those who died in German concentration camps, designed by the
Banfi, Belgiojoso, Peresutti, and Rogers firm (BBPR; Fig. 4.4).

These were the years of postwar reconstruction and of conflicts about appropriate methods for carrying it out. We, the organic, the Wrightian architects, did
not win. In 1946 I was invited to Cleveland by the American City Planning Institute to present the opening speech at the first postwar congress of that organization, and I chose a polemical subject: "Town Planning as an Instrument of an
American Foreign Policy." This problem of town planning was, in my view, urgent. The U.S. authorities in Italy had behaved in a way that damaged efforts being made toward the renewal of democracy in that country. Especially in the south,
they connected their initiatives to the official institutions of the Italian government, which, at the bureaucratic level, were still mainly Fascist. When it came to
establishing an American embassy in Rome, the authorities followed an appallingly
anticultural course: instead of producing a courageous modern building, designed
perhaps by Wright, they bought a royal palace in via Veneto, and then, in the name
of efficiency, they ruined it.

On the whole, we were defeated. But when one fights unconditionally, with no second line of defense, one is never completely defeated. In those years, not only did we create a number of buildings conceived in the organic spirit, but, what is more relevant, we also moved a new organic approach into urban housing programs and into rural villages, such as "La Martella" near Matera (Fig. 4.5). This spirit penetrated even into industrial architecture, as seen in the Olivetti factory at Pozzuoli, near Naples (Fig. 4.6). Luigi Cosenza, its designer, was an engineer and, for a short time, a partner of Bernard Rudolfsky; he was not an architect or, even less, a design professor, but he loved Wright and molded a factory, perhaps unique, where industry and nature would meet.

I come now to the fabulous year of 1951. A splendid exhibition of Wright's work was organized at Palazzo Strozzi in Florence by Oskar Stonorov, the Philadelphia architect for the worker's union CIO, and by the art historian Carlo Ludovico Ragghianti. A legendary antifascist leader, Ragghianti had in 1944 crossed, at night, the top passageway of Florence's Ponte Vecchio, which had been mined by the Germans, to ensure contact between the Allies, encamped on the other side of the Arno, and the resistance fighters inside the city.

The 1951 exhibition of Wright's work fascinated not only Italy, but all Europe. Recognizing Wright's immeasurable greatness, the old world thanked the new for its astounding creativity. The huge Broadacre City model (see Figs. 1.14, 3.11, and 5.1) was seen in the middle of the exhibition, and full-size photo murals gave the impression of being inside the buildings and moving fluidly through their spaces. A few hours after Wright's arrival in Florence, when he visited the

exhibition and suggested some little variations, Stonorov told him gently but firmly that nothing would be changed because it had been conceived as Wright's first posthumous exhibition, only the corpse was still alive.

Count Carlo Sforza, an antifascist leader who had found refuge in the United States during the war and later became minister of foreign affairs in the democratic government, made Wright an honorary citizen of Florence (Fig. 4.7). When the Medici trumpeters sounded their instruments, Wright's daughter Iovanna fainted. It could not have happened in any other part of the globe. In Palazzo Vecchio, a masterpiece of medieval architecture, in an immense hall covered by mannerist paintings, Italy celebrated one of the greatest personalities of architectural history, if not the greatest.

Figure 4.8
Bruno Zevi and Wright, Venice, 1951.

I was with Wright from early morning to late that night. He spoke not a word about the months spent in Fiesole in 1910, not a comment on Brunelleschi's cupola of the Duomo or on Michelangelo's chapel in San Lorenzo. He was interested only in the views of the city as seen from the top of the ninety-four-meter tower designed in the fourteenth century by Arnolfo di Cambio.

In Venice there was a quite different climate. Actually, in Florence nobody really cared about Wright, except for a few hundred people who came from all parts of the peninsula. But in Venice the Taliesin master was a popular myth because the school of architecture was composed of people with a passion for Wright, from the director, Giuseppe Samonà, to the design professor, Carlo Scarpa, and Bruno Zevi, the young teacher of architectural history (Fig. 4.8). When Wright walked in the *calli* or through the *piazzette,* or when he traveled by gondola, Venetians of all social strata recognized, greeted, and applauded him. Wright was surprised and happy—such recognition had never happened to him before; indeed, he liked that much more than the solemn ceremony in the Palazzo Ducale, where he was awarded the degree *honoris causa.*

Let me mention three more episodes in the trip to Venice: In Torcello there is a little bridge with no parapets, just in front of the basilica; Wright went up alone

Figure 4.9
Carlo Scarpa *(left)*, Wright, and students,
Venice, 1951. (FLWA 6808.0026)

and, in spite of risk, danced on the bridge for quite a while in a delightful way. Then we went to Murano, to visit the glass factory. In the vestibule was a selection of products fabricated over many years. Wright looked around almost absentmindedly, then said that he wanted to buy this, this, that: five or six objects. Believe it or not, they were all designed, long ago, by Carlo Scarpa. Without knowing, Wright had generated a poet, Carlo Scarpa, who lagged behind Wright not a century, like the majority of us, not even half a century, like the deconstructivists, but perhaps only twenty or thirty years (Fig. 4.9).

In Venice Wright discovered the message of the baroque. I had selected for him a room at the Hotel Gritti, just in front of Santa Maria della Salute by Baldassare Longhena. He was astonished by the octagonal shape of the church, by the crown of explosive volutes, and especially by the two cupolas. His hands followed slowly the different profiles from the top of the church to its base alongside the lagoon. For the first time, he grasped what, without knowing it, he had rejected a priori.

Finally, we reached Rome. There were no official engagements, almost nothing to do. His wife, Olgivanna, decided to visit the Vatican. He felt that he shouldn't. So we were free to spend the day, first in the atelier of the painter-writer Carlo Levi, who made a portrait of him, then at an exquisite lunch at the

MASIERI MEMORIAL   CANAL GRANDE   VENICE
STUDENTS' LIBRARY AND DWELLING
FRANK LLOYD WRIGHT ARCHITE

Gianicolo (but far from the American Academy) with the historian of Byzantine art Sergio Bettini, and later wandering much of the afternoon around Rome, where he met the architect I love most after Wright, the baroque master Francesco Borromini.

This report on Wright and Italy must be expanded: In 1952–53 he designed for the family of one of his disciples, who died in a road accident in New York, the Masieri Memorial on the Grand Canal (Fig. 4.10; see also Figs. 5.5 and 5.6), and we fought for years to have it built. However, we lost this battle, just as those for Le Corbusier's soft and gentle hospital and Louis Kahn's Biennale were lost. The 1960s and the 1970s, as you will remember, saw a process in which the Modern Movement was deliberately confused with its opposite, the International Style. The critics who had stood for the International Style against Wright, accusing him of being romantic, escapist, utopian, and so on, now started to attack the International Style with the same arguments Wright had used for decades. This did not, however, produce a much greater appreciation of Wright's creativity.

Then came the 1980s—Philip Johnson and Michael Graves, Aldo Rossi, Ricardo Bofill, and the postmodern nausea that ended only in 1988, with the "Deconstructivist Architecture" exhibit at the Museum of Modern Art in New York.

No doubt neoacademic and postmodernist shame touched Italy too, but the organic Wrightian reaction was decisive. As far as I know, no professional institute or magazine anywhere else in the world showed itself as consistently willing to fight neoacademism and postmodernism, no matter the cost, as did the Italian Institute of Architecture and the monthly magazine *L'architettura: cronache e storia*. Only in Italy, if I am not mistaken, did Wright's stature appear in its true Michelangelesque splendor, as something that belongs to a century or so from now. We feel that we have to work hard and cheerfully to reach, in a hundred years, that "architecture as space" that Wright himself created.

To end this recollection, I must mention the principles we absorbed from Wright. On the theoretical level, Wright grasped and developed all aspects of modern architecture. In Italy, in order to fight the classical language of architecture, an anticlassical language was codified, based on seven "invariant" principles or anti-rules:

1. Listing of contents and functions, derived from William Morris and the arts and crafts movement, to which Wright subscribed in the key of the machine.

2. Asymmetry and dissonance. Indeed, the Taliesin master is the Arnold Schoenberg of architecture.

3. Antiperspective, three-dimensionality, directed to deny the boxlike building as seen from a static Renaissance point of view.

4. Four-dimensional decomposition. Wright is the father of the Dutch De Stijl movement.

5. Cantilever, shell, and membrane structures, which join to end the schism between engineering and architecture.

6. Living, dynamic, fluid space. Herein lies the very identity of Wright.

7. Continuity between inside and outside, between building and landscape, in urban texture.

Seven invariants, all employed by Wright. There is no other architect in history as powerful or sublime.

FIVE: WRIGHT AND ITALY

THE PROMISE OF ORGANIC ARCHITECTURE

Maristella Casciato

In January 1910, Frank Lloyd Wright arrived in Florence. Marginal in respect to other European centers of modern architecture, Florence seemed an ideal refuge for Wright as he sought to distance himself from the criticism that accompanied his departure from the United States in the company of Mamah Borthwick. After two months in Florence, Wright moved to the Fiesolian hills; there, in the pleasant Villa of Belvedere, he would continue his voluntary exile for another six months. It was during this period that Wright developed themes elaborated in his long essay "The Sovereignty of the Individual in the Cause of Architecture," which served as preface to the Wasmuth portfolio.[1] "Of . . . joy in living there is greater proof in Italy than elsewhere," he wrote. "Buildings, pictures and sculpture seem to be born like flowers by the roadside, to sing themselves into being. Approached in the spirit of their conception, they inspire us with the very music of life."[2]

In May 1951, Wright returned once again to Florence on the occasion of the first exhibition of his work in Italy, this time accompanied by his third wife, Olgivanna, and their daughter, Iovanna (Fig. 5.1). The forty years between the two visits had wrought tremendous change, for now Wright was a venerable eighty-four years old and internationally famous. In Florence he was ecstatically described by one onlooker as standing straight, his gaze turned toward infinity, and as having the sweetest voice.[3] For the many architects, students, and friends who came to pay him homage, Wright powerfully embodied the fascinating figure of a creative pioneer.[4]

For these Italian admirers, however, Wright also incarnated an ideal of liberty and democracy that the young postwar republic was striving to achieve. In postwar Italy, only recently liberated from authoritarianism and whose economic rebirth was in part due to American aid, Wright's contribution to modern archi-

Figure 5.1
Wright and friends at the "Sixty Years
of Living Architecture" exhibition in
Florence with the model of Broadacre
City, June 1951. Pictured are *(left to
right):* Olgivanna Wright, Wright, Bruno
Zevi *(partly obscured),* an American
friend of the Wrights, Iovanna Wright,
Carlo Ludovico Ragghianti, Count Carlo
Sforza, Oskar Stonorov, and Licia Collobi
Ragghianti.

tecture was perhaps less important than his spiritual influence. Those crucial years between the end of the war and the economic boom will be the focus of this essay, as we explore how, in architecture as well as in life, as Cesare Pavese put it, Italians "discovered Italy while looking to the men and the words in America."[5]

Spurred by a sense of urgency during postwar reconstruction, many Italian architects, young and established alike, chose Wright as their *maestro* in their quest for a liberating freshness and vitality. But who was Frank Lloyd Wright for such diverse Italian architects as Luigi Figini, Gino Pollini, Giuseppe Samonà, Carlo Scarpa, Giancarlo De Carlo, Bruno Zevi, Angelo Masieri, Gino Valle, Bruno Morasutti, Edoardo Gellner, Luigi Pellegrin, Francesco Passanti, Marcello D'Olivo, and Leonardo Ricci? Apart from his personal charisma, to what measure and in what context did Wright's thought become a renovating force for their architectural expression?

Historians have provided veiled answers to these questions.[6] If their conclusions have been less than incisive, it is perhaps because some of the architects in question are still active professionals, which makes an accurate assessment of Wright's influence on their work difficult to determine. Some scholars have described the rediscovery of Wright in post–World War II Italy as merely a short-lived episode, a superficial infatuation.[7] The question of "Wrightism" has been better addressed by Ernesto Nathan Rogers, who states that Italian architecture first absorbed Wright's themes indirectly, then concretized his forms, ad hoc, into its own language.[8] Following Rogers's cue, in this essay I address the spirit of Wrightism rather than seeking examples of direct imitation.

CHRONICLE OF A DISCOVERY

Prior to World War II in Italy, interest in Wright's work was limited. It was not until 1921 that the name Wright (surname only) finally appeared in an Italian publication, in the first issue of *Architettura e Arti Decorative*.[9] Wright was not mentioned in the context of architectural developments in the United States, however, but in the discussion of the birth of "cubism" in modern Dutch architecture. Echoing J. J. P. Oud's earlier statements in *De Stijl*, the article linked the American architect and the Como-born Sant'Elia, visionary interpreter of the futuristic "città nuova," emphasizing the fantastic nature of both men's work. The article ultimately concluded that both architects were isolated "grand masters" and labeled them mere "precursors" of truly modern architecture.[10]

This judgment was still popular in Italy as late as 1933. That year the International Exhibition of Modern Architecture at the Fifth Milanese Triennale excluded Wright from the list of ten architectural greats who were to be featured in the show. Agnolodomenico Pica, curator of the exhibition, again placed Wright on a par with Sant'Elia, continuing to judge both solely as isolated forerunners.

Also in 1933, changes were made at the Milanese magazine *La Casa bella* that would have a great impact on Wright's future reception in Italy. Tossing aside the article at the beginning and fusing the main words of the title, the newly renamed *Casabella* acquired an equally new director, the Istrian architect Giuseppe Pagano-Pogatschnig, who was flanked by Edoardo Persico as editor in chief.[11] A courageous defender of rational architecture, Pagano sympathized with the ideals of the European modern movement but had not yet moved away from the generally accepted opinions concerning Wright.[12]

Persico, in contrast, brought a more sophisticated understanding of Wright to Italy.[13] In January 1935 he gave his most famous lecture, entitled "Profezia dell'architettura" (Architectural prophecy)—the prophet in question being none other than Frank Lloyd Wright. Persico observed that modern architecture was reduced to the fatal situation in which the only possible means of expressing modernity was through technical revolution, as represented by "the perfect trinity of modern construction: glass, iron, concrete." Instead he proposed moving the emphasis from the technical to the visual. For Wright's work of the Prairie years, this meant reducing its connection with Cubism: "Cubism is yet to come, not only because we are in 1901 or 1904, but also because to define the figurative elements of this construction we must refer to the Impressionist vision, to the vision of Cézanne. . . . Wright might be considered the Cézanne of the new architecture."[14] In reformulating his question on the destiny of architecture, Persico sought the answer "beyond architecture." Following in Wright's footsteps, he concluded that "the destiny (of modern architecture), its prophecy, is to claim the fundamental liberty of the spirit."[15]

Persico's interpretation of Wright's individualism and its relationship to the collective good coincided with Wright's own proposals for liberating man from the tyranny of efficiency. In the same year as Persico's lecture (1935), Wright included this concept in a message that his son, John Lloyd, read in his father's name in Rome at the International Congress of Architecture, organized by the Fascist National Union of Architects. Emphasizing the themes explored in his Broadacre City scheme, Wright stated that the conditions existed in Italy for applying "the principles of the new pattern home." Furthermore, he included a direct address to Mussolini and his architects, entreating them to "lead their country to a modern lease on life by abandoning the old academic order and to establish this more natural and humane order."[16]

In the years that followed, *Casabella* continued to be the only Italian magazine to present Wright's work. The first special issue dedicated to Wright appeared in 1938, after Persico's death; the art critic Raffaello Giolli penned the editorial introducing the issue. Unlike Persico, Giolli separated himself from the Wrightian myth, allowing the architect's buildings to speak for themselves.[17] Giolli did, however, openly identify with the aging Wright, and especially with his sincerity and courage, qualities the critic considered necessities for renovation in architecture as well as in life.[18]

AMERICANISM AND THE ITALIAN DEVELOPMENT OF ORGANIC ARCHITECTURE

The homages of Persico, a historian, and Giolli, a critic, elucidate the significance of the myth of American individualism in Italian culture of the late 1930s.[19] Wright, along with other American "individualists" such as Herman Melville, Walt Whitman, Sinclair Lewis, William Faulkner, and John Dos Passos, to name those best known in Italy, became symbols of the progressive America of Roosevelt and his New Deal. In the words of Italo Calvino, America represented "a disorderly synthesis of all that fascism claimed to negate or to exclude."[20]

In 1939 Pasquale Carbonara published his *L'architettura in America: La civiltá nordamericana riflessa nei caratteri dei suoi edifici* (Architecture in America: North American civilization reflected in the character of its buildings), which, as the subtitle indicates, examined the "civilizing force" that shaped America's history and architecture. Although it concentrated on typological analysis of buildings, Carbonara's book made frequent reference to Wright as the "ultimate exponent of nineteenth-century American individualism" and the grand interpreter of the American domestic ideal.[21]

After the war, interest in Wright's work grew. Translations of his books began appearing in 1945. *Architettura e democrazia* was the title given to *Modern Architec-*

ture, the compilation of Wright's influential Princeton lectures, and it included an excerpt from Persico's 1935 lecture as its introduction. *Architettura organica: L'architettura della democrazia,* edited by Alfonso Gatto and Giulia Veronesi, was the translation of *An Organic Architecture (The Architecture of Democracy),* which contained the four lectures given by Wright in London in 1939.[22] Bruno Zevi's book *Verso un'architettura organica* (Towards an organic architecture; see Fig. 4.1), which was to become a milestone work for the cultivation of interest in Wright and other American architects, also appeared in 1945.[23]

In 1946, as the echoes of war began receding into history, Giulia Veronesi wrote of "Wright's hour," and her brief but illuminating essay resounds with a sense of the epic: "The old American continues to be the man of the day; today no discourse concerning architecture can disregard reference either to his work or his word. Italy was late in becoming aware of him."[24] She also emphasizes Persico's contribution to Wright's notoriety, stating that ten years before, when Persico first mentioned Wright's name, "no one knew who he was," and even less what he stood for.

In this postwar climate of invigorated interest, two events accelerated the renewal of Italian architectural culture and its relationship to Wright's "organic architecture": the birth of the magazine *Metron* and the formation of the Associazione per l'Architettura Organica (Association for Organic Architecture), known by its acronym APAO. Both of these events had Rome as their stage and Bruno Zevi as their chief protagonist.

The magazine *Metron,* which existed for less than ten years (the last issue appeared in 1954), was fueled by the animating hope that characterized Italy during the years of postwar reconstruction.[25] The initial issues (nos. 1–24) were modest, but as time went on the magazine published a formidable series of contributions to critical analysis that enabled Italy to rejoin the international arena of modern architectural thought (Fig. 5.2). Of special note are the two double issues dedicated to Wright: one devoted to the Florentine exhibition, the second devoted to the Masieri Memorial project in Venice (Fig. 5.3).[26]

Metron served as APAO's propagandist, which is not surprising considering the influence Zevi exercised on both the magazine and the association. The group, which became officially operative on 15 July 1945 and met for five years,[27] was formed to promote a "liberal association of work and research" that would unite modern architects interested in the reconstruction of Italy. The meaning of Wright's term "organic" was the subject of much debate. For APAO generally, the organic was an abstract concept connected with the "search for reality" and the definition of a social ideal. For Zevi, it wasn't the visual motifs that were most valuable, but those that were more human because they permitted the individual to discover a unity of the spirit, thus forging both a new personality and a new culture.[28]

APAO's "Declaration of Principles" was published in the second issue of *Metron.*[29] The group called on its members to provide a bridge between ratio-

Figure 5.2
Cover of *Metron* (nos. 31–32,
September–November 1949) issue
on the masters of modern architecture.
Pictured are *(top row, left to right)*
Erich Mendelsohn, Alvar Aalto, Wright;
(middle row) Le Corbusier, Sven Gottfried
Markelius, Erik Gunnar Asplund;
(bottom row) Walter Gropius, Ludwig
Mies van der Rohe, Richard Neutra.

Figure 5.3
Cover of *Metron* issue (nos. 41–42,
May–August 1951) dedicated to the
"Sixty Years of Living Architecture"
exhibition in Florence, showing Crystal
Heights project.

nalistic and organic thought, with the organic being recognized as "a development and maturation of rationalism."[30] APAO's declaration also included a resounding, albeit weak, political appeal to democracy.[31] APAO did succeed in awakening the professional conscience of many architects throughout Italy; shortly after its founding, the mother association gave rise to a vast family of local branches.[32]

In his *Verso un'architettura organica* Zevi further discussed the ideals of organic architecture and its chief apostle, Frank Lloyd Wright. The title, which added the adjective "organic" to Le Corbusier's *Vers une architecture,* expressed the author's desire to go beyond European functionalism and Italian rationalism. The book was particularly useful for Italian architects who, "finally liberated from political imposition, [could now] return to reality, coming forth from an absurd and artificial world that confused the limits of architecture with those of life."[33] In the preface, dated February 1944, Zevi expressed himself clearly as being in favor of organic architecture, the contents of which he described so succinctly that successive debates have added little to the definition:

> The best architects are tending today towards a kind of architecture which has been called organic. This term, if it has no other merit, at any rate does not end in "ist" and thus indicates that it is to be understood as referring not to a programme or a dream of architecture but to an actual tendency discernible in buildings and in architects. . . . Its meaning in regard to architecture must be defined . . . as something equally opposed to the theoretic and the geometrical, to the artificial standards, the white boxes and the cylinders which distinguish so much of the first modern architecture and to its general nudism.[34]

Zevi's goal was to redeem the term "organic" from the linguistic definition that had been popularized by Wright, and thus to reestablish its architectural meaning. The growth of organicism was dependent on the fact that it had found vital nourishment in Wright's genius.

Zevi's contributions to the Italian understanding of Wright's thought and work through APAO, *Verso un'architettura organica,* and his 1947 book *Frank Lloyd Wright* were supplemented by *Metron*.[35] The magazine functioned as a sounding board for an Italian reformulation of Wright's architectural language; the call to embrace Wright's thought was also a call to social ethics. *Metron* published, along with its critiques of the new ideas that dominated Italian architecture immediately following the war, almost the full text of Wright's speech delivered at the *New York Herald Tribune*'s forum on postwar reconstruction, in which, speaking of architecture and democracy, he emphasized that "if they are organic, they cannot be separated."[36] Italian architects were just beginning to examine these same ideas.[37] Democratic rhetoric was potent in an Italy that was still trying to grasp the complexities involved in transforming a fascist bureaucracy into the liberal administrative structure so necessary to modern planning.

This passionate rediscovery of Wright, with Zevi as its animator, did not, however, occur without criticism. Wright's Italian critics were largely exponents of conservative, traditional Catholicism for whom the true enemy, hidden behind the rhetoric on Wrightian thought, was none other than Bruno Zevi himself. This antipathy had its roots in a curious mixture of anti-Semitism (Zevi came from a Jewish family) and opposition to the supporters of socialist thought who were then rallying around the banner of the Partito d'Azione, to which Zevi belonged along with other notable members of the intelligentsia who had fought in the Resistance.

In *Libello contro l'architettura organica* (Libel against organic architecture), published in 1946, Piero Bargellini addressed the "badly instructed know-it-alls"—in other words, Italian architects who had precipitously and too enthusiastically adopted the word "organic" without deep understanding or conviction. For Bargellini, this problem lay not with Wright, whom he considered worthy of great respect, but with the abuse of the term.[38] By contrast, in the journal *La Nuova Città,* Giusta Nicco Fasola and Giovanni Michelucci offered ongoing critical analysis of Wright's architectural theory, addressing in particular the problem of organic humanism, or the "natural, psychological, and social" aspects of the human being, and its influence on Wright's designs.[39]

"60 YEARS OF LIVING ARCHITECTURE": WRIGHT COMES TO FLORENCE

In 1947 *Metron* published Giulio Carlo Argan's essay "Introduzione a Wright" (Introduction to Wright), ushering in a new phase of critical investigation of Wright's work. The essay promoted public appreciation of Wright and spurred the flowering, in the first half of the 1950s, of a true Wrightian phase in Italian architecture.[40] Argan's essay responded to earlier criticism:

> This organic architecture, which monumental and reactionary architects
> have accused of being merchandise imported from abroad, of being
> pseudo-intellectual, and of other epithets with which those who don't
> think or who choose the easy way out attempt to liberate themselves from
> new movements and artistic themes, finds, instead, in our country not
> only a profound and natural reverberation but—what's more important—
> a critical maturation more precise in its investigations, more ample in its
> essential intuitions, and more able to open toward new perspectives.[41]

Argan's writings offered the supporters of organic architecture a new alternative to the principles of the idealist aesthetic. His favorable assessment of Wright was a key factor in creating the triumphant climate at Wright's show at the Palazzo Strozzi in Florence. Not only was this exhibition to be the apex of Wright's success in Italy, but it has remained to this day an epic event in the collective memory of Italian architects.

However, the idea of a Wrightian exhibition was born, it seems, a great distance away from any design tables, the fruit instead of a "new liberalism" that came to dominate American political life after the 1948 presidential elections. In the early months of 1949, Clare Boothe Luce, then a Republican member of Congress and subsequently, under President Eisenhower, the American ambassador to Italy (1954–56), and Arthur C. Kaufmann, executive head of Gimbel's Department Store in Philadelphia, had an important conversation. At issue was politics in postfascist Italy, where, in a turn of events unsatisfactory to the United States, the Communist Party had taken on a prominent role in the nation's reconstruction effort.[42] Finding themselves faced with an Italy perilously balanced between democracy and renewed authoritarianism, Luce and Kaufmann agreed on the necessity of promoting a cultural project that would serve a double purpose: to propagandize the creative power of an American genius and to demonstrate that this genius had developed as a result of life in a free country. That they chose Wright as their example is not surprising. His masterpieces were world famous, formidable vehicles for the diffusion of American democracy.

Kaufmann contacted Oskar Stonorov in Philadelphia to organize the exhibition. The European segment of the show would be launched in Italy, the objective being "to help cement among nations of the world the bonds of good will so much needed in these days."[43]

The Florentine art historian Carlo Ludovico Ragghianti, who was asked to coordinate the exhibition in Italy, conducted a rapid survey of Italian architects to discover their feelings about such a show. An indirect confirmation of these consultations is found in the response of Giuseppe Samonà, dean of the Istituto Universitario di Architettura (School of Architecture) in Venice and active participant in APAO: "I am so happy to hear that Wright will probably come to Italy; it will be a marvelous event for many of us."[44] Ragghianti, in his later invitation to Samonà to join the exhibit's executive committee, emphasized the "exceptional importance of this show, both for the cultural rapport between the United States and Italy and for the intrinsic significance of an exhibition dedicated to a living architect, but also for [its] impact . . . on the actual architectural culture of Italy and of Europe."[45]

"Frank Lloyd Wright: 60 Years of Living Architecture" was conceived as the largest one-man show ever realized for an architect.[46] To judge by the number of boxes sent to Florence, that objective was more than realized. But what funds supported such an extraordinary and surely expensive undertaking? Even today this is unclear. Wright himself on more than one occasion lamented the uncertain financial management of the operation.[47] In Italy, at any rate, the State Department, the United States Information Service, and the Italian Ministry of Foreign Affairs supported the exhibit at the very least in a political sense.

The exhibition was held in Florence under the auspices of its mayor, Marco Fabiani, and through the initiative of Ragghianti, who was the director of the Studio Italiano di Storia dell'Arte (Italian Institute of Art History), which had its headquarters in the Palazzo Strozzi, the site of the exhibition. Count Carlo Sforza, the minister of foreign affairs, presided over the exhibition's honorary committee. There were also a technical committee and an executive committee, both chaired by Ragghianti and including Bruno Zevi.[48] The inclusion of so many notable personages gave the Florentine event a certain importance, which was added to by the presence of Wright himself. After arriving in Florence, Wright, at the invitation of Samonà, traveled to Venice in the days immediately preceding the exhibition's opening. There he was awarded an honorary degree from the Venetian School of Architecture on 21 June in the Sala dei Pregadi at the Palazzo Ducale.[49]

Returning to Florence, Wright attended the exhibition's inauguration on Sunday, 24 June, an occasion that coincided with the solemn public ceremony, in the Sala dei Dugento in the Palazzo Vecchio, at which Count Sforza presented the American architect with the Gold Medal of the City of Florence. In the exhibition brochure, Wright addressed the organizers of the exhibit and seemed to connect with the hopeful energy of his hosts: "The essence of the Italian creative spirit that all artists love will always be alive. . . . To young Italy my best hope and wish: that Italy were young."[50]

The exhibition was enthusiastically trumpeted by Wright's Italian friends and sympathizers, who saw him as "the greatest artistic genius of our century . . . the last pioneer. . . . One day we'll say to our children with pride: we knew Wright in 1951."[51] The address by the editorial staff of *Metron* to Wright also contained tones of excessive adulation:

> Your architecture is the fruit of your genius and of a democratic life. We genuflect before your genius and defend democracy and the rights of the individual. From the night of fascist barbary was born a new republic conquered through the sacrifices of its best sons. . . . You represent, therefore, the true America that meets the cultivated Italy. This is a bond stronger than any political pact. We sign it with joy. God bless you.[52]

The exhibition occupied fifteen halls and covered sixty years, ranging from the first houses designed by the young Wright to the E. Kaufmann garage, designed in 1949. On exhibit were approximately eight hundred drawings, twenty-eight models, a full-scale model of the core of a small residence, several additional photographic panels, and a series of enlarged color transparencies. Text in the form of brief captions, longer comments, and passages extracted from Wright's own writings accompanied the images.[53]

The first hall served as an introduction to the complex personality of Wright the man and the designer. Included here was "The Hymn of Work," a poem written by Wright in 1896 that served as his personal "declaration of independence." There were also photographs of the architect at his work table, some draw-

ings, and a panel entitled "Point of Departure" that explained Wright's relationship with Louis Sullivan. Another panel, labeled "Potpourri," was a collage of
photographs of buildings constructed for the World Exposition of Chicago in
1893 (Fig. 5.4), meant to illustrate the architectural environment in which Wright
began to evolve his own vision.

A large wood and plastic model of Broadacre City, cleaned, repaired, and re-
painted for the occasion, was the pièce de resistance of the fourth hall (see Figs.
3.11 and 5.1), and it made a profound impression. On its explanatory panels the
curators synthesized Wright's thoughts about urban planning; other boards contained the principles of organic architecture as well as a series of aphorisms on
"una nuova libertà per la vita" (a new liberty for life) that were integral to his
thought. Because the ideas underlying Broadacre City could be applied in any
country, they were a potential source of inspiration for Italian urban planners involved in postwar reconstruction. This was certainly the hope of the exhibition's
organizers, who asked Wright to present a talk in which, imagining himself in
conversation with Stonorov, he discussed his concept of the modern metropolis.
In that talk, later published in Florence, Wright gave a passionate description of
Broadacre City, its harmonious relationship with nature and the countryside, and
its existence as a free city in the midst of modern life.[54]

In the last hall, the model of the Guggenheim Museum constituted the ideal conclusion to the exposition, for it epitomized, with its helicoidally ascendant form, Wright's concept of spatial continuity. This concept was to become one that many Italian architects adopted and used to produce uniquely expressive designs, something that would not have been possible if they had relied on direct imitation of Wrightian forms. The Sicilian work of Leonardo Ricci, as seen for instance in the village of Monte degli Ulivi near Riesi (1961), where he was responding to the beautiful landscape of olive trees, provides a definitive example of the sensitivity achievable through local interpretations of Wrightian space.

Despite the largely positive response to the exhibition, there were many who resented what they perceived as a subservient acceptance of Wright's genius.[55] Furthermore, Wright's ideas were received by Italian professionals with considerable skepticism. Most commentators criticized in particular the impracticality of Wright's scheme of urban development, as exemplified in Broadacre City, attaching these criticisms to a generic confrontation between the Ville Contemporaine of Le Corbusier and the "archipelago" city of Wright.[56]

Among the most lasting critical responses to the exhibition were those of Giuseppe Samonà and Giusta Nicco Fasola. The latter's analysis was so profound that her opinions still animate debates on the architect's merits.[57] Samonà's comments provoked Wright to respond with enthusiasm and even affection: "A competent English translation of your extraordinary criticism of my work has just reached me. I have enjoyed, for the first time in my life, comprehensive insight of the nature of that work."[58]

What interested Samonà was how Wright's poetic vision was expressed, not in the way a house interior was treated, but in the way the house was to be "lived in."[59] This subtlety accounted for the convincing unity of Wright's buildings, a unity evident in his Prairie Style houses and developed in the Usonian projects. However, said Samonà, Wright's idea of unity was based on oneness with nature and concerned the intrinsic harmony of the inhabitants and the building materials. Samonà intuited that Wright's true modernity lay in the spatial and material continuum of his projects, which were encompassed by an architectural concept that began with the world surrounding the house and finished with the person who lived within it.

Samonà's Wrightian thinking allowed him to cut the two Gordian knots of modernity: the concept of rationality as it was automatically linked to functionalism, and the dialectic between the abstract and the concrete. His conclusions are hardly surprising when viewed within the context of his directorship of the fertile didactic entity that was the School of Architecture in Venice.[60]

The school in Venice was a "new Bauhaus," the only Italian institution that succeeded in elaborating on Wright's themes and combining them with a renovating cultural initiative directed toward the professional world of architecture and the teaching of design. These twin aims were both expressed during a debate over whether the school should award Wright an honorary degree. Where Wright excelled, the Venetian school maintained, was as the champion of a new human-ism. It was around this aspect of Wright's work and character, to which Italian historiography attributed great importance, that the discussion undertaken by the professors in Venice revolved. The Florentine exhibition simply augmented Wright's influence, as did the architect's numerous publications, which had spurred "three generations of American and European architects to an awareness of their art and to a civic conscience."[61] In closing its debate, the faculty insisted on the importance to the profession overall of the Taliesin Fellowship, founded and directed by Wright, because it stimulated and inspired architects in every part of the world.

PRACTICING WRIGHT

Wright's visit to Venice in June 1951 led to one of the most clamorous episodes of cultural eclipse that twentieth-century Italian architecture has ever known. The controversy erupted around the project that Wright later developed for the Masieri Memorial, located along the Grand Canal, which for months filled the pages of newspapers both in Italy and abroad. In what appeared to be endless debate, the communal board of Venice quarreled with many important cultural and public figures over every imaginable aspect of the project. The outcome of the debate had an impact on a much larger issue: the fate of future planning and building in the old city center of Venice—in short, the fate of the "Venezie possibili" (the "possible Venices").[62]

The controversial project centered on Angelo Masieri, a thirty-year-old de-signer from Friuli and a former student of Carlo Scarpa's at the Venetian School of Architecture. Masieri loved Wright's architecture, and he owned a small, three-story house at the intersection of the Grand Canal and the Rio Nuovo.[63] This house also happened to neighbor the fifteenth-century Palazzo Balbi and face the Ca' Foscari, both important Venetian historical sites. Masieri asked Wright, on the occasion of the master's brief visit to Venice in 1951, to design, as a replace-ment for the existing house, an edifice which could be used both as a residence for himself and his young wife, Savina, and as Masieri's architectural office. This was a dream the couple had cherished for quite some time. Masieri also hoped to be able to work with his much-admired master on the design. Wright ac-cepted the proposal, but put off the definition of the task and of the characteris-tics of the project until a successive meeting could be arranged and held at Tal-iesin West.

Thus in the late spring of 1952 the young couple embarked on a Wrightian "Grand Tour" of America, with the double objective of admiring firsthand the architecture of the master and of approaching Wright once again about the Vene-tian project. However, the adventure ended tragically. On 28 June Angelo Masieri was killed in an automobile accident as he was returning from Arizona, where he had gone to meet Wright—though sadly, the meeting did not take place because of Wright's absence. Supported by the Masieri family itself as well as by friends at Venice's School of Architecture, Savina did not abandon the project, and six months after her husband's death she wrote to Wright: "He [Angelo] loved and worshipped you. It was his dream to live in a house of your creation. My husband's parents and myself still hope that dream may come true, though under changed circumstances. Such a building would lastly keep alive his remembrance, housing a beneficent institution for undergraduates of the School of Architecture, where he himself accomplished his studies."[64]

This new project, which proceeded under the auspices of the School of Architecture and in particular of Carlo Scarpa, provided Wright with two design options: an edifice with apartments that could be rented out, creating a fund for scholarships or other cultural activities that would be managed by the school's faculty; or a sort of house-hotel in which about twenty deserving architectural students could live. The second option was preferred by the Masieri family. Wright responded quickly. He accepted the project, which by now he felt honored to be charged with, and wrote to Savina: "I am indeed willing to plan a memorial building to him. . . . It seems to me the dormitory for students would be the best. . . . Nothing could please me more than to do something in Venice worthy of my good and gracious friends."[65]

The details were finalized within an extraordinarily brief period. In little more than a month after he had received Savina's initial letter, Wright sent her a telegram informing her that the design was ready and he was only waiting to hear from her as to the most suitable method for its shipment.[66]

The solution imagined by Wright for the Masieri Memorial was simple: a triangular edifice, mirroring the lot on which it would stand, composed of a two-story ground floor with mezzanine, two upper stories, and a garden terrace (Figs. 5.5 and 5.6; see also Fig. 4.10). The triangle's smallest side faced the Grand Canal; the other two sides paralleled the adjacent buildings. The new structure would not adjoin the Palazzo Balbi because Wright introduced a private-use lane between the two buildings. Wright's design for the principal facade was composed of marble pilasters, large windows, balconies, and two angular pillars that combined to produce, in a chiaroscuro effect, an interpretation, both personal and modern, of the essence of Venetian architecture. Explaining the motives that inspired his work, Wright stated: "Loving Venice as I do I wanted, by way of modern techniques, to make the old Venice tradition like anew."[67]

At first, excited arguments over the project were muted out of respect for the Masieri family, who, it was felt, were promoting an essentially noble initiative. Also, as the university took the first steps toward obtaining bureaucratic approval for the project, few people actually saw the plans. It was Wright himself who brought the Masieri Memorial to international attention.

The scandal exploded in the summer of 1953. In May of that year Wright displayed a perspective of the design in an exhibition at the National Institute of Arts and Letters in New York. The U.S. Information Service, which at that time

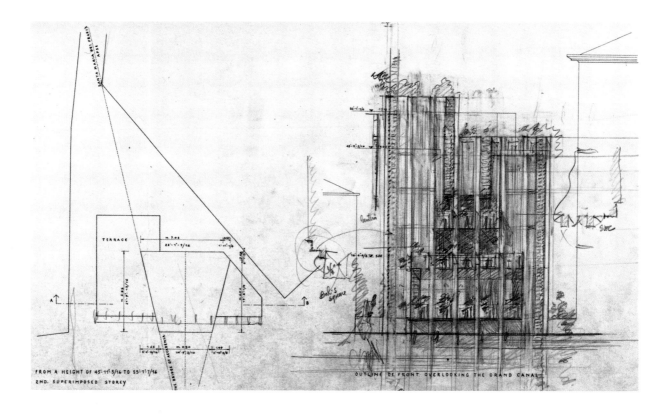

FROM A HEIGHT OF 45'-11" 3/16 TO 55'-1" 7/16
2ND. SUPERIMPOSED STOREY

OUTLINE OF FRONT OVERLOOKING THE GRAND CANAL

Figure 5.5
Site plan and elevation, Masieri
Memorial, Venice, 1952. FLW,
architect. (FLWA 5306.008)

Figure 5.6 *(opposite)*
Elevation, Masieri Memorial,
Venice, 1952. FLW, architect.
(FLWA 5306.025)

was very active in Italy, publicized the exhibit and reproduced the drawing—which in fact exaggerated the facade, making it appear at least as tall as the adjacent Palazzo Balbi—within the pages of its newsletter. The drawing ignited a fire in the debate between the illustrious defenders of the untouchability of Venice (Italian intellectuals and architects such as Cederna, Quaroni, Papini, and Bellonci) and the tenacious preachers of the gospel of organic architecture (including Zevi and the members of APAO, together with Pane, Ragghianti, Rogers, and Bettini).[68]

Daily newspapers and weekly magazines fanned the flames of controversy with defamatory articles, labeling the Masieri Memorial with epithets such as "casa-mostro" (monster-house) and publishing retouched photographs that falsified its appearance. But was all this excitement actually about Wright and his ideas? Or was the dispute about his project only a clamorous occasion for once again bringing to light old controversies, stifled interests, and calls for a return to Italian roots that had existed for some time?

The chronicle of the critical response has been reconstructed many times; it is therefore worthwhile to discuss only the most important points of the opposition to Wright's project. The crux of the problem lay in the seeming impossibility of combining the architecturally modern and the historical. Antonio Cederna repeatedly pointed to the danger that lay in offering an influential precedent

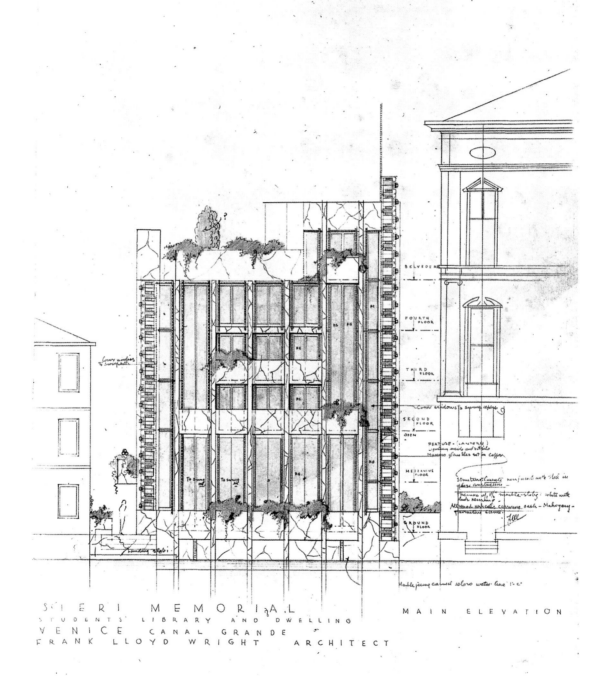

S I E R I   M E M O R I A L

STUDENTS' LIBRARY AND DWELLING

VENICE   CANAL GRANDE

FRANK LLOYD WRIGHT   ARCHITECT

MAIN   ELEVATION

"for a thousand little craftsmen who would transform Italy into the image and likeness of the E42 [meaning the classicizing architecture of the Esposizione Universale di Roma (EUR), planned to be held in 1942]."[69]

Among those who defended the project, Ernesto Rogers was most capable of looking beyond the immediate controversy. His commentary on the debate was a reproach against the overshadowing of the real concerns of contemporary Italian architecture by a project that was not itself that important.[70]

But perhaps the river of words that rained on Wright's "skyscraper" on the Grand Canal also served to wash away opponents of the status quo and bring new attention to the innovative designers at the School of Architecture in Venice. This irony was stated with perfect clarity by Manlio Brusatin, who noted that "the objective [of the critics], beyond everything that was said or written, was to attack heavily the tendencies of the Venetian School of Architecture," and therefore its direction by Giuseppe Samonà, its teaching staff, and its commitment to developing a new method for the preservation of Venice's historic center.

The events of the following two years belong more to the chronicle of city administration than to the history of architecture. Judgments were handed down by both the Building and Health Commissions of the Municipality of Venice; technical opinions were called for and given; urgent requests for calming words were sent to Wright by Savina Masieri; and interrogations were undertaken by the Società Adriatica di Elettricità (Adriatic Electric Company), owner of Palazzo Balbi. The dialogue, though, took place among the deaf. All of this activity served only to camouflage a fundamental aversion to Wright's project, and in the end it came to nothing. Wright's "Venice affair" was a closed case by the autumn of 1955.[71]

THE VENETIAN SCHOOL

This controversial chapter, while ending in outward defeat for Wright, nevertheless cast a spotlight on the inherent vitality of the Venetian School of Architecture and made abundantly clear the strength of its call to Wrightian architectural concepts. At the end of the war, the school showed its commitment to these concepts by giving political and cultural refuge to a group of "exiles," architects who might otherwise have felt themselves strangers in their own country, including Carlo Scarpa. In 1948 the director, Samonà, called Zevi to Venice, offering him the first chair in the history of art and the history of architectural style at the School of Architecture. There swiftly followed the recruitment of other "excluded" architects of the caliber of Franco Albini, Ludovico Barbiano di Belgiojoso of the group Banfi, Belgiojoso, Peresutti, and Rogers, and Ignazio Gardella (all of whom came from the Milan area and had been instrumental in developing Italian rationalism), the urban planners Luigi Piccinato and Giovanni Astengo, and the young engineer Giancarlo De Carlo, who had earned his second degree in architecture from the Venice school.

Zevi's propaganda in favor of Wright and organic architecture found an accepting audience at the Venetian school. Venice had remained, as it were, isolated from both the rationalist experience and the architectural vicissitudes of the Fascist regime. In some ways its isolated position made it an island of privilege where the contradictions and uncertainties of modern architecture could be studied, verified, and repaired. Thus it was able to demonstrate a sentimental inclination toward Wrightian spatial and environmental concepts. For fifteen years the Venetian School of Architecture remained a factory for new ideas. When in the second half of the 1960s the dissolution of the school began, Carlo Scarpa wittily invoked the names of those he considered to be the school's guiding lights: "For a perfect faculty of architecture one would need Wright as teacher of design, Le Corbusier for urban planning, Aalto for the architecture of the interiors, Mies for technology and the constructive elements . . . and finally Samonà to run it all."[72]

Without doubt, Carlo Scarpa was the architect who exercised the most influence on Wright's reputation in Italy. He regarded Wright with a measured deference and used the most original of Wright's models to develop the varied language of his own craftsmanship. In the 1950s Scarpa found a way to introduce Wrightian motifs and design principles (without discounting his attraction to Alvar Aalto's design methods) into his own methodology. As a university professor Scarpa nurtured many brilliant students in the study of Wright, some of whom went on to perfect their understanding, often by means of a trip to America.[73]

The influence of Wright's style of architecture on Scarpa's design projects is a favorite topic of historians, in particular Francesco Dal Co and Manfredo Tafuri. Inspired by Scarpa's achievements, Dal Co has proposed an investigation of the profound intellectual affinity between the two architects, both of whom he called "tenacious observers" and "collectors of images."[74] Their most important link can perhaps be perceived in the relationship each man established with his own cultural tradition. But differences existed there as well, Dal Co points out, noting that while Wright desired to establish new traditions and values, Scarpa rejected such "ideological" leanings.[75] Dal Co also notes that the only foreign tradition for which both Wright and Scarpa demonstrated enthusiasm was orientalism in general and Japanese architecture in particular. This was a "love from youth," according to Bernard Huet, one that created a profound tension in the mature works of both men.

Tafuri emphasized the cultural disparity between the two men rather than dwelling on Scarpa's interest in Wright's evolutionary style. Unlike many Italians, Scarpa was not interested in Wright's "American roots"; rather, Tafuri sees Scarpa's interest as lying in Wright's "art of discontinuity," as represented in works like the Ocatillo Desert Camp (1928). By the closing years of the 1950s Scarpa had distanced himself from the stricter Wrightism that had characterized his work in the late 1940s (typified by his 1949 design for an apartment building at Feltre;

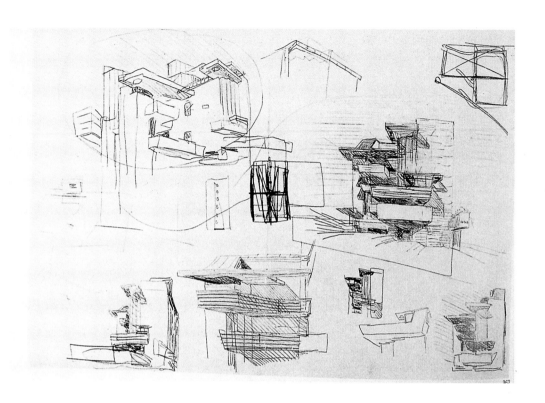

Figure 5.7 *(above)*
Sketches for a project for a four-story
apartment building at Feltre, 1949.
Carlo Scarpa, architect.

Figure 5.8
Sketches for the Venezuelan Pavilion
at the Venice Biennale, 1954–56.
Carlo Scarpa, architect.

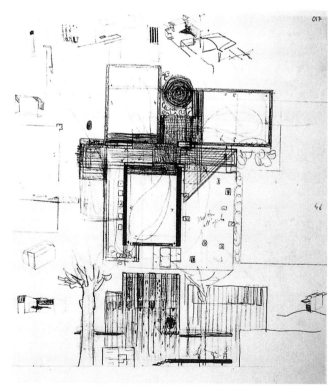

Fig. 5.7), declaring his independence through the development of his own "dissolved" syntax.[76]

One explanation for this divergence might lie with Wright's Usonian houses (1948–51), designs that represented both a semantic evolution in formalism and decorativism, and a maturation of the architectural values from the Prairie years. According to Brusatin, the presence of Wright in Scarpa's work must be traced backward from the Usonian houses to Unity Temple (1906), and then forward to Midway Gardens (1913) and the Imperial Hotel (1915).[77]

Two of Scarpa's buildings are significant examples of Wright's influence: the Pavilion of the Book of Art (1950) and the Venezuelan Pavilion (1954–56), both located at the Giardini di Castello at the Venice Biennale. The Pavilion of the Book of Art was saluted with great enthusiasm by *Metron,* which heralded it as "lightning from a clear sky" and a pure "act of courage" produced by the "best architect of Venice."[78] It was constructed in the manner of Taliesin West and influenced by the Wright of the Lake Tahoe experimental cabin designs (1922), yet it was also a showcase for its own unique attributes. The pavilion's linear structure reached outward, uniting interior and exterior and creating a continuity of space that was one of the most important postulates of organic architecture.

Scarpa's Venezuelan Pavilion (Fig. 5.8), one of the best-known buildings in modern architecture, according to Brusatin, constituted "the seal and the conclusive proof of the direct influence of Wright's architecture" on Scarpa's work. This project poetically implied a dynamic conversation between Wright and Scarpa, in which Scarpa masterfully absorbed the lessons of Wright's Unity Temple.[79]

Few episodes in the history of modern architecture have generated the idealist fervor that the Wrightian challenge brought to Italy. The most convincing echoes of that fervor can be found in the works of APAO's members and among the architects associated with *Metron* or those who were Zevi's friends. Many of their names have already been mentioned; among their buildings the following is a partial list: the Villa Giacomuzzi in Udine (1948–50), the Villa Bortolotto at Cervignano in Friuli (1950), and the Veritti tomb at the Udinese graveyard (1951), all designed by Masieri, which show very strongly Wright's geometric matrix in both squared and triangular forms; the Villa Scimemi at Mondello on the outskirts of Palermo, designed by Samonà (1950–54), a reinterpretation of Usonian architecture (Figs. 5.9 and 5.10); the palazzina in via Monte Parioli, Rome, by Silvio Radiconcini and Zevi (1950–52); schools in Urbino and in Sassari (1956), designed by Luigi Pellegrin; the Zigaina House at Cervignano in Friuli (1958), by Giancarlo De Carlo, another good example based on Wright's interpretation of the domestic universe.

Finally, the works of Marcello D'Olivo and of Luigi Figini and Gino Pollini merit special attention. In the case of D'Olivo, Wright's Prairie houses provided particular inspiration for a restructuring of his work. The Villaggio del Fanciullo, the most significant example of D'Olivo's Wrightian designs, was a large complex meant for orphans and displaced children, constructed between 1950 and

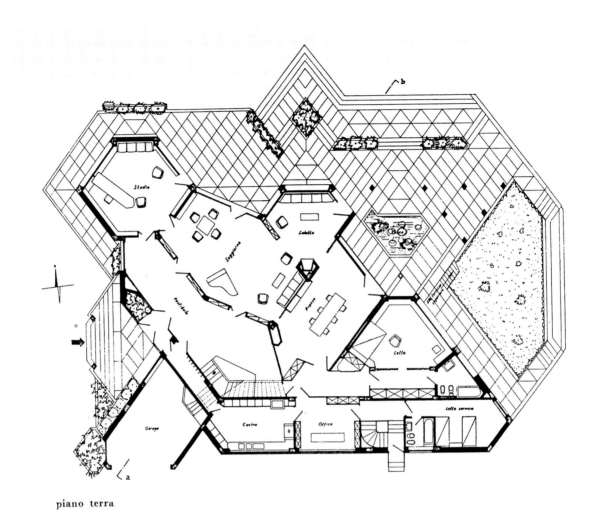

piano terra

Figure 5.9
Plan, Villa Scimemi at Mondello,
near Palermo, 1950–54. Giuseppe
Samonà, architect.

Figure 5.10 (opposite)
Exterior, Villa Scimemi at Mondello,
near Palermo, 1950–54. Giuseppe
Samonà, architect.

1955 at Villa Opicina, just outside Trieste. D'Olivo envisioned the villaggio as a small city in strict rapport with the barrenness of the Carsican plain. He centered his design on a large dining hall, with a rectilinear body and two diamond-shaped towers; a typesetting studio; and a central pavilion with dormitories and living rooms for its small guests. D'Olivo derived the site planning, spatial motifs, and decorative elements directly from Wrightian architecture, for example from the master's project for the Unitarian church in suburban Madison, Wisconsin (1947).[80]

In the Church of the Madonna dei Poveri in Milan (1952–54; Fig. 5.11) and in the social services complex for Olivetti (1954–57; Fig. 5.12) at Ivrea, by contrast, Figini and Pollini combined Wrightism with their own view of rationalism. The church, designed in the climate of postwar Italy and immediately labeled "neorealistic," was constructed along Corbusian "regulatory lines," starting from the hexagon of the chorus, with the intent of responding to the needs of both the officiating priest and the congregation. This care for the "human" was a value that Italian organic architecture always respected. At the opposite end of the scale is the "organic" solution proposed for the Olivetti building, which, seeming derived in part from the geometric polygon of the Villa Scimemi at Mondello by Samonà, indicates a will to unite the reality of organic architecture with the political reasoning of a great industrial giant.

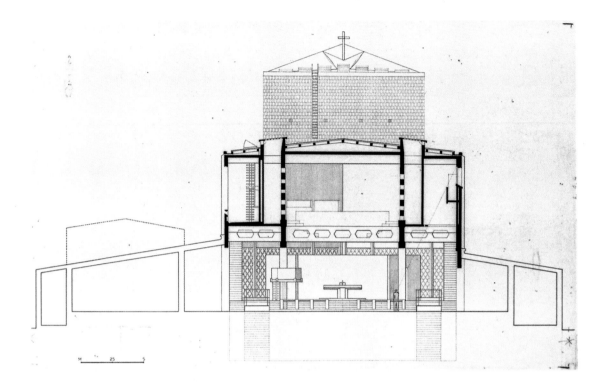

Figure 5.11 *(above)*
Section, Church of the Madonna dei Poveri, Milan, 1952–54. Luigi Figini and Gino Pollini, architects.

Figure 5.12
Plan and elevations, Olivetti social services complex, Ivrea, 1954–57. Luigi Figini and Gino Pollini, architects.

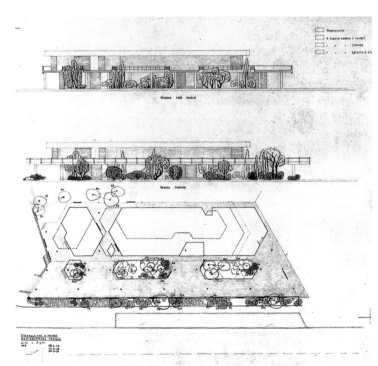

Figure 5.13
Wright exhibition at the Milan Triennale,
1960. Carlo Scarpa, designer.

The 1950s concluded with an explicit homage by Scarpa to Wright when he curated the architect's magnificent exhibition at the Triennale of Milan in 1960 (Fig. 5.13). Scarpa carved the galleries into fragmented spaces separated by panels marked with simple Wrightian decorative motifs, like the geometric shapes of the square and circle. He designed the lighting to create a magical atmosphere, carefully screening and focusing it to manipulate vision and space.

Now that some historical distance from these events exists, one may legitimately ask: What exactly is organic architecture? And did the study of Wright in Italy make the rediscovery of the organic Italian architecture more fruitful? Perhaps only Scarpa was able to interpret Wright's work in a way uniquely his own, while the majority of his colleagues, because of the orgy of eclecticism that invaded the profession, arrived at uninspired results completely antithetical to the promise of organic architecture.

SIX: USEFUL HOSTAGE

CONSTRUCTING WRIGHT
IN SOVIET RUSSIA AND FRANCE

Jean-Louis Cohen

The impact that Frank Lloyd Wright's first works had on German and Dutch architecture and their subsequent promulgation in Europe has been discussed and reexamined in these essays. The discovery of Wright by the leading figures of two of the principal scenes that affirmed the new architecture after World War I, namely France and Russia, however, has remained relatively unknown to this day. The concrete conditions of the circulation of Wright's works in Europe, and of his response to the European scene, are beginning to be better understood;[1] as we shall see, however, in Russia and France, where architects set as their goal the routing of art nouveau and eclecticism, the inspiration of Wright's Prairie houses and the Larkin Building was quite different from that which shaped the thinking of many of their European counterparts.

Whatever distance separates the Netherlands from Italy, or France from Russia, it must be emphasized that the European reception of Wright was determined by a phenomenon that affected all of Europe, namely, Americanism.[2] F. Rudolf Vogel discussed Wright's residential designs in *Das amerikanische Haus* (1910), for example, situating them within a general panorama of New World domestic architecture.[3] On the occasion of his 1911 trip to America, Hendrik Petrus Berlage also fixed his attention on the work of Wright, "the master who has created projects without equal in all of Europe."[4] Wright's buildings interested European architects not only for the novelty of their spatial solutions, but also because they manifested a new architectural style anchored in urban American culture.

Wright's influence was particularly intense and widespread in Germany and the Netherlands, but in other nations there was notable resistance to Wright's ideas; in these places it was not until the 1920s that Wright's buildings and projects received serious consideration. In certain cases, the resistance was overcome at the expense of a distortion of the meaning of Wright's work, which was newly invested with local concerns. But this "distortion" also revealed aspects of Wright's work that had previously gone unremarked. From this point of view, a look at the different scenes of Russia and France permits a grasp of the stakes linked to the discovery of Wright in two architectural cultures opposed to each other in many ways. Presented above all as an American "rebel," Wright was nonetheless discussed on the level of content and meaning in post-1917 Russia, whereas he was the object of a much more formalist reading in France until 1939.

WRIGHT AND THE SOVIET SCENE

Wright was incontestably one of the key figures of the *Amerikanizm* that gripped Russia even before the revolution of October 1917. There is no evidence to show, however, that Wright was truly known before World War I, despite S. Frederick Starr's claims of Wrightian traces in a Pantelejmon Golosov project of 1912.[5] Vogel's book was noted in the Russian architectural press, where the most recently presented works by an American were those of Louis Sullivan. The architectural production that developed in the USSR of the New Economic Policies has, of course, nothing in common with Wright's architectural agenda, since orders for villas obviously disappear after 1917. This did not prevent him from becoming a constant presence in the Soviet literature from the moment avant-garde theorists devoted their first commentaries to him. Was El Lissitzky familiar with Wright's works when he studied architecture in Darmstadt prior to 1914? They could not in any case have escaped the artist's notice during his stays in Western Europe between 1922 and 1924. His ties to the *Wendingen* circle, which devoted a monographic issue to Wright in 1925, have been demonstrated and are doubtless the direct cause of his knowledge of Wright.

In 1925, in the journal *Krasnaia niva,* Lissitzky critiqued the duality of the structure of American skyscrapers and their surface ornamentation, a contradiction discussed in 1923 by Le Corbusier in *Vers une architecture* and also denounced by Vladimir Mayakovsky following his trip to New York in 1925. Henceforth, therefore, Lissitzky found the sole authentically innovative place in the New World to lie in the American West, the place where Wright appeared as "America's only architect, who dared to discard all textbook precepts and to create a new type of dwelling, which has revealed him as the father of contemporary architecture."[6] When Lissitzky the following year published an analysis of the framework of industrial buildings and skyscrapers in Europe and America, he discussed Sullivan's and Wright's innovations, but only so he could then put their achievements at a distance by asserting that the new architecture's "center of gravity" was no longer to be found in America, but resided now in the work of the Taut Brothers, Mies van der Rohe, and Perret.[7]

Moisei Ginzburg, an architect who, like Lissitzky, was constrained by being a Jew and forced to study abroad, caught wind of Wright's work while at the Brera Academy in Milan. The first evidence of his discovery of Wright's work

XXIX. М. Я. Гинзбург и Н. А. Копелиович

Макет дома Локшиных в Евпатории 1917 год

are the plans he drafted for the Lokshin Villa for Evpatoria in Crimea upon his return to Russia in 1915 (Fig. 6.1).[8] With its broad, gently sloping, overhanging roof and the triple window of its central portion, the house resembles the 1901 Frank Thomas House, while the door set in a semicircular arch, the base in a course of carved stones, and the perron adorned with two large vases directly evoke the Arthur Heurtley House of 1902. The overall architectural conception, however, maintains a clear axial symmetry and a compactness that have nothing in common with the modular principle and horizontal extension of Wright's Prairie Style houses.[9]

In 1926, by now the principal theorist of Constructivism, Ginzburg took an interest in Wright's domestic architecture, addressing the Robie House in a commentary in *Sovremennaia arkhitektura* (Fig. 6.2). Despite his judgment that Wright's architecture belonged to a fruitful but outmoded period, Ginzburg found Wright to be representative of the American "farmer-pioneers" and placed him in an important position, alongside the airplane, as a model for "new work methods" in architecture.[10] To Ginzburg, Wright's Robie House offered "an entirely new plan, simple, open, suffused in air and light, and developing freely in space."[11] For the Russians, judged to be "even more pioneers than the Americans," there is in this assessment a challenge comparable to that of machine technology, in reference to which Ginzburg cites analyses of Wright that were then already old. When in 1933 he addressed the question of dwelling spaces in a global vision, Ginzburg once again presented the Robie House, the plans for the Avery Coonley House, and

ФРАНК ЛЛОЙД РАЙТ
FRANK LLOYD WRIGHT

ПРОЕКТ ДОМА В ОК-ПАРКЕ. ЧИКАГО

ФАСАД. STRASSENANSICHT

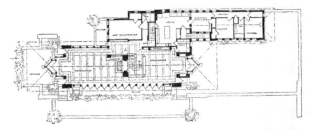

ПЛАН. HAUPTGESCHOSS

Научная теоретическая разработка функционального метода—одна из важнейших задач современной архитектуры. Тем громаднее для нас значение проверки теоретических положений этого метода на каждом конкретном примере материальной деятельности человека. Именно с этой целью мы поместили в **СА 3** аэроплан и методы его конструирования. И точно с такой же целью мы считаем необходимым упомянуть об американском архитекторе **Франк Ллойд Райте**, около четверти века тому назад давшем примеры применения в конкретной деятельности зодчего новых методов работы.

Один из немногих, почти единственный в свое время, **Райт** понял особенности тех условий, в которых ему пришлось работать, увидел новые предпосылки, из которых слагается современная архитектура.

Прежде всего бытовой уклад американских фермеров-новоселов, с его промежуточным положением между бытом городского особняка и деревенской фермы,—натолкнул **Райта** на изобретение совершенно нового плана простого, открытого, омываемого светом и воздухом, свободно раскинутого в пространстве.

„Я требую от архитектурного сооружения того же, что и от человека: искренности и внутренней правдивости, и только с этим связаны для меня все качества архитектуры“,—говорил **Райт**,—и это привело его к четкому функциональному членению своего задания. Стоит взглянуть на приводимый здесь дом в **Ок-парке**, чтоб убедиться в том, что расчленение общего пятна плана — есть расчленение по функциям: жилая часть, служебная, помещения для гостей и пр.

Точно также с большой ясностью оценил **Райт** те возможности, которые давал ему новый материал—железо-бетон. Все части сооружения, начиная от распределения стенной поверхности и окон, пропорций этих окон и кончая сильно выступающими горизонтальными плитами— все это естественное следствие новых свойств материала—железо-бетона и нового бытового уклада, скрывающегося за этим железо-бетоном.

И когда в наше время находятся люди, не знающие „в каком стиле им сегодня работать“ и уповающие на спасительную силу отмерших форм,—хочется с особой настойчивостью противопоставить им слова, сказанные более 15 лет тому назад **Райтом**:

„Архитектор нашего времени не имеет более важной заботы, чем возможно полнее использовать плоды нового орудия производства нашей эпохи—машины, этого истинного пионера демократии. Но что же делают вместо этого архитекторы? Они употребляют эти орудия производства на воспроизведение форм, созданных другими временами, другим небом, форм—сегодня мертвых, и они делают это при помощи машины, действительное назначение которой именно эти отмершие формы уничтожить“.

Задачи, стоящие перед нами, современными архитекторами СССР, еще более очевидны, чем они были у **Райта**. Мы еще более новоселы, чем американские фермеры, — новоселы нового социально-бытового уклада, строители новых форм человеческой жизни. Возможности новых строительных материалов и роль нашего „орудия производства“—машина, возросли во много крат раз за истекшие 15 лет. Нужно овладеть этими новыми предпосылками и воплотить их в нашей конкретной работе.

Если многое удалось в своей области сделать четверть века тому назад одиночке **Райту**, то, конечно, больше нужно сделать нам в наше время—коллективу, ясно ставящему себе свои задачи, настойчиво овладевающему новым методом работы.

ERSTE AUSSTELLUNG DER ARCHITEKTUR DER GEGENWART SA

MITGLIEDER-VERZEICHNISS:

M. BARSCH, G. BARCHIN, BAUHAUS (Dessau), VICTOR BOURGEOIS (BRUXELLE), A. BUROFF, VAN-DER-VLUGT (Amsterdam), WEEGMANN, A. WESSNIN, V. WESSNIN, L. WESSNIN, W. WLADIMIROFF, B. WELIKOFFSKY, ALEXEJ GAN, MORICE GASPARD (Bruxelle), GALPERIN (Leningrad) WALTER GROPIUS (Dessau), M. GINSBURG, J. GOLOSSOFF, P. GOLOSSOFF, HOFFMANN (Berlin), R. GUEVREKIAN (Paris), A. IWANITZKY, N. COLLEY, S. KOJIN, ANNA KAPUSTINA, J. KORNFELD, KREUTZAR (Prag), KROGA (Prag), P. KOSINSKY (Warschau), A. KORSCHEWSKY (Warschau), A. KAWETZEWSKY (Warschau), A. KARYNSKY (Warschau), B. KORSCHUNOFF, A. KRESTIN (Leningrad), G. KRASSIN, W. KOKORIN, W. KRASSILNIKOFF, G. LUDWIG, GUSTAV LUDECKE (Hellerau), J. LEONIDOFF, ANDRE LURCAT (Paris), MALLET-STEVENS (Paris), MORET (Paris), J. NIKOLAJEFF, A. NIKOLSKY (Leningrad), A. OL (Leningrad), J. J. P. OUD (Rotterdam) ALEX PASTERNAK, M. PARUSNIKOFF, J. RAICH, G. RIETVELD (Utrecht), J. SSOBOLJEF, L. SLAWINA, SIRKUS (Warschau), SSYNJAWSKY, MAX TAUT (Berlin), FISSENKO, A. FUFAIEFF, D. FRIEDMANN, ZARNOWEROWNA (Warschau), A. SCHUSSJEFF, S. TSCHERNISCHOFF, T. TSCHIJIKOWA, TSCHOUKA (Warschau), IRENE WILLIAM, NINA WOROTYNZEWA. HOCHSCHULEN ZU MOSKAU, LENINGRAD, KIEW, ODESSA, TOMSK U. A. BAUFIRMEN: TECHNOBETON, ASBOSTROM, MOSKWOTOL U. A.

56. Жилой дом в Ок-парке. Чикаго. Фр. Л. Райт.

57. Дом Фреемана в Лос-Анжелосе. Фр. Л. Райт.

Figure 6.3 *(opposite)*
Robie House, Chicago, 1906, and
Freeman House, Los Angeles, 1923.
From Moisei Ginzburg, *Zhilishche*
(Moscow: Gosstroyizdat, 1934), 39.

Figure 6.4
Urban scheme for Magnitogorsk, 1930.
Ivan Leonidov, designer. From *Sovremen-naia arkhitektura* 5, no. 3 (1930): 5.

views of the Freeman House, but this time without commentary (Fig. 6.3).[12] Some of the illustrations were drawn from the Russian edition of Richard Neutra's book *Wie baut Amerika* (How America builds), published in 1929, in which Soviet readers were able to learn about certain of Wright's Californian constructions.[13]

Points of convergence between Constructivist ideas and Wright's own thinking appear in the course of the debate on the ideal form of the socialist town that opened with the meeting to devise the first Five-Year Plan in 1929. Not long before Wright began his reflections on the future planning and division of the American territory, which would lead to the Broadacre City project, the "de-urbanists"—advocates of territorial spread—intervened in the debate on urban and town planning to reject, as Wright would later, both capitalism's dense metropolitan conglomerations and the radical solutions proposed by architects like Le Corbusier. Just like the precepts Wright would formulate in 1932, the linear mechanisms for community planning proposed by Mikhail Okhitovich and his comrades at the 1929 convention rested on a model of regional control based both on the introduction of the individual home and on the mass availability of the automobile of Henry Ford, who in the 1920s was a great popular hero in the USSR.[14] In certain projects of like inspiration, such as Ivan Leonidov's plan for Magnitogorsk (1930), there was even a limited visual resemblance to Wright's designs: towers were articulated in a decentralized arrangement, as they would be at Broadacre (Fig. 6.4).[15] But there the similarities end.

One of the most astonishing episodes in the Soviet reception of Wright is linked to the American visit in 1930 of filmmaker Sergei Eisenstein, the sole representative of the Russian avant-garde of great standing to go to the United States since Mayakovsky's 1925 trip. While in New York, Eisenstein undertook the prepara-

Статья Ф. Л. Райта написана- для „Архитектуры СССР" в ответ на анкету редакции (см. № 6 за 1933 г.).

КАК Я РАБОТАЮ

ФРАНК ЛЛОЙД РАЙТ

Изложение и теоретическое обос- нование процесса творческой работы архитектора является само по себе творчеством. Попытаюсь все же от- ветить на поставленные вами вопросы.

В условиях каждого задания сле- дует искать метода его решения. План, форма и общий характер проек- та предопределяются характером уча- стка, характером применяемых мате- риалов, способами применения их, природными данными и, наконец, назначением данной постройки. И всегда творческая индивидуальность

их великими памятниками, способ- ствует и в наши дни созданию великих архитектурных творений. Но те зда- ния, которые должны воздвигать мы, естественно, резко отличаются от них.

Редко бывает, чтобы методы кол- лективной работы распространялись и на область подлинной творческой работы архитектора, если не считать тех случаев, когда один архитектор выполняет то, что задумал другой. Но даже в этих случаях высшего со- вершенства нельзя достигнуть.

В искусстве архитектуры замысел

Figure 6.5

Wright, "Kak ia rabotaiu" ("The way I design"), *Arkhitektura SSSR* 2, no. 2 (February 1934): 71.

tion of a film entitled *Glass House,* the idea for which he initially had in Berlin in 1926. In his working scrapbook he glued a view—clipped from the 29 July 1930 issue of *New York* magazine—of one of the towers studied by Wright for St. Mark's-in-the-Bouwerie. The filmmaker saw in the tower project the material- ization of the "glass skyscraper" he had imagined four years earlier, which was to serve as the central theme for a film he would never bring to light.[16] While this is not an instance of direct influence, it illustrates the spirit shared by artists in very different circumstances.

With Russian architecture's turn toward socialist realism in the 1930s, interest in Wright did not cease, but its nature changed. If the Communist Party daily, *Pravda,* addressed him on two occasions, in 1932 and in 1933, it was in order to draw anticapitalist comments from him about the situation of architects in a West struck by the Great Depression. Since Le Corbusier was practically persona non grata, it fell to Wright to incarnate the figure of the famed "architect friend" of the USSR. Wright did not deny himself the opportunity to denounce the state of intellectuals in the United States, characterizing them as "hapless beneficiaries of a success system they have never clearly understood, but that has worked mir- acles for them while they slept." Although he stated that in America "the pres- ent economy has practically eliminated our profession, such as it was," Wright did not hide his reservations regarding the Soviet system.[17]

Several months later, the Union of Architects' journal *Arkhitektura SSSR,* founded in 1933, questioned Wright on the subject of his work methods. In an extended investigation of the design process of Western architects, Wright's creative technique was presented (Fig. 6.5) alongside those of the Frenchmen Robert Mallet-Stevens, André Lurçat, and Raymond Fischer, the Dutchman J. J. P. Oud, the Austrian Josef Frank, the Belgian Victor Bourgeois, and the Swiss Hannes Meyer and Hans Schmidt. In the text, Wright deems that the notion of "composition," about which he is questioned, is "dead" from the moment the building is thought of as an "entity."[18] Invited to take a position on the issue of relations to the classical "heritage" that underlay the doctrine of socialist realism then being introduced in Soviet architecture, Wright resisted all nostalgic postures on the matter and warned against the indiscriminate use of classical forms.[19]

The architect and critic David Arkin, who solicited this contribution from Wright, played a particularly important role in the Russian discussion of Wright's theories and projects. In 1932 he included Wright's post-1918 works in his panoramic study *Arkhitektura sovremennogo Zapada* (Modern Western architecture; Fig. 6.6), drawing the attention of the Russian public to Wright's solutions to urban problems and providing a translation of the text on the "third dimension" published in *Wendingen* in 1925.[20] Arkin also emphasized Wright's influence on the modern architects of Western Europe and noted that the "clearest formulas in the work" of Wright do not escape the "contradictions of the new architecture."[21] In 1932, in *Iskusstvo bytovoi veshchi* (The art of the everyday object), a book devoted to domestic space and furnishings, Arkin likewise mentioned Wright's 1901 lecture entitled "The Art and Craft of the Machine."[22]

In 1936 Arkin discussed the question of the relationship between aesthetics and the machine in his preface to the Russian edition of Lewis Mumford's 1927 book *Sticks and Stones,* as translated from the German edition. This encomium to the architectural culture of the United States purports to be a study of the culture itself, stating that "nowhere else but in America has the capitalist city set before the architect so many complex and contradictory problems, nowhere else have the very methods of the architectural project, and the very type of the architect himself, known changes as substantial as in America." Underlining this condition, Arkin stressed the marginal character of the works of Sullivan and of that "most recent of innovators, Frank Lloyd Wright," whose work fell outside the mainstream.[23]

Ever considered by Soviet Russia to be an anticapitalist "rebel," whose abstract sympathies for the USSR could be put to profitable use, Wright was one of the few foreigners invited to participate in the 1937 Conference of Architects (Fig. 6.7). This solemn visit to Moscow certainly won over his wife, Olgivanna, who served as interpreter during the trip. The meeting served as a high mass intended to consecrate definitively the "new course" of architecture in the USSR, one to be achieved both by the public humiliation of the old Constructivists and by the use of foreign "guests," criticism of whom would be of the most veiled sort.[24]

только не ослаблявший влияния его концепции, но, наоборот, сделавший эту последнюю особенно привлекательной для определенных тенденций и течений в новейшей европейской архитектуре. Райт был одним из первых и ранних деятелей архитектуры, выбросивших лозунги борьбы со стилизаторским пассеизмом традиционного зодчества, с его каноническими «стилями», с орнаментально-декоративными началами модерна—со всем прикладническим наследием буржуазной архитектуры доимпериалистической поры. Один из первых Райт призывал архитекторов и художников-прикладников сойти с антииндустриальных позиций рескинской эстетики, пойти на выучку к машине, ориентироваться на машинное производство и считаться с индустриальной техникой как с важнейшим фактором архитектурного и художественно-промышленного формообразования. Об этих своих первых выступлениях, предвосхитивших позднейшие лозунги конструктивизма, Райт сам рассказывает в своем «Третьем измерении»—программной статье, вошедшей в настоящую книгу.

Райт объявил войну декоративизму задолго до Корбюзье, и в этом молодое поколение европей-

ф. л. райт. операционный зал фирмы ларкин

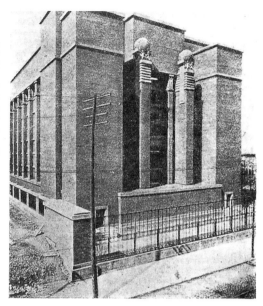

ф. л. райт. здание фирмы ларкин

ских архитекторов видит историческую его заслугу; причем райтовское влияние в позднейшие годы оказалось особенно сильным еще и потому, что оно исходило из Америки, материка, в чью сторону обратились взоры всех ревнителей «европейской культуры», лишь только выяснилось, что единственным победителем из мировой бойни вышел доллар. Из-за океана начали ожидать не только спасительных займов для укрепления падающих европейских валют, но и заветов и поучений по части «нового мировоззрения», в частности, новой эстетики. Это возросшее значение американских образцов сыграло свою роль в укреплении влияния Райта на европейскую архитектуру.

Однако, как мы уже отметили (и это является важнейшей чертой для всей характеристики Райта и райтовского влияния), его архитектурная практика обнаруживала чрезвычайно резкие противоречия с тезисами и лозунгами, им же самим провозглашенными. И что особенно примечательно, именно эта противоречивость художественно-идеологического облика Райта послужила опять-таки притягательным моментом для определенных течений послевоенной европейской архитектуры, ибо соответствовала собственным противоречиям этой последней.

Отталкивая все старые «стили», всю подражательную прикладническую архитектуру конца XIX века, призвав архитектора к выучке у индустриального производства, Райт в то же время культивировал в своей архитектурной практике самый

87

д. аркин

Ф. Л. Райт
в кулуарах Дома союзов

F. L. Wright dans les couloirs
de la Maison des Syndicats

Figure 6.6 *(opposite)*
Larkin Building, Buffalo, New York,
1902–6. FLW, architect. From David
Arkin, "Frank Lloyd Wright," *Arkhitek-
tura sovremennogo zapada* (Moscow:
OGIZ-IZOGIZ, 1932), 87.

Figure 6.7
Wright at the Architects' Congress,
Moscow, 1937. From *Arkhitektura SSSR*
5, nos. 7–8 (July–August 1937): 50.

In his conference talk, Wright warned against the excesses of Americanism and criticized "false and artificial" eclectic skyscrapers, thus revisiting points stressed in Arkin's analyses as well as in those formulated during the 1920s by Lissitzky, Nikolai Ladovskii, and Ginzburg. In a passage that does not appear in versions of his speech published in *Izvestia* and *Arkhitektura SSSR*, he attacked in the same stroke the project for the Palace of the Soviets, then being designed by Iofan, Gelfreikh, and Shchuko, which was to be dominated by a giant statue of Lenin.[25]

In condemning the course of the avant-garde and of the conservatives, Wright did not differentiate himself greatly from the dominant discourse of the Soviet leadership, except, of course, when he pitted organic architecture against the mega-lomania of Russian state projects.[26] Wright was seen in the conference halls with Boris Iofan, who earlier had visited the United States to find techniques that would permit the realization of his colossal Palace of the Soviets. In the analysis of American architecture that he published at the close of his trip, Iofan praised Broad-acre City (Fig. 6.8), a "utopian project for an agricultural village" that promised "to save humanity from capitalism."[27]

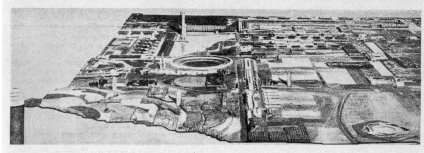

ных фасонных частей, в том числе мраморных и гранитных колонн и разных архитектурных деталей. Следует подчеркнуть, что карьеры снабжают своей продукцией целые города, что придает многим американским городам общий колорит, столь характерный, например, для Рима и Парижа.

В зданиях менее капитального типа, а также в деталях сложного рисунка нашли широкое применение искусственные материалы. Многие образцы представляют большой ин-

опыт в деле организации проектирования, и во многих случаях нам не мешает этим опытом пользоваться. Ряд консультационных фирм специально занимается вопросами планировки, устройства жилищ, больниц, всевозможного оборудования зданий и т. п. Важнейшим моментом архитектурного проектирования массовых зданий является отбор и комбинирование стандартных элементов, предлагаемых строительными фирмами. Правда, все это не может дать

План Бродекр-Сити. Арх. Ф. Л. Райт. 1935
Broadacre City. Arch. F. L. Wright. 1935

3   33

Figure 6.8
Illustration of Broadacre City model, 1935. From Boris Iofan, "Materialy o sovremennoi arkhitekture SShA it Italii," *Akademia arkhitektury* 3, no. 4 (1936): 33.

When Wright's turn came to address an audience at the Moscow Center for Architects, he proposed taking forty young Soviet apprentices to Taliesin. He also recalled the 1930 call of Le Corbusier, suggesting that Moscow—a conservative and obsolete city—be left to rot, and that the capital be rebuilt elsewhere.[28]

Upon his return to America, Wright cast a look back "across the Pole" at Moscow, criticizing its gigantism but lauding the human qualities of his interlocutors. In the two versions of the article he subsequently published, Wright balanced criticism of the official architecture with praise for "comrade Stalin."[29] Until 1943 he corresponded with Arkin, whose interest in Western architecture and Jewish origins would lead to his being accused, after 1945, of "cosmopolitanism" and, along with Alabian, the secretary general of the Union of Architects, of being a mercenary for Stalin's normalization.[30]

The Central Asian architects who, even before the end of World War II, began to lay the groundwork for the reconstruction of Russia did not take up the regional principles of Broadacre City as such, but the Wrightian plan did figure among the points of reference used to conceive of the postwar Soviet Union. In 1937 the satirical writers Ilya Ilf and Evgueni Petrov had published a hilarious account of a trip to the United States, entitled *Odnoetazhnaia Amerika* (literally, *One-Storied America*). In this tale, the Americanist vision of the metropolis no longer dominated; instead, a region fitted out with the automobile and whose standard theme was not the skyscraper but the roadway junction became the norm.[31] Echoing the words of Ilf and Petrov, who also reported an interview they conducted with Henry Ford, the urbanist Andrei Bunin imagined an architectural, "one-storied Russia," based on increased use of the automobile and the individual dwelling. Reflecting these opinions, models of American homes were at this time often the subject of publications concerning reconstruction projects.[32]

In other respects, Wright's influence remained discernible in the few expressions of propaganda organized in Moscow before the political climate between America and the USSR froze again in late 1945 at the onset of the cold war. His works were included, for example, in the photography exhibition "The Architecture of the U.S.A.," organized by Harvey Wiley Corbett and mounted in June 1944 at the Center for Architects,[33] as well as in the much more ambitious exhibition of 350 photographs selected by the editor of *Architectural Record,* Douglas Haskell, which was sent to Moscow in 1945 in an exhibit designed by Frederick Kiesler.[34]

Invited again in 1949 to receptions at the Soviet embassy in Washington, and apparently very pleased to be so, Wright was nevertheless completely shut out of the talks on twentieth-century architecture given by the USSR's postwar Socialist Realist ideologues. The "rehabilitation" of modern architecture carried out under Nikita Khrushchev beginning in 1954 would have to arrive before he would be considered an interesting creator once again. Presented as a destroyer of classicism in the 1920s, then as an anticapitalist rebel in the following decade, and ultimately forgotten, he would reoccupy a fitting status in the histories of Soviet architecture only once modern themes regained pride of place.

WRIGHT IN FRANCE: AN AMBIGUOUS READING

Wright's reception in France came even later than in Russia.[35] It produced, between 1920 and the early 1950s, different themes than those found in the conflict of the Soviet movements. The echo of Wright was practically indiscernible in France of the 1920s, as demonstrated by Lewis Mumford's remark that he was astonished that the first French monograph devoted to Wright should be entrusted to the novice historian Henry-Russell Hitchcock Jr. Mumford saw in this choice "an act that can attest to the French lack of familiarity with the work of Mr. Wright, for his influence in France has been negligible."[36]

At first, the superiority complex of the graduates of the Ecole des Beaux-Arts obliterated the potential for the first generation of Wright's works to be discovered. Thus, Jacques Gréber completely obscures the work of both Sullivan and Wright in *L'architecture aux Etats-Unis: Preuve de la force d'expansion du génie français* (Architecture in the United States: Proof of the expansive power of French genius), his 1920 work intended to be of encyclopedic scope.[37] To be sure, Wright's works are difficult to present as such "proof," given the American architect's unceasing criticism of the Beaux-Arts method of composition.[38]

Le Corbusier, the other opponent of Ecole des Beaux-Arts conventions, had a certain familiarity with the works of Wright, but it is linked to his visits to Ger-

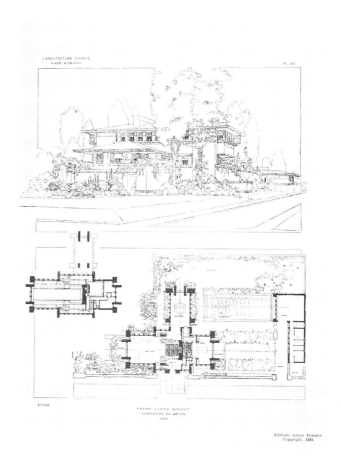

Figure 6.9

Plan and elevation, H. J. Ullman House, Oak Park, Illinois, 1904. FLW, architect. Illustration from the Wasmuth folios, erroneously dated 1920 and reproduced as "Habitation en béton" in *L'Architecture vivante,* winter 1924, n.p.

many prior to 1914. In a text from the first volume of the *Oeuvre complète,* he indicates that it was at Peter Behrens's office that "one day in 1913, a magazine arrived bearing the works of Frank Lloyd Wright, that precursor, and student of Sullivan's, a greater precursor still."[39] He was doubtless referring to issues of the *Schweizerische Bauzeitung* containing articles published by Berlage on his return from his trip to America, or perhaps to the *Ausgeführte Bauten* of Wright.[40] Invited by Hendricus Theodorus Wijdeveld to contribute to the 1925 *Wendingen* volume dedicated to Wright, Le Corbusier recalled the powerful effect the Prairie houses and the Larkin Building had had on him.[41]

The young Jeanneret not only thus discovered Wright, but he also conveyed his admiration for him to his mentor Auguste Perret. In 1915 he sent documents to Perret about the American's work.[42] Retrospectively, though, Le Corbusier settles accounts with Wright by classifying him as one who ignored the "essential rhythm" of building materials. In other respects, Jeanneret seems to use Wrightian themes at once in the 1912 home built in La Chaux-de-Fonds for his par-

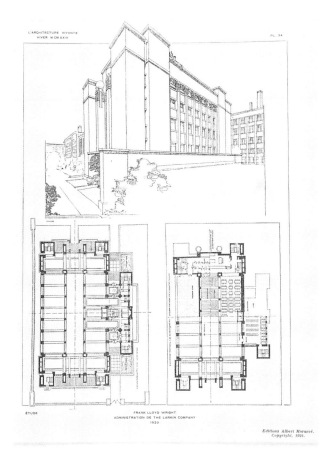

Figure 6.10

Plan and elevation, Larkin Building, Buffalo, New York, 1902–6. FLW, architect. Illustration from the Wasmuth folios, erroneously dated 1920 and reproduced in *L'Architecture vivante*, winter 1924, n.p.

ents, in the Schwob House, completed in 1917, and, beginning in 1914, in the conception of the Dom-ino projects.[43]

Other architects working in Paris gained access to knowledge of Wright not by way of Germany but through the "Dutch connection." In 1924 Jean Badovici, who was in contact with the various Dutch groups interested in the work of "one of the great creative forces of our era," presented the first French reproductions of the Wasmuth portfolio in the pages of *L'Architecture vivante* (Figs. 6.9 and 6.10).[44] The principal agent in the circulation of Wright's work at this point was Robert Mallet-Stevens, who also contributed to the 1925 *Wendingen* volume. His essay in that work refuted J. J. P. Oud's commentary, which incorrectly claimed that Wright's "influence" extended to "Holland, Germany, Czechoslovakia, France, Belgium, Poland, Romania, etc."[45] Mallet-Stevens stated that Wright "was one of the first to dare to break with routine tradition in order to create" and called his work "grand, rich, and logical." When he stressed the importance of concrete for industrial constructions "of original and healthy line," as found in

Wright's work, his analysis was similar to Le Corbusier's. It is as if in Wright the Parisians found justification for the celebration of concrete as a building material, reaffirming in a self-congratulatory way France's contribution to the birth of concrete.

Mallet-Stevens, again like Le Corbusier, judged Wright's plans and elevations to be comparable "to the great classics." He considered that Wright "masterfully sets his volumes to play within space, without falling into a sorry search for the picturesque," and that his "compositions" thus "possess an originality of imagination that radiates an impression of gaiety and well-being." Although according to Mallet-Stevens the American's "task" was "easier" than that of the current generation in Europe, he did not conceal his apprehension that "architects without ideas" would copy Wright's buildings. While "works with the power of Wright's" are "impossible to plagiarize," he confessed to sensing "with terror the efforts made by these architects to seize them, and to exploit this theft." On the whole, Mallet-Stevens made no attempt to conceal an admiration he admitted was already "of long standing."[46]

In a lecture entitled "Les raisons de l'architecture moderne dans tous les pays" (The reasons for modern architecture in all countries), Mallet-Stevens places the work of "the renowned American architect" within the context of a new global architecture. Commenting on a view of the Robie House, he declared himself struck by "this desire for long horizontals, lines whose realization only reinforced concrete permits." Likewise, presenting the "very geometric, very regular facade"

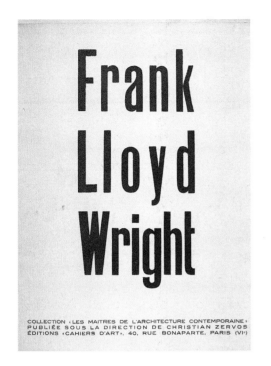

Frank Lloyd Wright

COLLECTION «LES MAITRES DE L'ARCHITECTURE CONTEMPORAINE»
PUBLIÉE SOUS LA DIRECTION DE CHRISTIAN ZERVOS
ÉDITIONS «CAHIERS D'ART», 40, RUE BONAPARTE, PARIS (VIᵉ)

Figure 6.12
Front cover, *Frank Lloyd Wright*
(Paris: Editions Cahiers d'Art, 1928).

of what he designates a "casino" of Wright's (doubtless Midway Gardens), he contended that "this symmetry and this repetition of elements considerably enlarge the edifice without the aid of arbitrary horizontals."[47] Mallet-Stevens thus closely associated the theme of concrete with Wright's works. His Cavroix Villa in Croix near Lille, built in the early 1930s, contained echoes of the Prairie Style in the horizontal elaboration of its geometry, while maintaining a more traditional sense of overall massing (Fig. 6.11). In fact, although the process of "enlarging" a building toward the exterior that Mallet-Stevens noted in Wright's houses can be seen in the villa's elongation, the compartmentalized character of the interior has little in common with American models.

Beginning in 1927, the Parisian journal *Cahiers d'art* announced a series of works "intended to popularize, using means of reproduction as perfect as possible, the most prominent figures in architecture and the laws that guide this architecture." The announcement was stated in terms standard to the thought of the young architect André Lurçat, who was put in charge of the collection by Christian Zervos, the series' founder.[48] The first two volumes of "Les maîtres de l'architecture contemporaine" (Masters of contemporary architecture) were to be devoted to Wright and Oud. The former is the only work of standing to be devoted to Wright in France prior to 1945 (Fig. 6.12). In announcing the publication, Lurçat took care to position Wright within a broader landscape, presenting "the slow and sure development of a mind that knew marvelously how to combine the facts of reason with the surprises of the imagination, and with the subtlest of sensibilities."[49]

In the correspondence that marked the preparatory stages of the book, as Lurçat negotiated shipment of the photographs to be included, Wright vaunted the "new principle of employing reinforced concrete" then being used in his California houses, and announced his delight at seeing himself, at last, given recognition in Paris, stating: "It *will* be good to see myself in France."[50]

The text for this work was entrusted to the young Harvard graduate and historian Henry-Russell Hitchcock Jr., who paid a visit to Lurçat on the recommendation of Oud.[51] The selection of illustrations was expressly credited to Lurçat, who likewise conceived of the book's layout, according to Willi Boesiger, then a draftsman in his studio. Boesiger shortly thereafter patterned his design for Le Corbusier's *Oeuvre complète* after Lurçat's.[52]

The book's forty-eight plates correspond in large part to the images that appeared in the 1925 *Wendingen* monograph, revisiting the cycle of the Prairie houses, which are illustrated with plates from the 1910 Wasmuth edition. Lurçat also included Wright's California experiments, represented by the Hollyhock and Millard houses, Midway Gardens, the Imperial Hotel, and Taliesin.[53] In his essay, Hitchcock compared Wright's work to current European work, taking into account Wright's manner of discourse—which Hitchcock aligns with both Walt Whitman and Le Corbusier's *Vers une architecture*—as much as his constructive thought.[54] If he here reasserts the dominant theme of French analyses that praise especially the constructive dimension of Wright's work, in other respects Hitchcock is careful to warn the reader against architecture's penchant for ornament, the mark of a certain lack of "restraint."[55] In the following year, Hitchcock elaborated on this critical vision in his book *Modern Architecture: Romanticism and Reintegration.*[56]

In 1929, Lurçat published *Architecture,* a manifesto modeled on Le Corbusier's satirical tracts, in which he hoped to consolidate his own position in the French scene. Once again he invoked the figure of Wright, taking particular note of the Millard House and comparing it to his own work. He recalled that "the effort at renewal can be found even in America, where Frank Lloyd Wright, after Richardson, works to rediscover beneficial laws."[57] However, Lurçat scarcely introduced Wrightian themes in his own creations prior to the early 1930s. The Hefferlin Villa, built for an American client in Ville d'Avray in 1932, is the earliest example of an attempt to capture the spatial fluidity of Wright's houses. To some degree, the elongation of compositions he began to develop during his stay in Moscow between 1934 and 1937 is indebted to Wright's modular plans.

In about 1930 French analyses of the American architectural scene began to include Wright's designs more consistently. The art historian Louis Gillet observed that Wright was a "leader of modern architecture, an equal of Perret and Le Corbusier," and described the Larkin Building as one "of severe composition and admirably readable, whose bare masses stylize the components and spell out its purpose as clearly as would the labels of a file."[58] Myron Malkiel-Jirmounski, in a more refined observation, described Wright as the "first and only American architect," and suggested that his influence in Europe was even more immense and

116 | JEAN-LOUIS COHEN

profound than in his own country. Malkiel-Jirmounski emphasized the effect of the Far East upon what he described as Wright's "Cubist conception of masses and of deftly distributed volumes," as well as his "intimate" bond "with nature."[59]

Despite this period of making up for lost time, Wright's presence in France remained marginal between the wars. In 1926 Jean Badovici described Wright's journeys and his "exile" from America, and emphasized Wright's influence in the Netherlands;[60] like so many other critics, however, he considered Wright to belong to the past, and thus relegated him to the status of a precursor out of touch with the current scene.[61]

Four years later, in a special issue of *L'Architecture vivante,* the only journal to give detailed attention to Wright, Badovici suggested a different reading of Wright's work. This issue, dedicated to Wright, focused largely on the buildings presented in the 1925 *Wendingen* volume and contained the plates from the Wasmuth portfolio. Overall, though, the issue downplayed the relevance of Wright's buildings and declared it to be limited to American soil, even though Badovici identified Wright as "one of the greatest, if not the greatest of modern architects."[62] In the end, Badovici subordinated his reading of Wright's buildings to the defense of Le Corbusier's architecture. He emphasized Le Corbusier's practice, noting that his use of materials like "concrete, steel, and glass" was not "unequal to his theory, however much a product of genius this theory may be." Publication of *L'Architecture vivante* was interrupted in 1933, at which point the principal French journal became *L'Architecture d'aujourd'hui,* headed by André Bloc and Pierre Vago, which had begun publication in 1930. The latter journal's silence on Wright is deafening; travel notes on America such as those by Eugène Beaudouin remain mute about Wright's work, of which, granted, only rare fully constructed examples were to be found until 1936.[63]

French journals did not overlook Wright's response to the 1932 Museum of Modern Art exhibition on the International Style, curated by Hitchcock and Philip Johnson, or his general reactions to the rise of the new European generation of architects. In 1932, in *Cahiers d'art,* the Zurich critic Sigfried Giedion discussed remarks made by the "precursor" (as he termed Wright) the preceding year in a Swiss journal.[64] He took up Wright's warning "against the new formalism that would result from use of the surface, line, and triangle." Wright, he noted, claiming "the rights of the individual," demanded above all an "*organic* evolution." Giedion rejected the "Wright vs. Le Corbusier" disjunction and recalled that without painting, and Cubism in particular, "architecture would have remained subservient and slavish"; he ended by stressing, though not without a certain element of finesse, various impasses in Wright's aims.[65]

The figure of Wright was henceforth recognized by intellectuals outside the field of architecture, such as the writer Jean Prévost, who in 1939 included Wright's biography in a book whose title, *Usonie: Esquisse de la civilisation américaine* (Usonia: sketch of American civilization), demonstrated Wright's centrality—together with the great orchestra leaders and Walt Disney—among emblematic figures of

"American civilization."[66] Moreover, Prévost recognized all the ways this "man of tyrannical genius" stood in opposition to the American establishment—this man who "imposes upon his clientele—in addition to using his own size as a measure—his tastes as a man of distinction and a man of progress, his extreme demand for unity." Wright, in the face of engineers and skyscrapers, advanced with his "homes" a different "sort of spirit," one that opposed "geometric form" to the "vertical line," thus heralding a new role for architecture.[67] Despite the title of his book, however, Prévost does not discuss the Usonian house, a true, if recent, reformulation of Wright's domestic architecture.

After World War II, a polar inversion emerged in the French attitude toward Wright. French functionalists now fixed their sights exclusively on the technical dimension of his works, reserving their full enthusiasm for Richard Neutra;[68] from that point on, consequently, Wright was taken over by the conservatives, who subjected his work to closer scrutiny than ever before. André Remondet, winner of the Grand Prix de Rome and Perret's successor at the Ecole des Beaux-Arts, for example, paid special attention to the Johnson Wax Administration Building (1936; Fig. 6.13) and Research Tower (1944) when he provided the French public with the first panoramic overview of postwar America.[69]

The high point of Wright's French reception is the Paris showing of the exhibition "Sixty Years of Living Architecture" and Wright's visit to France in April 1952. The journal *L'Architecture française* also published Wright's positions in a special issue (Fig. 6.14).[70] Founded in 1940 with a clearly antimodern bent, this journal was long directed by Michel Roux-Spitz, and did not spare criticism either of Le Corbusier or of Neutra, both of whom were sponsored by *L'Architecture d'aujourd'hui*. In the special 1952 issue, *L'Architecture française* countered the architecture of the "moderns," dubbed fetishists of technology, with organic architecture and published an address by Wright to the French nation.[71] Upon his

L'ARCHITECTURE
FRANÇAISE

123-124
(800 ITS)

FRANK LLOYD WRIGHT

Figure 6.13 *(opposite)*
Interior, Johnson Wax Administration
Building, Racine, Wisconsin, 1936–39.
FLW, architect. As published upside
down in *Techniques et architecture* 5,
no. 11 (November 1945): 178.

Figure 6.14
Cover, special issue dedicated to Wright,
L'Architecture française 13, nos. 123–24
(1952): 3.

return to the United States from France, Wright drafted a text (subsequently unpublished) entitled "Massacre on the Marseilles Waterfront"; in it he poured out his criticism of what he perceived as Le Corbusier's "conscienceless façade-wrecking" at the Unité d'Habitation at Marseilles (1946–52), and decried the treatment of "native culture" as a "rubbish heap."[72]

Within the space of twenty years, then, a reversal occurred in the French estimation of Wright. Initially identified as a "precursor" and summoned as a supporter by the radical moderns, he was thereafter opposed by them in the name of a humanism whose cultural aims were, in fact, of the most conservative sort. In both of these critical circumstances, the formal spatial dimension of Wright's work remained unaddressed. It would be taken into account only with the publication of Bruno Zevi's *Towards an Organic Architecture* and *Frank Lloyd Wright* (1946–47) and with its explication by numerous young architects with Taliesin training.[73]

TWO PARALLEL USAGES

Certain features do establish a parallel between Wright's Russian and French ventures. In order for a new generation to recover its critical dimension, it had to rediscover—during the crisis of the hegemony of modernized academicism in the early 1960s—Wright's buildings. In both France and Russia, the specific local configuration of "Americanism" shaped reception of Wright. In Russia, the programmatic strangeness of his structures, but above all the force of *Amerikanizm,* prevented his ideas from moving toward production. In France, the masking effect created by the Beaux-Arts superiority complex delayed his reception to the point of permitting him, paradoxically, to be used against the very "excesses" of those who had first discovered him in the 1920s.

In Russia of the Brezhnevian "stagnation" years, Wright's architecture remained a kind of exotic curiosity, quite remote from the preoccupations of professional architects and critics alike. It was not the same in France, where knowledge of Wrightian buildings was spread through schools, and where original research—such as that of Jean Castex on the Prairie houses, part of the investigations carried out by the short-lived group "Syntaxe"—began to appear.[74] The Parisian public's astonishment upon viewing the model and drawings of Broadacre City, presented in the spring 1997 exhibition "Les Années 30" at the Musée National des Monuments Français, attests, however, to the hazy nature of knowledge about Wright in France, as if the initial distance has in some way persisted to the end of the twentieth century.[75] In the end, the separate interpretations developed by each country reveal an abundance of meanings that have been projected onto Wright's work. In Moscow as in Paris, the rule seems to have been a sometimes cynical exploitation of the architect in turn by radical movements and conservative institutions, at the expense of a profound understanding of his architecture. A rebel used by the Russians in their denunciation of American capitalism, Wright was first seen by the French architectural press, in contrast, as the pioneer of reinforced concrete, then, paradoxically, as a traditionalist.

SEVEN: WRIGHT AND GREAT BRITAIN

Andrew Saint

In 1963 Sir John Summerson, that shrewdest of English architectural historians, gave a paper at the Twentieth International Congress of the History of Art in New York entitled "The British Contemporaries of Frank Lloyd Wright."[1] It is salutary to look back upon the way in which Summerson tackled the subject, at a date when Wright's death four years before was fresh in memory. Departing from the point of his birth in 1867 and with sparing allusion to his architecture, Summerson shifts straight away into a quick survey of Wright's British contemporaries: C. R. Mackintosh, born in 1868, whose reputation (inflated since then beyond any measure that could have been anticipated) he softly disparages; C. R. Ashbee, born in 1863, Wright's one faithful English friend and admirer during the early and wilderness years; and others whom time and fashion may have rendered less familiar in the United States today.

Summerson's method is juxtaposition rather than comparison. For he was too alert a commentator, too aware of the depth of British insularity, and too steeped in the mysterious, magpie processes that inhabit the unconscious mind of creative architects to suppose that much could be illuminated by pressing the connections too hard. Instead we are presented with a foreground picture of two architectural cultures divided by a common zeitgeist. Behind this lies the backdrop of a British modern architecture only now at last being fulfilled (recall that we are in 1963), and of a nation for whom the nimble Lutyens, Wright's closest equivalent in authority and standing, has proved a noble but ultimately retrograde example.

In fact, Summerson is careful not to compare Lutyens directly with Wright, slipping him in only at the end. Did he know that Wright in 1951 reviewed the memorial volumes on Lutyens's work in glowing terms, praising "the love, loyalty and art with which this cultured Architect, in love with Architecture, shaped

HOUSE OF JAMES CHARNLEY, ESQ., ASTOR STREET, CHICAGO, ILL.

Figure 7.1
Charnley House, North Astor Street, Chicago, 1891–92. FLW for Adler and Sullivan, architects. From *American Architecture and Buildings News* 31 (December 1892).

his buildings"?[2] Whether he did or not, it would hardly have coloured his view of the matter. The lesson of the essay is that community of aim and milieu should never be confused with conscious influence or exchange.

Just one fleeting comparison between buildings slips into Summerson's paper. It remains as tantalizing today as it did at the time, might still upset current ideas about Anglo-American architectural exchange if something could be proved, and draws us naturally into looking at the first of a set of overlaps and misunderstandings between Wright and the architectural culture of Great Britain. The familiar starting place is Wright's beliefs in the 1890s and whether it is reasonable to identify them with the Arts and Crafts movement, British or American. The less obvious counterpoint, as we shall see later, concerns British architects' very particular reactions towards Wright down the generations—and vice versa.

There is a compelling resemblance, Summerson remarks, between the pavilion-flanked front of the Charnley House of 1891–92 (designed and published under the name of Adler and Sullivan but claimed by Wright for himself) and that suavest, most American-looking of Arts and Crafts buildings in London, Dunbar Smith and Cecil Brewer's Mary Ward Settlement of 1896–97 (Figs. 7.1 and 7.2).[3]

A link between the two is not impossible. There was, for the first time, lively if episodic fascination with American architecture in Britain during the 1880s and 1890s, as David Gebhard was the first to document.[4] The Charnley House was illustrated in the *American Architect and Building News* at the end of 1892.[5] Ar-

Figure 7.2
Mary Ward Settlement, Tavistock Place,
London, 1896–97. A. Dunbar Smith
and Cecil Brewer, architects.

chitectural and decorative-arts magazines crossed the Atlantic in both directions
(the Mary Ward Centre was published in the most international of all English
magazines, *The Studio,* in 1899). Yet so far as we can say, Smith and Brewer had
no knowledge of the United States when they designed their building. Later, in
1911, Cecil Brewer visited the United States and made friends with Bertram
Goodhue.[6] No contact with Wright is known, nor can any coincidence of idiom
be gleaned from Smith and Brewer's later work. An alternative explanation for
the apparent Americanism of the Mary Ward Centre has even been hazarded:
influence upon its architects by James MacLaren, that short-lived Scot whose
houses seem sometimes to take cues from H. H. Richardson.[7]

Nothing can be proved, then. Yet the points of convergence will not go away
so easily. The Mary Ward Settlement was a product of the "settlement movement,"
vigorous in the 1890s on both sides of the Atlantic, with an English power-house
at Toynbee Hall in London's East End and an American counterpart in the shape
of Jane Addams's Hull House, Chicago. There were close connections between
the institutions. Toynbee Hall was where C. R. Ashbee first developed the social
ideas about art which led him to set up his Guild of Handicraft; and it was at the
sister foundation of Hull House that Ashbee stayed when he first visited Chicago
and got acquainted with Wright in 1900.[8] Hull House was a hotbed of Anglophilia
and arts-and-crafts values around the turn of the century.[9] Here the Chicago Arts
and Crafts Society—of which Frank Lloyd Wright was a paid-up member—was

founded in 1897. Shortly after Ashbee's visit, Hull House was also the venue where Wright delivered the original version of his fierce anti-Ruskinian manifesto, "The Art and Craft of the Machine," in March 1901.[10]

There were other lines of contact between Hull House and England besides Ashbee. One was with the arts-and-crafts architect and theorist W. R. Lethaby, whose American brother-in-law, Ernest Crosby, wrote to his sister from Hull House in 1905 that "Lethaby's name is held in great reverence and I am looked upon with awe by reflection."[11] Lethaby had been party to the competition for the Mary Ward Settlement and was friendly with Smith and Brewer, then eager young men involved in the settlement movement.[12] Much later, in 1957, the painter and art teacher William Johnstone, who had been to see Wright at Taliesin, could claim to a London lecture audience that Wright had once said to him: "Johnstone, we got it all from Lethaby, you know."[13] No doubt this was a casual piece of flattery, trotted out for an impressionable English visitor and referring to community of educational aim, not architectural attitude. Yet the hint of connections, or at least tangents, persists.

Leaving this minor enigma aside, can we be more specific about Wright's cultural debt to Britain, and in particular to the English house? This question has

Figure 7.4
C. R. Ashbee, photographic portrait
taken by Frank Lloyd Wright during
Ashbee's visit to Chicago in 1900.

been well and succinctly addressed in Richard Guy Wilson's summary of the architectural relationship between Chicago and the Arts and Crafts movement, but may be worth rehearsing in a little more detail.[14] The difficulty in establishing Wright's affiliations and commitments lies, as always, in picking the truth from his obsessive later attempts to rewrite the record and convince himself that he stood alone against the world.

Pevsner claimed in the original edition of *Pioneers of the Modern Movement* that Wright was not unmindful of his debt to English ideas.[15] His membership in the Hull House circle appears at first sight to prove it. Yet if we ask to what extent in the fluid 1890s Wright really attended to developments in British art and architecture, the answer seems to be: very little. He had picked up an idealized grasp of Ruskin and Morris through reading and was alert to the American arts-and-crafts debate. In their unevenness of expression and range of styles, the early houses are on all fours, inside and out, with the wide-ranging mixture of motifs and ideals already found in the homegrown domestic revival of the Midwest. Doubtless Wright rummaged through the magazines, as young architects do, and could produce a passable half-timbered, "English" house when one was asked of him (Fig. 7.3). But it is idle to suppose that he had any real feeling about such a thing, much less that his path towards maturity was influenced by Shaw or Voysey or even Greek Thomson, as has been hazarded.[16] Nor did he meet any British architect or artist first-hand before Ashbee met him in 1900, so far as we know (Fig. 7.4).

If there was as yet in these years any real ideological difference between Wright and the English, it must be sought in the domain of process, not product. In 1894 he was happy to recommend Morris and Liberty fabrics, but he was also already talking in general terms about "the machine."[17] A divergence between British and American arts-and-crafts attitudes towards politics, labour, and machinery has often been remarked upon.[18] In reality, a spectrum of views can be found in either nation around 1900, from a hankering for primitive rural socialism and handicraft to a welcoming of capitalist modes of production and the division between design and manufacture.

In Chicago's case, the industrial nature of the city prompted its arts-and-crafts community to reach an accommodation with local manufacturers. That is what the short-lived Industrial Art League of Chicago, founded in 1899, was all about. Wright must have welcomed this move. Given the positive, almost boosterish attitude towards ornament and machinery articulated by Sullivan, it is unlikely that his famous assistant would ever have identified with the handworking wing of the movement. What is striking is that Wright came to identify this latter tendency, willy-nilly, with English influence.

In his first conversations with Ashbee in 1900, Wright was already lauding the machine, as the former recorded in his journal:

> He threw down the glove to me in characteristic Chicagoan manner in the matter of Arts and Crafts and the creations of the machine. "My God," said he, "is machinery, and the art of the future will be the expression of the individual artist through the thousand powers of the machine, the machine, doing all that the individual workman cannot do, and the creative artist is the man that controls all this and understands it." He was surprised to find how much I concurred with him, but I added the rider, that the individuality of the average had to be considered, in addition to that of the artistic creator himself.[19]

It is the Englishman's consent, coupled with his rider, that is most striking in this passage. It reminds us that Ashbee, Lethaby, and the best of their British arts-and-crafts contemporaries—even Morris before them—had their own developed and balanced attitude towards the uses and abuses of machinery. Yet it was to become their fate to be branded by Wright (and, in due course, the world of scholarship) as uncompromising, old-world Luddites.

In the original lecture "The Art and Craft of the Machine," given three months after his talk with Ashbee, Wright reassured his Hull House audience that "all artists love and honor William Morris . . . together with Ruskin, the great moralist." But, he went on, all artists who feel as they did "had best distinctly wait and work sociologically where great work may still be done by them. In the field of art activity they will do distinct harm. Already they have wrought much miserable mischief."[20]

Wright's target here was evidently the Morris-loving, handworking wing of the American arts-and-crafts community—the likes of the sententious Elbert Hubbard and his Roycrofters. Where Wright would have drawn the line about "sociological" work is a moot point. The general community activity of Hull House was clearly sociological; but Ashbee saw his Guild of Handicraft, in the depths of deprived East London, as sociological rescue-work too.

Wright's position, as was his wont, became more strident with time and repetition. By the 1920s he was alleging that the Anglophile arts-and-crafts and university intelligentsia at Hull House had conspired back in 1901 against his stand on behalf of the machine. This was unfounded. He had delivered "The Art and Craft of the Machine" at his own request; it contributed to a debate then being fostered by the Industrial Art League of Chicago, and there is no reason to believe that he was repressed or "voted down and out by the enthusiastic disciples of Ruskin and Morris," as he claimed.[21] Nonetheless, the consistency of his position is clear. By 1900–1901 at the latest, Ashbee concluded, Wright—as one might expect from an admirer of Sullivan's—was taking a more positive attitude towards machinery than the one which the average Arts and Crafts Englishman or American was prepared to take. This too-often simplified debate entailed differing attitudes not just towards style but also towards the whole process of procurement and control in architecture.

Similar overlaps and misunderstandings between the cultures are illuminated by the history of Wright's first-hand experiences of Britain.

Frank Lloyd Wright's first visits to Britain took place in October 1909 and September 1910.[22] He had a sole English friend and champion at that time: Ashbee, who together with his wife, Janet (Fig. 7.5), had come to know the Wrights more intimately during the second of their visits to Chicago, in 1908. This four-sided, uxorious friendship and the correspondence it elicited are among the main clues we have to Wright's moods and movements during these years.[23]

During their stay of 1908, the Ashbees became aware that the Wrights' marriage was in trouble. They had repeatedly asked Frank and Catherine to England, but the invitation was never taken up. Instead, Wright's early visits were solo stopovers after the marital separation from Catherine, as he escaped to and made his way back from continental Europe by liner. On the outward journey in the autumn of 1909 he was travelling with Mamah Borthwick Cheney, who with her husband, Edwin, had been one of Wright's clients. We know that Wright was demoralized or at least embarrassed, because when he finally broached the subject of the breakup with Ashbee, he told him that while in London he had not had the heart to call: "I passed your little home in Chelsea with a longing and disappointment hard to bear," he wrote.[24]

No strangers to emotional complexity, the Ashbees persisted in their invitation. So in September 1910 Wright spent the best part of a fortnight in Britain on his way home. (Mamah remained in Europe.) This included an excursion, prob-

Figure 7.5
C. R. Ashbee's mother, Mrs. H. Ashbee
(left), and his wife, Janet Ashbee *(right)*.
Portrait taken by Wright during the
Ashbees' visit to Chicago in 1900.

Figure 7.6 *(opposite)*
Silversmith's workshop at the Guild of
Handicraft, Chipping Campden, ca. 1905.

ably of some days, to Ashbee's country fiefdom at Chipping Campden in the Cotswolds.[25]

We know nothing of what Wright saw on this visit. Ashbee would have tried to enthuse him about the building and craft traditions of the Cotswolds, and indeed Wright praised Cotswold buildings on his trip to England forty years later.[26] But it is worth noting that Wright made the first moves towards establishing Taliesin soon after his return to Chicago from Chipping Campden. For in 1902, in a proto-Wrightian gesture of effrontery and courage, Ashbee had removed the whole of his Guild of Handicraft, lock, stock, and barrel, out of the East End of London and reestablished it in Chipping Campden (Fig. 7.6). Significantly, it had failed to prosper there and was formally disbanded three years before Wright arrived.[27] Nevertheless, many stalwarts from the guild stayed on and were still to be found in their workshops. The vestiges of a country-based collective for healthy making, doing, and living, inspired and controlled by an architect-ideologue and uncorrupted by urban distraction, were there before Wright in Campden to contemplate. Campden represented just one of many attempts to pioneer new patterns of communal living and working all over Europe and America in the early years of the century. But here, at any rate, Wright saw such an initiative at first hand. It seems to have helped him formulate the embryo of an idea, one that offered freedom and escape from the embarrassments of Chicago and Oak Park.

At the end of this visit there was some sort of quarrel between Wright and the Ashbees, seemingly occasioned by the draft introduction Ashbee had written for *Frank Lloyd Wright: Ausgeführte Bauten,* the so-called *Sonderheft*.[28] On the face of it, the disagreement concerned individualism and the extent to which Wright would acknowledge influence from and community with others, an issue that always brought out the aggressive side of his personality. Underneath lay the broader divisions regarding personal credit for and control over buildings which had already surfaced between the two men in 1900–1901. Ashbee stood, at least in theory, for a collective ideal of work, while Wright wavered between absolute individualism and the upholding of a common cause. Later, Wright confessed to "ungracious manners" on this occasion.[29] But Janet Ashbee had now begun to take a definite dislike to him. Henceforward she was Catherine's friend, while her husband's relationship with Wright became more episodic. The two men met again only twice after this encounter: at Taliesin in 1916 and in England in 1939.[30]

Apart from a possible further short stopover in 1911, more than twenty-eight years elapsed before Frank Lloyd Wright visited Britain again. Whereas in 1910 no one to speak of in England but Ashbee knew who he was or took any notice of him, in 1939 he was a celebrity: he expected to be, and was, lionized. During a week in London he and Olgivanna sped from dinner to lecture to broadcast performance and even to an appearance on that new marvel of technology, the television.[31] This was Britain's first taste of the international architect-megastar lecture-tour that so muddles and distracts architecture today. But whereas students nowadays never dream of arguing with the megastars or of telling them where they are going wrong, that in part is what happened to Wright in London.

May 1939 was a tense time in Europe. It fell between Hitler's effective repudiation of the Munich agreement in March, with the German move into Czechoslovakia, and the fateful invasion of Poland in September. Everyone in Europe knew that war was imminent. In America, not least in the Midwest, there was a clear conviction that the effete British had made a mess of things and were in a bad way. That was the feeling in Britain too, not least among young professionals. In the smarter schools of architecture, notably Liverpool and the Architectural Association in London (AA), students had become politicized—to a degree that was later played down. At the AA there had been open revolt against the atelier system of teaching; the students clamoured for "group practice" and social relevance in their project work. High-minded graduates were spurning jobs with private firms of architects in favour of New Deal–style bodies like the Miners Welfare Commission and city and county architects' offices. That was the supply side. On the demand side, programmes of slum clearance and school construction became the priority of a little British building boom that enlivened the late 1930s, before the government diverted money back into armaments.[32]

It was not just modernism or the so-called International Style that was being clamoured for, but socially directed modernism. If Lutyens had still been the leading British architect in 1930, by 1939 he was overshadowed by the philosophical Marxist emigré Berthold Lubetkin and his collective practice Tecton, whose more ardent partners spent their spare time running an agitprop group. Few architects under the age of forty were untouched by this mood, which persisted into the war and beyond. Even Summerson echoed the spirit, arguing in 1942 that "the next thing to be done is to render architecture *effective* in English life." This he construed as the task of getting the mass of ordinary buildings well designed and built, rather than "trying to fly level with the poet-innovator Le Corbusier."[33] He might have substituted the name of Wright, but it was Le Corbusier rather than Wright who inhabited the forefront of avant-garde British architects' minds at the time.

Into this perturbed climate breezed Frank Lloyd Wright, wafted by an invitation to give the annual Sir George Watson lectures for the Sulgrave Manor Board. Sulgrave Manor, a venerable stone mansion in Northamptonshire, had been built by a Washington in Elizabethan times. The Anglo-American Society bought the house after the First World War, as a base from which to foster friendship between the two nations, trading on the magic of the Washington name. Sir George Watson was a dairy owner who had endowed a London lecture series wherein distinguished and respectable Americans were to explain their politics and culture to the British.[34] It is a mark of how distinguished and respectable Wright had become by 1939 that his invitation to give the lectures had emanated from the British ambassador in Washington, Sir Ronald Lindsay. (Wright was the third choice following refusals from Henry Stimson and Van Wyck Brooks, two notables all but forgotten in Britain today.) Even five years before, such an invitation would have been improbable. But in the later 1930s the East Coast establishment of the United States had welcomed the wayward genius back into favour. Wright sufficiently enjoyed the fleshpots of civilization, against which he so often inveighed, to reap what he could from the consequences: hero worship, plentiful stays at the Plaza Hotel in New York, and jaunts abroad. Hence the 1939 trip to England.

It seems self-evident now that Wright must already have been famous in Britain. In fact, however, that fame was of very recent origin. *Ausgeführte Bauten und Entwürfe* of 1911 and its little companion volume, the *Sonderheft,* despite Ashbee's foreword, seem to have made almost no British headway. Both were German-language publications issued not long before the First World War, a catastrophe that inoculated most Britons against the products of German culture for a decade and more.[35] The *Wendingen* articles published in Holland took no firmer hold. Yet an intense English interest in Dudok and his Dutch, brick-building contemporaries after 1930 meant that architects came by degrees to know about Wright's work through the filter of those he had animated and influenced in Holland.

In interwar Britain, excellence in American architecture meant the East Coast Beaux-Arts tradition, commercial urbanism, and the skyscraper. These are the kinds of building admired and endorsed in, for instance, Manning Robertson's popular *Laymen and the New Architecture* (1925), which has not a whisper of Wright. Liverpool, under C. H. Reilly the leading architectural school, sent its best pupils to big East Coast offices with pride.[36] The New Yorkers Hastings, Corbett, and Hood all enjoyed landmark commissions during the 1920s in London (Fig. 7.7), where there was a widespread feeling that only Beaux-Arts–trained Americans knew how to plan modern city offices properly.[37]

In planning circles there was another set of links between the English garden-city movement and another East Coast power base, the Regional Planning Association of America—between Raymond Unwin, for instance, and Lewis Mumford, a self-acknowledged disciple of Patrick Geddes.[38] It was from Mumford, notes Alvin Rosenbaum, that Wright learnt in the late 1920s to articulate those arguments for urban decentralization and dispersal to which he had long been inclined by instinct. They got their first airing in Wright's Princeton lectures of 1930; were explored to the full in Broadacre City, the vague land-tenure proposals that seem to have been coloured by another Englishman, the social-credit theorist A. R. Orage; and were to be vehemently asseverated by Wright during his London visit of 1939.[39] But for British planning intellectuals, reared on Ebenezer Howard, the garden city, and the land-reform theories of Henry George, this was old hat by the 1930s. Broadacre City, if they knew about it at all, would have appeared a visionary irrelevance; Henry Wright of Radburn fame meant more to them at this time than Frank Lloyd Wright.

Figure 7.7
Ideal House (now Palladium House),
Great Marlborough Street, London,
1929. Designed by Raymond Hood
with C. Gordon Jeeves, architects, as
the "little sister" of the American
Radiator Building in New York City.

The Architectural Association in London was probably the first place where Wright's work was regularly appreciated and debated in England. Here a more outward-looking culture began to emerge under the energetic partnership of Howard Robertson, principal from 1926, with secretary-photographer Frank Yerbury. Robertson, who had an American mother and traces of an American accent, was a critic of sophistication, broad sympathy, and an insatiable appetite for travel. None of Robertson's copious American articles of the 1920s focussed exclusively upon Wright. But he published a plan of the Imperial Hotel in *The Principles of Architectural Composition* (1924), illustrated Midway Gardens in 1927, and gave Wright space and praise in his *Modern Architectural Design* of 1932, which included a personal sketch of the Ennis House.[40]

The first edition of Wright's *Autobiography,* published in 1932, seems to have earned the American architect a coterie of British admirers. Ashbee wrote its author a fan letter—though not without criticizing the book's "slovenliness of structure," which appeared so different, he pointed out, from Wright's own buildings.[41] Summerson acquired his copy in November 1935, sticking in it a Whitmanesque review of the book by John Dos Passos, and in the following year excerpts were published in the *Architects' Journal.*[42]

It was in this year, 1936, that Nikolaus Pevsner published his *Pioneers of the Modern Movement,* with its unequivocal ordination of Wright as protomodernist. The first edition illustrates just the Winslow House, the William R. Heath House in Buffalo, the American Luxfer Prism project of 1894, and the Larkin Building. The conscientious Pevsner made it his business to try and find out through an intermediary (probably Henry-Russell Hitchcock) about the sequence of the early buildings. Back came the answer from Wright, "Damned if I know," which Pevsner duly inserted in the text.[43] From this time on, Frank Lloyd Wright's name was more or less a household word in British architectural circles. Yet Pevsner still felt it necessary at the time of the 1939 visit to write an article saying how sluggish Britain had been on the uptake compared to other European nations.[44]

So, to the events of the visit. Wright duly descended upon London with Olgivanna and "an amazing colour-film of life at Taliesin and of his recent buildings." He enjoyed himself no end, feasting, orating, extemporizing, showing off, and exercising his combative skills at a breathless pace. At this juncture Wright had no more respect for the antifascist mood of the moment than he did for metropolitan values, so one may well imagine the tenor of his contribution to an English-Speaking Union debate on whether London's architecture was "more in danger from builders than bombers."[45] For the first and only time he met Lutyens and Voysey, both older than himself, and liked them both. But he had time for faithful Ashbee only once and ducked out of an invitation to address the Art Workers' Guild.[46] That relic of the William Morris era no doubt looked lacklustre and antediluvian to the creator of the Johnson Wax Building, as it did to the young at the time.

The lectures themselves, four in number, were held at the Royal Institute of

British Architects (RIBA). Widely advertised, they attracted unprecedented audiences—in some cases more than a thousand people.[47] A book of them had been planned and was promptly published by Lund Humphries as *An Organic Architecture*. But that did not prevent Wright from speaking impromptu. His words were taken down, he recalled, by an "old court reporter . . . it was amazing, and was the only time when a speech that I had made did not sound like the ravings of a drunken man. He had it straight, and I had very little to do with it, and so it was published, when the bombs were falling on London, in one of the nicest little books I have seen."[48]

The text of the talks offers as lively and witty a source as any for Wright's mature views on architecture and society. He made a point of speaking broadly, on the grounds that his invitation came from the Sulgrave Manor Board rather than the RIBA, and he tempered his remarks a little to his English audience. In general, the lectures were brilliantly and emotionally received. Wright added to the sense of occasion, as Peter Blake remembered, "looking very much like a Victorian character actor, or, more ominously, like Richard Wagner, with his flowing white locks and billowing cape."[49] Yet the younger architects lining the walls were dissatisfied. This emerges to some extent from the published text, which incorporates a modicum of anonymous questions and Wright's answers, but more from contemporary comments.[50] After the second lecture the *RIBA Journal* sounded a coded note of cool English warning, doubtless penned by the left-leaning E. J. (Bobby) Carter. He hoped that the Wrights' full programme would leave them time to "penetrate the unrevealing wall of adulation to the qualities of us and our architecture. Probably what he thinks of us is much more important than what we think of him." Listening or talking to Frank Lloyd Wright was one-way traffic, implied Carter; and what he had to say seemed unhelpful to a Britain on the brink of war.[51]

Two weeks later, with Wright safely on board his liner, Carter returned to the subject with a sense of frustration. The meetings, he said, had been "charged with feeling"; but Wright and his critics had got at constant cross-purposes, with

> Mr Wright presenting a formula, a general pattern of development,
> in a Marxian way, extending rationality in human problems to include
> spheres of life in which radical changes are all the time taking place;
> the critics all the time looking for an exactitude of solution which this
> extended reasoning could not allow. All along, mystics have been asking
> such questions as, "Please, Mr Wright, where do I put the soil pipes in
> organic architecture?"[52]

Wright himself must have been a little stung by his reception, for, once back at Taliesin after a Dalmatian holiday, he shot back a volley at his British critics. The objections of his juvenile opponents had been, essentially, that he had failed to get beyond the promise of his early career and was oblivious to the genius, vitality, and validity of cities. If the former complaint was ignorant, the latter one hit the mark. Asked about London, Wright had proposed to keep the historic centre as the middle of a great park but to "destroy the rows and rows of commonplace houses in which people try to live"; he was sure they would opt for dispersal. Now and again he would allow them back to their old environs: "We occasionally go to the graveyards of our ancestors, so why not to the remains of our cities?"[53]

Wright's philosophy of dispersal was no more drastic than proposals being dangled at the time (with the spectre of mass-bombing in mind) before the British government's Barlow Commission on the distribution of the industrial population. But the callous candour of his words infuriated his left-wing urban critics. For the gritty Londoners, the Taliesins as featured in Jimmie Thompson's seductive colour film were a romantic irrelevance; Wright was accused of betraying his early allegiance to the machine. One especially priggish respondent went so far as to claim that there was "no better man than the Cockney soldier and no one who can bear hardship with greater fortitude and cheerfulness," attributing this virtue to the experience of "battleship existence through living in crowded quarters."[54] Wright demolished this sinister argument coolly enough, and on the whole defended himself with accuracy, along with the customary egotism and panache. The machine, he argued, was now using man instead of being used by man:

> What I started to do, with high faith, and confidence in human-creative forces, I see giving way to certain sterilising factors in my original equation. Instead of mastering those factors on the side of creation, Europe has seen only a new aesthetic for academic consumption in a foolish attempt to establish a contemporary vernacular. . . . I said that the only way man can use his machine and *keep alive what is best of him* is to go by means of it to the larger freedom the machine makes possible—go towards *decentralisation* instead of continuing the centralisation the machine exploits and, so far as any great human benefit goes, will soon explode. Simple enough? Do I continue to befog the issue? If so the Machine itself will prove me right. Meantime I can wait and work.[55]

As Bobby Carter remarked, the combatants in this argument had got at cross-purposes because they were stereotyping one another, as so often occurs in cultural exchange. Abetted by Pevsner's interpretation and Wright's own imprecision, the British had scant idea of the effort Wright had put into standardization in the textile-block houses of the 1920s, or of the strides he was now beginning to make with the smaller Usonian houses, which Wright did show but did not explain precisely. They knew little of Fallingwater or the Johnson Wax Building. For his part, Wright had neither the temperament nor the time to grasp what Europe's urban and architectural problems really were and to modify his message accordingly. "Like Marie Antoinette . . . he offered us cake," snorted one critic.[56] In these circumstances, the chances of mutual understanding and beneficial influence were slim. One thing, however, this visit achieved: it convinced audiences that a professional architect could have public presence and charisma—something never seen in Britain before.

Wright's later visits to Britain, in 1950 and 1956, may be more briefly described. The grant of the RIBA's Gold Medal in 1941 had tickled him and dug him out of isolationism a little. Nor was Wright utterly immune to the sense of amity engendered by wartime alliance. So when he arrived in London in 1950 he was inclined to be politely sentimental about a war effort that had left him unmoved or hostile in 1939 and even 1940. He came at the behest of a telegram from Robert Furneaux Jordan, a left-wing architect and teacher and then the inspiring head of the AA. Jordan's rationale was simple, as he put it at the reception for the Wrights: there was only one really great architect in the world, and he felt that his students ought to see him. The school could not afford the visit, but that was Jordan's way.[57]

Wright duly played the great man with less provocation than he had shown when he had dropped into the AA eleven years before and told the students that they were boys and girls, not ladies and gentlemen, and that they needed weeding out by perhaps five to one (Fig. 7.8).[58] Presenting prizes in a marquee set up in Bedford Square, he pronounced that few if any of the prize winners would come to any good, and that you could never be any good at architecture until you had learnt to "shake it out of your sleeve."[59] On decentralization, he stuck to his hobbyhorse. His ideas for bomb sites were simple: "I do not care where it fell, even if it was on Buckingham Palace: plant grass."[60]

On this occasion, a prissy critic in *The Builder* summarized continuing British reservations over Wright's message:

> The thoughts of 99% of architectural students are devoted to planning
> the lives, the homes, the hospitals, the schools and the crematoria of the
> ordinary citizen. But when Mr Lloyd Wright last week accompanied his
> plea for an architecture of democracy by suggesting that that desirable end
> could be obtained only through organic architecture, we began to wonder
> at what point we came in, for he defined organic architecture as "some-
> thing which comes from within and spreads outwards." We read that as
> meaning a return to individual thought and action, and wondered what
> it had to do with an architecture of democracy which, in Great Britain
> at least, is girt round with the shackles of committees and group working,
> in which the individual is apt to stifle though the mass survive.[61]

Again, though, Wright enjoyed himself. He bought top hats "in the plural" in St. James's Street. Conducted by Jordan to the South Bank to see the rising Royal

Festival Hall, he could not be bothered with the site and went instead to see the drawings at County Hall, the London County Council's offices close by (Figs. 7.9 and 7.10). "Boys, boys," he is supposed to have reproved Robert Matthew and Leslie Martin, as he scrawled across a sectional drawing of the auditorium, "it won't work; it's got to be in the section of a trumpet." Thus did he recall Adler's pre-Sabinian science of acoustical design from the Chicago Auditorium of sixty years before. "So you fear, Mr Wright," said someone, "that we might get a little too much reverberation." "Fear! I don't fear, I know. I'm telling you. Sullivan and I built 26 concert halls [a gross exaggeration] and I know."[62] On this visit Wright also pilgrimaged to the Wales of his ancestors; eyewitnesses recall him urinating against the half-completed, nine-domed Brynmawr Rubber Factory, the other smart British building of the moment. By way of striking back on behalf of the European Modern Movement, the emigré architect Arthur Korn is remembered riding a child's tricycle round one end of a large North London living room and shouting a derisory "toot, toot" while Wright at the other end recounted to hushed admirers how it all began years ago amid the long green grass of the prairie.[63]

Figure 7.8
Wright with students at the Architectural Association during his visit to London, July 1950.

Figure 7.9 *(above)*
Wright with Leslie Martin *(left)* and
Robert Matthew *(right),* County Hall,
London, July 1950.

Figure 7.10
Wright in the doorway of County Hall,
London, with Leslie Martin *(left)* and
Robert Furneaux Jordan *(right),*
July 1950.

Figure 7.11
Wright with Clough Williams-Ellis
at Plas Brondanw, Wales, 1956.
(FLWA 6806.0001)

The last British visit was in 1956, when Wright received a doctorate of law from the University College of Wales at Bangor. On this occasion he stayed with another veteran architect, Clough Williams-Ellis. There are delightful photographs of them in the garden of the latter's beautiful home, Plas Brondanw (Fig. 7.11). They had met en route to Moscow in the headier days of 1937; now, in the year of the Hungarian Revolt and the Suez Crisis, they looked like nothing so much as a pair of amiable, elderly country squires, each with his own eccentric views and dotty domain—Taliesin for the one, the make-believe village of Portmeirion for the other. And indeed, Wright took in Portmeirion "without a blink," recalled Williams-Ellis, "seeming instantly to see the point of all my wilful pleasantries, the calculated naiveties, eye-traps, forced and faked perspectives, heretical constructions, unorthodox colour mixtures and general architectural levity."[64]

Back in London, the *Architects' Journal* solicited the eighty-nine-year-old Wright to hold forth for an hour in the Bride of Denmark, the whimsical private pub housed in the basement of the Architectural Press. He sat at the bar while

Figure 7.12
Wright in the Bride of Denmark, the
private pub of the Architectural Press,
July 1956. At the bar, facing him, is
the engineer Ove Arup; Maxwell Fry
is right of center, holding a glass;
R. Fello Atkinson is in the center.

the young and not so young duly asked him yet again about organic architecture, Le Corbusier, London, Eero Saarinen's new American embassy there, and so on (Fig. 7.12). "Literature tells about man," said Wright, "but architecture presents him. What you get is the man, in spite of him, whatever he thinks he is giving you . . . in organic architecture you have the man; he cannot hide." Then one of the party had to chauffeur Wright away to the BBC afterwards for a television interview. On his way he kept up a stream of remarks about cars and buildings ("a scornful remark about Hyde Park Screen, a mere wince at the Farmers Union in Knightsbridge, a joke about the 'suicide tenements' in Earls Court"). Arriving late, Wright was greeted by a harassed-looking BBC executive,

who led him away through a sordid-looking, pipe-infested passage. "Ah," he said to unamused ears as he ambled away. "I see the corridor is inextinguishable."

Half an hour later a pale-looking announcer introduced viewers to Frank Lloyd Wright. "Architecture," said FLW, "is going down a one-way street . . ."

"What do you . . . ?"

" . . . a one-way street to a dead end. Literature tells us about man, architecture presents him." The great Showman was beginning again. Desperately the announcer managed to slip him a question. "Have you been influenced," he asked, with childlike innocence, "by other countries?"[65]

Figure 7.13
St. Mary's Church, Twyford, Ealing, London, 1958. Nave by N. F. Cachemaille-Day, with columns in the style of Wright's Johnson Wax Building (Fig. 6.13).

It remains to say something about the few traces of Wright's protean achievement that can be found in British architecture of the postwar period.

By the 1950s, knowledge of Wright's work and thought was at last, albeit incompletely, in the public realm. But if visible influence is sought, it will disappoint in both quantity and quality. A few blatant instances only go to prove its sparsity. Nugent Cachemaille-Day built a church, St. Mary's, Twyford, in West London, with mushrooming nave columns hamfistedly reminiscent of the Johnson Wax Building (Fig. 7.13). Robert Townsend, an architect of heterodox enthusiasms, built a few houses bearing the incontrovertible marks of Prairie school inspiration. The Midlands firm of Yorke, Harper, and Harvey built Wrightian houses at much the same date in Coventry. But Alan Powers's investigations into British domestic architecture of the period have turned up little else of this type.[66]

Much earlier and in a category of its own is the unique White House, Hyver Hill, Barnet, built in 1934–35 for a cameraman from one of the film studios just

Figure 7.14
The White House, Hyver Hill, Barnet, London, 1934–35. D. E. Harrington, architect. Perspective drawing by Harrington, 1935.

outside London (Fig. 7.14). It was designed by a young architect named Dennis Harrington, who had travelled to the United States on scholarship and studied Wright's work with care. Fittingly for a house linked to the film industry, the Hyver Hill house picked up on Wright's textile-block houses in California. Literal and rather lumpy, it had no successor and has long since had its "Mayan" features toned down. More recently, in about 1984, a house designed by David Dodge of the Frank Lloyd Wright Foundation was built in suburban Camberley (Surrey); with some inevitability it has since been claimed by estate agents for Wright himself, as a selling point.[67]

Wright himself hated copying and the slavish imitation that goes towards the formation of any widespread style of architecture. So the British disinclination to copy him, though half-rooted in ignorance and insularity, was no particular discourtesy to his genius at all. Architectural circumstances in Europe and the United States, as his critics of 1939 and 1950 had remarked, were very different, far more so than they had been at the turn of the century. Up to the time of Summerson's paper in 1963, the developing program of welfare-state buildings was dominant in Britain. Privately sponsored buildings took a back seat; the individual, architect-designed house was uncommon, and very small when it was built.

It must also be remembered that Wright was a marginal figure, even if a celebrated and busy one, in American architectural culture during the last decade of his life. Though, as ever, he had plenty to say and do, his activities were still at odds with those of orthodox East and West Coast opinion formers. Just as they had done in the 1920s, British architects and efficiency experts of the 1950s went to the United States to study American offices and factories and American building productivity. If it was now the frame and curtain-wall system of Lever House and IIT which were admired rather than the disciplined planning and ashlar elevations of the Beaux-Arts era, the principles of ordering were not dissimilar, and more readily grasped than the rebellious organicism of the Guggenheim.

In due course a trickle of young British architects percolated as far as California, thirsting for adventure, openness, ease, and an escape from the austerity of the building programs at home. Yet even they seem almost always to have been drawn at first to the rectilinear framing of the Case Study houses rather than the big-handed, unpredictable freedoms and big gestures of late Wright, let alone Bruce Goff. As yet they could not quite escape the puritan discipline of Mies. Not till Reyner Banham arrived at UCLA in the early 1960s and began to interpret the West Coast for friends and readers back home did the more libertarian side of America's architectural virtues slowly unfurl for the British. There is a world of difference, for instance, between the abstract and very European reading of Wright offered by Banham in his *Theory and Design in the First Machine Age* of 1960 and his later championing of radiators under windows as the key to Prairie house planning.[68]

As collectivism receded, Wright's subversive instinct crept slowly yet surely into British architects' consciousness. A first muted stand against the admired postwar American architectural orthodoxy (and indeed the first independent British comment on Wright's work after Pevsner) came from the astringent pen of Colin Rowe. In a well-known article of 1956, Rowe paid lip service to Wright's early impact on Europe ("a plastic statement of the very highest relevance"). But he then added that the adulation of the Chicago frame had never been shared by Wright, who had every reason to know about it from Adler and Sullivan days. Was not the St. Mark's Tower design of 1924, asked Rowe, "a most elaborate evasion of a normal and standard structural fact? The frame, by so many modern architects, has been received almost as a heaven sent blessing. Why, one enquires, has it been so distinctly rejected by Mr Wright?" The Chicago frame was not so much an idea, he added, as "an accumulation of symbolism around the steel or concrete frame . . . without any desirable significance." Wright, in other words, was being used in the year of his last British visit to tilt cautiously against the prevalent trend.[69]

The rigorous Rowe is not usually thought of as a Wright enthusiast. But among those he taught at Cambridge, several became passionate about the more disciplined and spartan aspects of Wright's work, notably the mathematician-architect Lionel March; John Sergeant, who has written the standard book on the Uson-

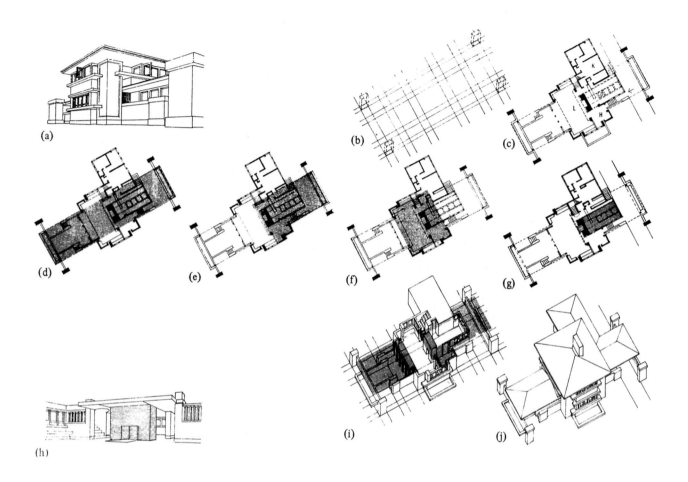

(a)

(b)

(c)

(d)

(e)

(f)

(g)

(h)

(i)

(j)

Figure 7.15

Drawings by Richard MacCormac of the Robert W. Evans House, Chicago, Illinois, 1908. FLW, architect. From *Environment and Planning B* 1 (1974).

ian houses;[70] David Lea, whose work subsequently developed in a refined, vernacular direction; and Richard MacCormac.

It is telling that this little group emerged from an English preoccupation during the 1960s with numeracy in architectural research. In history, for instance, this was the heyday of enthusiasm for Wittkowerian investigations into ratio in Renaissance plan-forms. In the sphere of design, the ebullient March set up the Centre for Land Use and Built Form at Cambridge, in the belief that optimal aesthetic as well as efficient configurations in planning could be delivered by mathematical analysis; Christopher Alexander began his missionary quest for an underlying "pattern language" founded upon number that was to deliver the key to architectural form.

To some few of those caught up in this search for numerical certainties, Wright's loyalty to the module promised blessed escape from the sterility of the postwar box—a return to feeling, complexity, richness, and individualism without loss of

Figure 7.16
Sainsbury Building (student accommodation), Worcester College, Oxford, 1983. MacCormac, Jameson & Prichard, architects.

geometrical discipline. Richard MacCormac has proved the most creative of these architects. In 1965, influenced in part by Banham's new obsession with the United States, he undertook a master's thesis on "space and form in the architecture of Frank Lloyd Wright." This offered a first analysis of the Prairie house plans in terms of the Froebel "gifts" on which Wright laid such stress in *An Autobiography,* illustrated by elegantly layered diagrams (Fig. 7.15).

The articles MacCormac subsequently published have been taken to task for imposing too precise a frame of thought on Wright's planning procedures—specifically, for detecting the complex "tartan grid" in houses bearing little true trace of it, and for suggesting that his sense of architectural space followed almost entirely from manipulation of the Froebel gifts.[71] From a British standpoint, however, MacCormac's investigations have a quite different significance. Like Colin Rowe's protest against the Chicago frame, they show an Englishman straining emotionally against the limitations of a technocratic straitjacket, yet able to do so even as late as 1965 only in the name of a superior, objective, elaborated mathematical order of grids and modules which were supposed to release the key to feeling.

And that indeed in his own personal manner of designing is what MacCormac has consistently delivered as an architect. Both in his early housing work for public authorities and in his highly praised private practice since 1970, a profound debt to Wright, always combining fierce geometrical discipline with romanticism, shines through (Fig. 7.16). He by no means stands alone. In the pluralist architectural world we now inhabit, along with him might be cited an assortment of British admirers of Wright from varying schools of thought. Romantics like Edward Cullinan (who met Wright), brutalists like Denys Lasdun and Peter Chamberlin, brutalists turned postmodernists like James Stirling, high-tech architects like Foster and Rogers, have all avowed or betrayed something of Wright's inspiration. What unites them is that their homage has been thoroughly digested. It does not often appear on the surface of their designs, as did the too-imitable examples of more tarnished heroes of modernism.

To that extent Wright still stands for the free spirit rather than the dead letter of architectural invention. If, as another member of the Cambridge generation of the 1960s, Patrick Hodgkinson, has recently claimed, the example of Wright has since his death been received for the most part in British architectural schools with "provincial nihilism," perhaps we should be glad of the fact.[72] For what this really reveals is how mercifully difficult it is for a British architect to be a blind follower of someone whose passion and inspiration were always profoundly specific to the circumstances in which he found himself. It is from the work of many independent-minded individualists rather than the tributes of a few literal-minded imitators that Wright's British legacy can best be appreciated today.

EIGHT: WRIGHT AND SOUTH AMERICA

Alberto Sartori

To understand the development of Latin American architecture and its connections to the ideas of Frank Lloyd Wright, it is necessary to understand the spatial feeling of the Latin American region. The enormous tract of land, extending from the Rio Grande in the north to Tierra del Fuego and on to Antarctica in the south, is a large and heterogeneous entity that is impossible to understand as a unit. For foreigners, and Europeans in particular, this area will seem to be of enormous proportions, its geographical and environmental development unimaginable. This great conjunction of geographically diverse places, united by a discovery and conquest that assure a common political and cultural base, has developed with many economic and social differences, as well as with a strong religious unity among multiple ethnic groups that, in some areas, have remained in the majority.

Before the Conquest, Latin America produced works of architecture comparable to those in the great cultures of ancient Egypt, Babylon, Greece, and Rome. The year 1492 represents a turning point for America and the subsequent development of its architecture. The conduct of Latin America's conquerors was varied, and in some cases forces acted in opposition to each other: the differences among Pizarro, Cortés, and Vespucci, for example, are great. Surely the only thing they had in common was their Christian faith, which imperialism had declared a universal truth to be imposed on all pagan communities. Christian Europe, the land of the conquerors, was the product of a long Roman Christian tradition. It was the Christianity of the Italian Renaissance that arrived during the Conquest, catching fire with gothic mysticism, exploding in the difficult mannerist spirit that was a great success in the New World. José Luis Romero described the situation succinctly: "For the conquerors, Europe was the only valid world among inferior worlds submerged in obscurity."[1]

This conviction of superiority permitted the destruction not only of the spiritual beliefs of the conquered, but also of their buildings and monuments. As part of the effort to erase the grand Latin American tradition, the Europeans built churches and convents on the foundations of antique and magnificent structures, symbols of the importance and superiority of the new culture they were imposing.[2] In architecture there are some particularly notable instances of this obliteration: the church constructed atop the great pyramid in Cholula, Puebla; in Mitla, Oaxaca, a church implanted inside a pre-Hispanic building, much as the Córdoba Cathedral was constructed inside the great mosque; and the cathedrals of Mexico City and Cuzco, Peru, or the convent of San Francisco in Quito, Ecuador, built on the foundations of important indigenous sites.

Thus in Latin America we cannot speak of a single "style." The ancestral eclecticism that characterized the region before the Conquest produced a mixed artistic expression, derived from an evident mannerism that, after the Conquest, led to a Baroque period of combined European and pre-Columbian architecture.[3] The countries of Latin America are inhabited by Indians and by the children of immigrants—the Spanish conquerors as well as settlers of English, Italian, German, Israeli, and many other backgrounds. The multiethnic eclecticism that resulted is of great significance. Growing as it did from the abundant mixture of landscapes, races, and aesthetic visions, this eclecticism is, I believe, a beautiful element in the design of our future because it expresses our varied and original cultural foundation.

This fertile and heterogeneous land, a product in part of communication with Europe principally, could not, as the twentieth century progressed, remain outside cultural relations with the United States. Frank Lloyd Wright's ideas, expressed in his written works and speeches, echoed in Latin America—particularly in Brazil, Uruguay, and Chile, and to a lesser degree in Argentina. Architects in these countries tried to assimilate the teachings of the man from Wisconsin. Over ninety years after the first public exhibition of his work at the Architecture Club of Chicago in 1900, his ideas and designs are still important in the ideological foundation of many works of the architects of Latin America.

BRAZIL AND URUGUAY

Wright visited Brazil in 1931 as a judge for the design competition for the Columbus Memorial, by invitation of the Pan-American Union of Architects (Fig. 8.1). At the time, it was believed that this one visit would be enough to initiate a powerful movement in Wright's tradition in the giant Amazon nation. In the end, however, the influence of Le Corbusier, who in 1946 worked with Brazilian architects on the Ministry of Education and Public Health, had a greater impact on the profession. Nevertheless, Wright's theory was recognized by various groups of Brazilian architects, who adopted and maintain it today.

In his early designs the São Paulo architect Juan Bautista Vilanova Artigas used

Figure 8.1

Wright with Lúcio Costa *(left)* and Gregori Warchavchik *(right)* at the Copacabana in Rio de Janeiro, Brazil, 1931.

many of Wright's ideas, though later on his creations transmitted Wright's organic message in a more veiled fashion. One also cannot forget the generous and elegant contributions of Miguel Fortes and Galiano Ciampaglio, who became acquainted with Wright's work through numerous trips to the United States. In 1943, Miguel Fortes spent three days in Wisconsin, on a visit that proved very beneficial to his architectural education. He returned to the United States in July 1947, and together with Galiano Ciampaglio and Jakob M. Ruchti he began to build on his knowledge of Wright's work. The trio had the privilege of meeting Wright himself. Between 1947 and 1948, Fortes built his own house that bears Wright's influence, adapted gracefully to the tropical climate of São Paulo.

Uruguay, too, provided fertile ground for Wright's influence on the country's architecture. In the book *Arquitectura renovadora en Montevideo, 1915–1940,* the architects Mariano Arana and Lorenzo Garabelli highlighted the work of architect Roman Fresnedo Siri (1938 and 1939), notably his house in Barreira on Artigas Boulevard, as well as the designs of J. C. Montes Rega, Ildefonso Aroztegui, and Hector Vignale.[4]

Along the Atlantic coast of Uruguay near Montevideo, in cities like Punta del Este, Atlántida, and Punta Ballena, the landscape and climate caused architects to

Figure 8.2
Casa de Piedra, Laguna de Sauce,
Punta del Este, Uruguay, 1986.
Horacio Ravazzani, architect.
(Photograph by author)

look abroad for their formal destiny, and in the work of Wright they found a co-herent motivating theme. Throughout the Uruguayan territory one encounters beautiful anonymous designs that are noteworthy for their elegance and their com-patibility with the environment. Great horizontal eaves, brick, and wood make possible an architecture with honest and beautiful features that evokes the most profound characteristics of the western rain forest and that demonstrates the influence of Wright in this part of the world. For example, Samuel Flores's Po-seidon House in Laguna del Diario, with its broad roof beams and low horizon-tal profile, bears resemblance to Wright's Suntop houses. The architect Horacio Ravazzani says of his summit-top House of Stone (Casa de Piedra; Fig. 8.2), sit-uated in a place called Laguna de Sauce: "I tried to make it so the work was not an obstacle, a barrier, but that its transparency would allow it to integrate into the landscape." The architecture that resulted from these expressions combines materials from the site, such as stones, with the landscape and historical notions of indigenous architecture.

CHILE

In Chile, the architectural culture has evolved and developed to a high level. Chile's geographical isolation has not been an obstacle to outside influence; various me-dia have provided access to the various architectural movements of the twentieth century, including the ideas and works of Frank Lloyd Wright. The architect Josué Smith Solar, born in 1867, was an exact contemporary of Wright's. As a youth, Smith studied in Philadelphia, beginning his work in a Wilmington, Delaware, office in 1891. There he learned of the early projects of Wright, who opened his first office in Chicago in 1893. I am not certain if Smith knew Wright personally, but the formal and volumetric similarities of his designs, as well as his use of materials, indicate a familiarity with the Chicagoan's work. Smith's Las Vizcachas Administration Houses (1905) and a pavilion for the 1910 Agricultural and Industrial Exposition for the Compañía Maderera Malva are two examples of his Wrightian production.[5]

The career of Josué Smith Solar had a great impact on Chile, culminating as it did a cycle that began with basic housing and continued with more complex buildings, university campuses, and urban planning. The plan for a Santo Domingo summer resort, the first large-scale resort project in Chile, was indirectly influenced by the 1911 design for the new Australian capital of Canberra, by the Chicago architect Walter Burley Griffin, Wright's former employee and collaborator. Santo Domingo is a good example of a garden city project. The golf course, situated on the edge of the town, interlocks with housing lots installed liberally on the neighboring pine-covered hill and is integrated to the north with the Maipo River; in the distance are Tejas Verdes and the southern hills of Llolleo.

Wright's impact would not be fully felt in Chile, however, until after World War II, when his ideas began to spread quickly throughout Latin America thanks to the arrival of more published material and the return of young architects who had journeyed to the United States and Europe to study. Accomplished professors, scientists, and architects from abroad also traveled to Chile during this period, from the mid-1940s into the 1960s. Through the teachings of such men as Arnold William Brunner, Cornelis van Eestern, and, later, Kenneth Frampton, architectural thought from all over the world was shared with Latin America.

In the United States after the war, the International Style and the ideas of Le Corbusier and followers of Mies van der Rohe and Walter Gropius reigned without challenge. In Chile, too, the functionalist aesthetic found acceptance. After the earthquake of 1939, Le Corbusier studied the architecture of Santiago, offering a reconstruction plan for the cities of Chillán and Concepción that, although it was not carried out, led the majority of architects and students to embrace his ideas freely. Many years were to pass, however, before works could be realized and leaders would come forward and build a successful architectural movement.

During this time, Latin America experienced a period of social and political effervescence. Although Chile did not see significant economic development, it was considered an up-and-coming country. In this milieu, Wright's philosophy found much favor. In contrast to the emphasis on materials and form embodied in the work of Le Corbusier, Wright's ideas were a guarantee of democracy's quality and strength, as exemplified by his view of the architect's role:

In this sense I saw the architect as savior of the culture of modern American society; his services the mainspring of any future cultural life in America—savior now as for all civilizations heretofore. Architecture being inevitably the basis of an indigenous culture, American architects must become emancipators of senselessly conforming human beings imposed upon by mediocrity and imposing mediocrity upon others in this sanitary but soulless machine-age.[6]

For the students in the architecture schools, at the University of Chile in particular, where I began my architecture studies in the early 1950s, the arrival and reading of Henry-Russell Hitchcock's *In the Nature of Materials* had the force of a bomb.[7] The ideas in this book encouraged the young students to take up a new challenge: the noble cause of understanding the rationality of the architectural principles proposed. Students now professed a faith in Wright's principles, where once they had embraced the principles of the Bauhaus more or less exclusively.

Ricardo Alegría, Jose Covacevich, O'Higgins Palma, Karin Hoffmann Rivadeneira, and myself, without prior agreement, made it our goal to disseminate at any cost in the University of Chile Architecture School—indeed, throughout Chile—the words that had so deeply penetrated our young minds. Under the auspices of Professor Reyes's studio, we sought to transform and ground Wright's words in the context of our own country. We took our work seriously, though we understood there was a risk that it would be misunderstood and confused with simple, youthful whim, intended only to shock with its daring new spirit and therefore ease our progress toward graduation.

Consistency between ideas and practice, place and environment, was the first of our proposals to provide a solid foundation for the acceptance of Wright's philosophy in our school. Geographically, Chile is in many ways similar to North America, both having vast and beautiful regions. The Arizona desert and the Atacama are alike not only in their geological characteristics but also in their flora and fauna. Chile's central valley and central-northern region resembles California, and the Chilean south in general—with its rolling landscape, lakes, rivers, and streams—is similar to Wisconsin and the coast of Lake Michigan. For us, natives of a region where the land was the only thing of value to conquerors, this surprising environmental correspondence only seemed to confirm the magical words of Frank Lloyd Wright; therein lay, we hoped, an especially appropriate foundation for the development of Chilean architecture, the models for which had previously been transplanted from England and France, countries quite dissimilar to our own.

Our journey began as a student's adventure but ended in the production of many Wrightian works, both by the architects mentioned above and by many others who were less overtly influenced by Wright. If today it is difficult to continue spreading the word, the veiled potential of Wright's architectural message remains present, and has continued to spread, even though many now do not recognize it. By analyzing the works of important Chilean architects, I have discovered traits that denote the subtle traces of Wright's influence, suggesting that indeed, his ideas did penetrate and take root in the collective memory.

In my own case, my teacher, the Chilean architect Roberto Dávila, did not build many works, nor did he actually discuss Wright's work. Dávila tended to focus instead on the work of Le Corbusier, with whom he had studied and worked in the rue de Sèvres architectural office in Paris. Dávila explained his own architectural philosophy as follows:

> In my classes I give the following definition to Architecture, for which I assume full personal responsibility: Architecture is a solution for material and spiritual problems through tangible mediums and solid and spatially sensitive forms that produce immobile works; it takes into account not only economic and social concerns but also the region, the race, the country, the environment, and local idiosyncrasies, as well as tradition and the history of the people.
>
> It is, above all, a work of creation, more closely related to art than to science, and therefore it is in permanent evolution, paralleling general progress.
>
> It requires artistic intuition, imagination, inventive capacity and creativity, knowledge, and intelligence. But it is more.
>
> With these definitions I have expressed, in principle at least, my line of thought regarding my work, for which I am fighting within our school because I believe it to be right. This line of thought includes the cultural and historical value of architecture and creation, without limiting it, but rather helping to find a true architectural expression.[8]

To me, his definition of architecture is similar to Wright's conception of organic architecture. In synthesis, they express the same concept. Wright wrote: "I believe in an architecture that embodies total quality, the present time, beauty, and that is in harmony with every region or country—its landscape, climate, race, materials, culture, tradition, and history."[9]

Roberto Dávila, like Wright, worried little about the professional achievements of his students. It was much more important to him to arouse architectural passion among us; his approach to teaching was such that it was very difficult for us not to be bewitched and fall in love with our academic work. Consequently, he was an educator of the highest order.

In the 1940s, there had existed in our country two architecture schools: that at the University of Chile, which was secular and state-owned, and the Architecture School of the Catholic University. Of the first, I already mentioned a group of students who began to promote the first theories and early manifestations of Wright's ideas. In the middle of the 1950s, an admirable generation of young architects was also produced at the latter school. The majority of them were the students of two elderly professors, architects Emilio Duhart and Sergio Larraín

García Moreno, who had been both teaching and designing magnificent works of architecture.[10]

Motivated by their personal passion for architecture, two of those students, Horacio Borgheresi and Hugo Gaggero, gave us, in their residential designs, singular interpretations of Wright's organic architecture. Gaggero's design for his own home shows, in its clear geometry, the unmistakable influence of Wright's Prairie houses (Fig. 8.3). Borgheresi lived in the United States for two years, where he came in direct contact with Wright's influence. From his position as dean of the Architecture School at the Catholic University, Borgheresi was capable of transmitting his interest in Wright to a whole generation of architects. Borgheresi's later works are marked by the marvelous style of the Usonian houses, and his latest work in Santo Domingo shows Wright's indirect influence, again by way of Walter Burley Griffin.

THE "CARACOL" EARTHQUAKE AND THE UNCONDITIONALS

There is another side to Wright's influence in Chile. After the inauguration of the Guggenheim Museum in 1959 (Fig. 8.4), very shortly after Wright's death, great controversy unfolded worldwide regarding this work. Much of the criticism was voiced by architects who did not understand how one could appreciate works of art in this moving space, which tries to subjugate everything in its path. In Chile, however, a group of architects wholeheartedly embraced the mu-

Figure 8.4
Perspective, Guggenheim Museum,
New York, 1943–59. FLW, architect.
(FLWA 4305.017)

Figure 8.5
El Caracol de los Leones, Santiago,
Chile, 1959. Melvin Villaroel, architect.
(Photograph by author)

seum's form by copying Wright's work, constructing a similar building, called "Caracol" (meaning "snail"), at an important intersection in a new district of Santiago. The resulting building, white and with a coiled ramp like that of the Guggenheim (Fig. 8.5), was intended as a commercial structure to house small local businesses. In his written works, Frank Lloyd Wright tells us that the real origin of architectural form is implicit in the act of "making" the work. Here, the Chilean architects made the ancient error of copying a design without understanding it.

Upon its completion, a great wave of uncultured people visited the building,

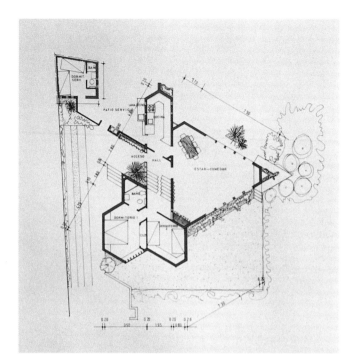

Figure 8.6 *(above)*
Plan, Casa Habitación, Santiago,
Chile, 1960. Sepp Michaeli, architect.

Figure 8.7
Exterior, Casa Habitación, Santiago,
Chile, 1960. Sepp Michaeli, architect.

which thereby took on the status of a spectacle, becoming an attraction for the entire city. Its design scheme was then appropriated and further developed by different architectural firms that wanted merely to join in the tremendous commercial success of the first building. It was very sad, to say the least, to witness the multifarious replication of our beloved Guggenheim reinterpreted by a whole generation of commercial architects.

Even while this fiasco was unfolding, however, the talented generation of the 1960s, to which I belong, left the university to encounter the challenges of professional practice. Some of us chose to work with a passion that, for us, represents organic architecture in its essence; others did so intermittently, such as Christian Boza, whose summer house in Los Vilos shows both his eclectic style and his ties with Wright. Cristián Fernández and Patricio Schmidt truly love Wright, and their destinies have been marked by his lessons. A highlight of Fernández's work is the Curanurín Restaurant in Curacaví, on the road to Viña del Mar; in its expression of foundation, reminiscent of Taliesin West, it demonstrates a deep-rooted love of our land.

Patricio Schmidt has created a significant number of works in Chile, and in all of them he has applied the principles of organic architecture, confirming his admiration and respect for Wright. He states:

> Since I became imbued with his work, Wright had a profound impression on me because of his . . . unwavering fidelity to his principles. It is not a trivial thing that the pillars of his work—the founding of his ideas in observation of the natural world; the searching out of the roots of his country and its people; his innumerable innovative concepts like "horizontality," the "broken cube," among others; structural liberty; the study of previous cultures, both Eastern and Western—led him to develop such a strong architectural position vis-à-vis the present and the future, even under heavy criticism from his contemporaries. This marvelous consequence of honest Architecture-Response has influenced me and my work, throughout my entire life.[11]

Sepp Michaeli, an architect who lived in Europe for many years, once told me emphatically, "I cannot understand the garbage-level quality of the buildings that were made in the Bauhaus period; they are unhealthy centers, difficult to live in." Michaeli's work embraces the ideas of Wright, as shown in his "Casa Habitación," whose wide eaves and rotated polygonal plan recall the Usonian houses (Figs. 8.6 and 8.7).

José Covacevich, a 1955 graduate of our old school and today part of a major architecture office, states:

> Frank Lloyd Wright was a decisive discovery in our student years, in the 1950s. [While we were] still dreaming of the word "Modernism," intro-

Figure 8.8
Casas Parrón, Santiago, Chile,
1979. Enrique Browne, architect.

Figure 8.9 *(below)*
Hanna House (also known as the
Honeycomb House), Palo Alto, California,
1936. FLW, architect. From *Architectural
Forum* 68 (January 1938).

duced in the 1930s by Europeans, Wright came along and was different. He was human and an innovator, his organic architecture was familiar to us, suitable to our idiosyncrasies, deeply rooted in the land and in the American tradition. My thesis project was a virtual homage to Wright. It was a "Price Tower," that took for its form the structure of a tree, with a central trunk and branches that conquered the heights.[12]

Enrique Browne, in addition to dedicating himself to writing about architecture, has founded his professional work on great originality and a purity within, in addition to an inherently American eclecticism. Browne seems to vacillate between a poetic rationality similar to that of Emilio Ambaz and a strong "high tech" sensibility, as demonstrated in the Casas Parrón in the Las Condes district of Santiago (Fig. 8.8). From the geometrical and essentially formal point of view, the Parrón houses have an organic nature of great expressive character that conveys much of the truth of Wright's proposals.[13]

In 1953, the January 1938 issue of *Architectural Forum* fell into my hands. In it, among other works, I discovered the Hanna House in Palo Alto (1936; Fig. 8.9), which made a great impression on me. At that moment, I realized, I understood the truth about architecture. The hexagonal form and the light and dark values, shown so well in black-and-white pictures, allowed me to dream how architecture could be without ties or scruples, and revealed a true place where it could be possible to have a family and live like a human being. Since those years, my partner and I, the late Mario Recordón, produced in our architectural office (1964–94) more than a million and a half square meters of built space. Although a generation gap meant that our positions on design were completely opposed, I tried to sustain within our work the vision and projection always present in organic architecture, which I later came to know personally through wandering voyages in the United States, where I visited many of the works of Wright. Indeed, I continued making those voyages until just a short time ago, in order to reinforce my design principles and my future work trajectory.

I want to highlight some works that are my own allusions and responses to Wright's ideas, but adapted to my own country, including homes, stadiums, apartment buildings, and public buildings. In the first category, I should point out my first important work: Casa Figueroa (1970; Fig. 8.10), a structure soaring out from a small hill that dominates the El Golf district of Santiago. The house is most like Wright's Pew House (Shorewood Hills, Wisconsin, 1939; Fig. 8.11), with a hexagonal form and a terrace that projects into space as a hanging platform twelve meters high.

More recently, a client asked me to design an "Italian villa," but, guarding my principles, I convinced him to let me design a Prairie Style house. The Corbo House (1993; Fig. 8.12), in an enclave of Santiago created from the sale of older suburban plots, is an exercise in style and a direct homage to Wright. It is, to be specific, a reinterpretation of the Winslow House, the first house Wright made

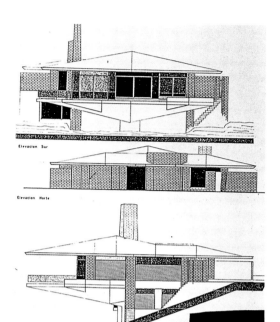

Figure 8.10
Elevations, Casa Figueroa, San Luis Hill, El Golf District, Santiago, Chile, 1970. Alberto Sartori, architect.

Figure 8.11 *(below)*
Elevation, Pew House, Shorewood Hills, Wisconsin, 1939. FLW, architect. (FLWA 4012.015)

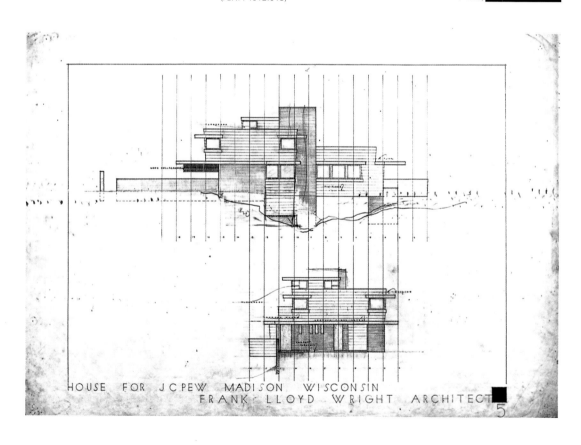

HOUSE FOR J C PEW MADISON WISCONSIN
FRANK·LLOYD WRIGHT ARCHITECT

Figure 8.12
Villa Corbo, Santiago, Chile,
1993. Alberto Sartori, architect.
(Photograph by author)

for a client, in 1893 (see Fig. 2.12). One hundred years later, I celebrated by making this house in my country, as a sincere dedication to the man who changed so many of our lives and made possible my career as an architect.[14]

Among my apartment buildings, the Travesia Building on the beach at Viña del Mar is designed in curved terraces that take possession of the reef and the undulating, ruptured form of the bay. In section, this building's stepped floors are similar to Wright's Arizona project for Dr. Alexander Chandler, San Marcos in the Desert (1927).

Of my large-scale works, the most significant are the Sport Frances Golf Club and the Medialuna de Chile at Rancagua, both of which follow Wright's principles. The golf club (Fig. 8.13) is situated between Santiago and the bank of the Mapocho River on sixty hectares of gardens and hills, near dense forests and a mountain range five thousand meters high with eternal snow. The club's enormous roof hosts activity with a great openness, hovering birdlike on its supporting beams. The design is suitable for our geography and fulfills the Wrightian philosophy, acting as a witness to the greatness of his message in a place far from its origin.

Figure 8.13
Sport Frances Golf Club, terrace and bar, Santiago, Chile, 1995. Alberto Sartori, architect. (Photograph by author)

I have left for last the Medialuna de Chile (Figs. 8.14 and 8.15), which was completed and dedicated in 1997. It is a stadium for Chilean rodeo, the national sport, in which I was able to concretize organic architectural teachings in massive form. The Medialuna is a circular arena for twelve thousand spectators excavated in this Chilean land, evoking a volcano's caldera and surrounded by a wooden pergola of great dimension. It integrates sport within an urban landscape in a structure of tremendous plastic richness.

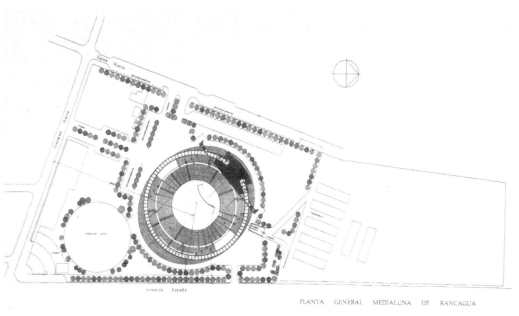

PLANTA GENERAL MEDIALUNA DE RANCAGUA

Figure 8.14 *(above)*
Plan, Medialuna de Chile rodeo arena,
Rancagua, Chile, 1997. Alberto Sartori,
architect. (Photograph by author)

Figure 8.15
Medialuna de Chile rodeo arena,
Rancagua, Chile, 1997. Alberto Sartori,
architect. (Photograph by author)

If we enunciate in summary Wright's basic principles in the form of a testament, we get a lesson of such tremendous power that the results could be considered "universal standards of design." Because organic architectural principles are independent of particular stylistic strictures, they appear in almost all of Latin America's architecture, but disguised such that they take on a different character from that suggested by Wright's own work:

Earth line	Affinity between construction and land; a natural quality
Tension plus continuity	(traction)
Continuity	Elastic and cohesive stability
The third dimension (thickness)	The exterior that enters and the interior space that goes out; depth, the other dimension of space; appropriation of the space outside the building
Form	The essence of the building, in contrast with the objective geometric figure
Organic unity	Building and environment summed into a single entity, using machines and artifacts as parts of the whole, not as motives
Shelter	Incorporating the human factor in all designs
Nature of materials	Considering each type of material and its unique expression; the independent dignity of the material being used
Decentralization	The war against massive and harmful centralization

These concepts are used widely by architects all over the world, not only those who claim allegiance to organic architecture.[15] The negation of these principles implies a serious regressive movement in architectural thought as we stand on the brink of the third millennium.

Wright's proposals for the city and the countryside and his insight into what the automobile would represent in the future of human settlements today have application to the entire social body in Latin America. He taught a generation of architects, well before the environmental movement of the 1980s, a love for nature, the importance of one's own country, its people, and their origins, and a knowledge of liberty. The concept of horizontality, articulated by structures in tension, and attention to the inherent nature of raw building materials are enduring premises for the open design of American architecture.

With his constructive inventions, derived from his love of technology in the service of mankind, Wright accompanies us silently, protecting architects all over the world who understood that his message would not be affected by fleeting trends. This understanding guaranteed his permanence and made us more mature as people. His protecting eaves allowed Latin America to believe that we are slowly creating our own great architectural force, an architecture that is simple, free, and democratic, that takes possession of a place, making it more beautiful and helping to make real our grand dream of transforming nature into culture.[16]

NINE: TOWARDS AN ORGANIC ARCHITECTURE IN MEXICO

Keith Eggener

Frank Lloyd Wright's interest in Mexican and Central American architecture has long been acknowledged, even by Wright himself; his own reception in these regions, however, has received little notice.[1] While Wright's influence was certainly less pervasive than that of his European contemporary Le Corbusier, it can be seen in the work of such men as Paul Ehrenberg of Costa Rica and Calvin Stempel of Panama, and among Caribbean designers like Antonin Nechodoma and Henry Klumb of Puerto Rico (the latter of whom worked with Wright from 1929 to 1933) and Walter Betancourt of Cuba (who worked with Richard Neutra in Los Angeles during the late 1950s). In most of these cases the borrowings were fairly overt, from Nechodoma's Puerto Rican Prairie stylings to Stempel's translation of Wright's Price Tower (1952) in his 1964 Atalaya Apartment Building in Panama City.[2]

The situation in Mexico, however, has always been less clear and even more critically neglected. In 1967, looking back on the functionalist movement he helped initiate during the late 1920s, the architect and painter Juan O'Gorman said, "It was unfortunate that Le Corbusier, and not Frank Lloyd Wright, caught our attention. Wright would have helped us stay closer to our true American tradition."[3] Though it came later and in a more limited way than did Le Corbusier's, Wright's influence did reach O'Gorman and a few of his compatriots. In Wright, and particularly in his 1936 house for Edgar Kaufmann, Fallingwater (see Fig. 9.8), O'Gorman and colleagues Max Cetto, Diego Rivera, and Luis Barragán saw a means of breaking the perceived impasse of International Style functionalism. In short, Wright's work provided a model for how one might fuse architecture with place to create a distinctly localized modernism.

Yet as O'Gorman's comments indicate, for most Mexican modernists before World War II Le Corbusier was the man to watch. News of his revolutionary ar-

Figure 9.1 *(far left)*
Diego Rivera House, San Angel, Mexico
City, 1929–30. Juan O'Gorman, architect.
From *Architectural Record*, April 1937.

Figure 9.2 *(left)*
House and studio for Amédée Ozenfant,
Paris, 1922–23. Le Corbusier and
Pierre Jeanneret, architects.

chitecture arrived soon after the worst of the violence associated with Mexico's decade-long revolution ended. In 1924, the same year President Alvaro Obregón succeeded in putting down the last openly mutinous elements of the army, the second French edition of *Vers une architecture* was published, and José Villagrán García, a young professor at Mexico City's National Academy of San Carlos, introduced the book to his classes on architectural theory.[4] Villagrán's students, including O'Gorman, Alvaro Aburto, Enrique del Moral, and Juan Legarreta, devoured Le Corbusier's message.[5] With his emphasis on mass production and universally adaptable forms, and his messianic weaving of rationalism and romance—"Architecture or Revolution," he concluded in *Vers une architecture*— Le Corbusier proved irresistible to these idealistic, reform-minded young designers. At the same time, the optimized production techniques he prescribed appealed to the technocrats, bureaucrats, speculators, and other bottom-line types who would pay for much of Mexico's new functionalist architecture. They saw the bare-boned forms of the International Style as an economically and ideologically sound course for postrevolutionary Mexico, providing structures that were frugal, forward-looking, and free of unwanted historical bulk. By the early 1930s, under the direction of O'Gorman and his peers, stripped-down, reinforced-concrete housing, schools, hospitals, and factories (several of these financed by the federal government, which, not coincidentally, held a monopoly on cement production and saw tremendous profit potential in the new architecture)[6] were rising throughout the country. Many of these early efforts borrowed unabashedly from Le Corbusier's work. O'Gorman's 1929–30 San Angel studio for Diego Rivera (Fig. 9.1), for example, though painted a deep earthy red and surrounded by a cactus fence, featured an exterior spiral stair and a sawtooth roofline quoted directly from the 1922–23 Ozenfant House in Paris (Fig. 9.2). Explaining such

formal importations in 1936, O'Gorman referred to "noble technological architecture, architecture that is the true expression of [contemporary] life" and said
that "architecture will have to become international for the simple reason that
every day man becomes more universal, collective."[7]

In that same year, Luis Barragán moved to Mexico City. During the previous
nine years in his native Guadalajara he had planned a public park and built or re-
modeled nearly two dozen mildly modernized Spanish colonial–style houses (Fig.
9.3). Once in the capital, however, he immediately adopted the fashionable Corbusian form-language, with borrowings almost as blatant as O'Gorman's. Over
the next four years he built another two dozen houses and small apartment buildings, most in collaboration with others such as the engineer José Creixell and the
German-born architect Max Cetto.[8] The 1939 building housing four painters'
studios at Plaza Melchor Ocampo is typical of such efforts (Fig. 9.4). Notable
here are the membranous facade, metal-framed factory windows, and walled roof
terrace opened by an unglazed, "punched-out" rectangular void—a device adapted
from projects like Le Corbusier's Savoye and Stein villas near Paris, and from his
Weissenhof-Siedlung houses in Stuttgart.

While the influence of the dynamic and relatively young Le Corbusier loomed
large in Mexico during the 1930s, Wright, nearing age seventy by 1935, was widely
seen as past his prime.[9] His recent preoccupations—the pre-Columbian–flavored
Los Angeles houses of the 1920s and the antiurbanism of Broadacre City (a low-

Figure 9.4
Painters' studios, Plaza Melchor Ocampo,
Mexico City, 1939. Luis Barragán with
Max Cetto and José Creixell, architects.
(Photograph by author)

density scheme incompatible with both traditional and contemporary Mexican residential patterns)—held little appeal for the new generation of builders.[10] Nor did his organic method, with its focus on the individual situation and its implications of costly and time-consuming analysis, much interest them either. The younger Mexicans, alert to the responsibilities and the opportunities inherent in the reconstruction of their country, undertook building projects with a sense of urgency. Even as late as 1967, Mario Pani, who graduated from the University of Mexico in 1934 and four years later began the magazine *Arquitectura México*, pounded his desk as he spoke of the needs of his people: "We must build for all of them. Plan! Build! Plan well! Build now!"[11]

Finally, whereas many Latin American architects read French and could identify with Le Corbusier's Mediterranean sources, Wright was a *yanqui*. Because the United States had invaded their country on more than one occasion, most recently in 1916–17, many Mexicans still viewed the U.S. and its products with caution, if not outright hostility. As a 1947 article in *Architectural Record* put it, "The Mexican temperament is rather unresponsive to what it considers the austerity and coldness of . . . non-Latin movements. Almost unanimously, Mexican architects ignore or dismiss the architecture of Frank Lloyd Wright."[12] Max Cetto later explained, "Being an immediate neighbor of the USA and economically dependent on her, Mexico is naturally more exposed to the so-called Coca-Colonization than any other people. Every Mexican is more or less painfully aware of this situation, and the architectural profession is no exception."[13] Consequently, whereas progressive Mexican architects remained open to European influence, they tended to resist ideas and images from the United States. *Arquitectura México,* for example, from its inception in 1938, published relatively few articles on architecture from the United States, while coverage of Europe frequently equaled and sometimes exceeded that of Mexico itself. Wright's death in 1959 received only a mention in *Arquitectura*'s "Notas y Noticias" section; Le Corbusier's death six years later occasioned an entire commemorative issue.[14]

Nonetheless, by the end of the 1930s it was becoming apparent that some of Le Corbusier's most ardent Mexican acolytes were burning out. In 1938 O'Gorman retreated from architecture altogether and devoted himself to painting, claiming that he "did not know where to turn from functionalism."[15] Two years later Barragán also withdrew, citing his "demoralization" over the practice of architecture.[16] Both O'Gorman and Barragán, however, soon returned to building, and at about the same time, around 1944–45, at which point their new work was seen to diverge significantly from their earlier efforts. They and others in Mexico, such as the former functionalists Aburto and del Moral, had begun to question the technological, utilitarian, and international orientation of modern architecture as it had proliferated in Mexico since the 1920s; they now saw such efforts as sterile, alien, and adverse to humane and local concerns.[17] While many still described their work as shaped by the utilitarian and economic imperatives of a developing nation, they experimented with forms that they and their critics characterized as responding to local culture, landscape, and materials and to traditional built forms and methods of production. According to O'Gorman, "Today the task is to try to produce an architecture which, irrespective of all functional rules, will be more functional, that is to say, with a better adaptation to climate, to customs and to site. It should be planned for its regional use and not as a universal utility."[18] Projects like Barragán's Parque Residencial Jardines del Pedregal subdivision (1945–53, hereafter "El Pedregal"; Fig. 9.5) and the contemporaneous Ciudad Universitaria (Fig. 9.6) were seen as emblematic of the shift.[19] Located side by side within a bizarrely picturesque two-thousand-year-old lava field south of Mexico City known as the Pedregal ("stony place"), these developments made more or less direct allusions to Mexican history through the medium of built form. At El Pedregal, in houses like the one he built for Eduardo Prieto López in 1949–50, Barragán subtly evoked the architecture of Mexico's colonial-era convents and haciendas. Nearby, O'Gorman's university library

Figure 9.5
Advertisement for El Pedregal. From
Arquitectura México, no. 41 (March
1953): back cover.

Figure 9.6 *(below)*
Main Library, Universidad Nacional
Autónoma de México, Mexico City,
1950–52. Juan O'Gorman, Gustavo
Saavedra, and Juan Martínez de Velasco,
architects. (Photograph by author)

Figure 9.7

Hotel, San José Purúa, Michoacán, 1939.
Max Cetto and Jorge Rubio, architects.
From *Architect and Engineer*, September
1945. Photograph by Nelson Morris.

Figure 9.8 *(opposite)*
Kaufmann House (Fallingwater), Bear
Run, Pennsylvania, 1935. FLW, architect.
Photograph by Bill Hedrich, 1937;
published in *Architectural Forum* 68
(January 1938), and in *Time,* 17 January
1938. (Chicago Historical Society,
HB/4414/D3)

tower was enveloped by figurative stone mosaics representing an intellectual history of the region, from ancient to modern times. Architectural historian Carlos González Lobo recently concluded that "it was within a collective consensus [during the 1950s] that [El Pedregal and University City] balanced both modern and regional traits and . . . managed to establish a national expression."[20]

Since the 1950s, the modern traits that González Lobo mentions have typically been linked by critics and historians to European architecture.[21] As I have suggested, there are sound historical reasons for this; yet Wright did figure into the rise of the new Mexican architecture, initially through personal contacts. When Barragán's future collaborator Max Cetto left Germany for the United States in 1938, one of his first stops was at Taliesin, Wright's home in Spring Green, Wisconsin. Shortly thereafter he requested a professional recommendation, which Wright granted. By 1939 Cetto was working for Wright's former assistant Richard Neutra on such projects as the Kahn House in San Francisco.[22] Later that year, as a German national fearing deportation with the outbreak of war in Europe, Cetto left for Mexico. He carried impressive credentials. In addition to being connected with Wright and Neutra, he was also a former student of Hans Poelzig, a former employee of Ernst May, and a founding member of CIAM, the Congrès Internationaux d'Architecture Moderne. This pedigree helped Cetto quickly find work with Villagrán, Creixell, Barragán, and Jorge Rubio.[23]

A project that he and Rubio designed during that first year in Mexico, the Hotel San José Purúa in rural Michoacán (Fig. 9.7), suggests the sensitive siting of Taliesin East, or of Fallingwater, which was just then being published to international acclaim (Fig. 9.8).[24] Working on a remote and rocky hilltop site, the architects devised low-slung pavilions—some rectilinear, some curvilinear in plan—that were terraced down and wrapped around the hillside. It has been said that Cetto drew full-scale plans directly on the ground with chalk so as to obtain the best possible integration of site and architecture.[25] The resultant layout was well suited to the resort function of the rural hotel, providing rambling walks and unobstructed views of the surrounding mountains, and it kept down construction costs by obviating the need for extensive grading.

Within a year of Cetto's visit to Taliesin, Juan O'Gorman was himself in the United States, in Pennsylvania, as a guest of Edgar Kaufmann Sr.[26] O'Gorman later recalled how the invitation came about. Kaufmann's son, Edgar Jr., had come

to Mexico in 1937 to study painting. As a painter the young Kaufmann was apparently unsuccessful, but upon seeing O'Gorman's recent murals at the Mexico City Airport, he arranged to have the artist visit Pittsburgh to paint a series of murals for a Jewish youth center that his father supported there. For six months in 1939 O'Gorman worked on the project. On weekends he and his wife left the city to stay with the Kaufmanns at Fallingwater. Although his murals were eventually rejected by the youth center's advisory board,[27] O'Gorman gained intimate knowledge of Fallingwater, and by his own account, he was mightily impressed. "The building is one of magnificent beauty," he later said, "probably one of the most beautiful buildings in the world. . . . I thought it would be very important for Mexico to have a house, one building, applying the general principles of Wright's organic architecture."[28]

After the war O'Gorman sought to implement these principles in the design of his own house, which he began in 1949 on a site at the northern edge of the Pedregal (Fig. 9.9). Except for the mosaic-clad stone wall shielding the site from Avenida San Jerónimo, the house was destroyed by its owners in 1970. Wright's influence upon it is difficult to see in photographs. Set into a natural grotto within the Pedregal's lava flows, the building was covered inside and out with brightly colored mosaics and sculptural elements made of the rough local stone: Aztec gods and warriors, jaguars and monkeys and butterflies in motion, a writhing snake forming crenellations along the roofline, an eagle above the main door, and giant toy soldier–like guardian figures posted on either side. Strangest of all was the effect produced by the placement within these walls of tidy metal-frame factory windows, the same sort of gridded openings to be found in O'Gorman's earlier functionalist buildings, only now, peering out from the rough-hewn, polychromed chaos, they seemed as if overtaken by some peculiar breed of petrified fungus. It is not surprising that the house was thought "bizarre" by some.[29] Nonetheless, O'Gorman claimed that it was "the most complete and satisfying work that I have done in architecture. It is an example of Organic Architecture, and I think it can be called modern and Mexican. . . . It could be the beginning of a new regional tradition."[30] (It was not, much to his dismay.)

Just what did O'Gorman mean when he spoke of organic architecture? His model, he said, was Wright; yet acknowledging this in light of the building just described raises other questions. Did he really understand Wright's organicism at all, or did he simply get it wrong, whether unintentionally or willfully? It is clear that O'Gorman's Pedregal house looks like nothing designed by Wright (instead works by Antonio Gaudí and, perhaps, Bruce Goff come to mind). Still, it seems most productive to regard this building not as some bizarre anomaly, a distortion or misreading of Wrightian organicism, but, rather, as a highly selective and deeply inflected variation on it, a displacement and amplification of one of its central themes, a sort of test case or thesis statement of rather limited resonance.

More than Wright's systems of ornament, his geometrized abstractions of natural forms, his demand for unity between building and furnishings, his ideas about truth in materials and form's expression of function—all components of his organicism—it was Wright's call for the integration of building and site that engaged O'Gorman.[31] And beyond the functional, structural, or economic implications of this linkage, it was the ideological potential, as expressed through built form, that O'Gorman underlined. On one level his plea was for a "regional" architecture seeking to establish harmonious relations among building, users, and the land on which both stood.[32] More profoundly and polemically, he presented his work as a simultaneous affirmation of the indigenous, the American, and a rejection of the imported, the European. He now dismissed Corbusian functionalism (which he termed "Abstractionistic") as aggressively as he had once advocated it, and he defended his new "organic" work as the "opposite of international-type architecture . . . [which] imposes itself from above . . . [and] has no social human base."[33] "Organic Architecture," he wrote,

[finds] purpose in its relation with nature and can be understood
as a naturalistic realism. . . . In realistic architecture . . . style is not
imposed but produced by every region as a consequence of the need
[for] expression . . .

Figure 9.10
Wright, in porkpie hat, in front of
the Broadacre City model at the "Sixty
Years of Living Architecture" exhibition,
Mexico City, 1952. (FLWA 6808.0039)

[It] is born from the bottom as a natural process in the creation of
Architecture as a collective expression. In Realistic Architecture . . .
different styles indicate the differences in social conditions and in the
natural physical background; this necessarily produces other forms of
expression with national and typical character[istics].[34]

It is then because of, rather than in spite of, such formal divergence that we might
regard O'Gorman's organicism as closer in spirit to Wright's than that of those
whose work more superficially resembles Wright's. Unlike, say, Puerto Rico's Antonin Nechodoma, who transplanted Wrightian forms to a field far from their
place of origin, O'Gorman translated an idea, a "general principle," he called it,
that he believed would give rise to an indigenous Mexican form.

As the inventor of "the truly organic architecture of our time," Wright, said
O'Gorman, was "the supreme architect of this century."[35] Yet he qualified his admiration by claiming that Wright had developed his approach through long study
of ancient Mexican architecture.

Many of his buildings, definitely influenced by ancient, pre-Hispanic
Mexico, are the best examples of American architecture. His house,
Taliesin [West?], is the greatest modern house built in this century, and is
one of the most important works of art of all times. It has a recognizable

Figure 9.11
Left to right: Wright, Diego Rivera
and Oscar Stonorov in Mexico City,
1952. (FLWA 6808.0050)

Mexican character. It revives the Meso-American tradition. It was Wright,
a frequent visitor to our archaeological sites, who understood organic
architecture as related to the human being in his geographical and historical content.[36]

While his visits may not have been as frequent as O'Gorman suggests, Wright did
indeed admire Mexico's ancient architecture.[37] Furthermore, he spoke favorably
of some of the country's more recent buildings, particularly the stadium at the
new University City with its enormous mosaic by Diego Rivera.[38] Wright had
seen this in October 1952, when he and his wife, Olgivanna, attended the Eighth
Pan-American Congress of Architects as guests of Carlos Lazo, then president of
the Mexican Society of Architects. The international exhibition "Sixty Years of
Living Architecture," with, according to Wright, twenty-three models, one hundred photographs, and eight hundred original drawings, was displayed at this time
in Mexico City (Fig. 9.10).[39] Upon his return to the United States Wright wrote
to Lazo to congratulate him on the convention's success and to say, somewhat
hyperbolically and with a triumphant dig at Le Corbusier, "More than ever [I
am] sure that American Architecture needs only American influences originat-
ing in the Toltec area as the great basis of all future Architecture if we are to carry
on to a great life of our own in our own time. Swiss or French influence is now
behind the American lighthouse and I hope it stays there."[40]

While in Mexico Wright also met Diego Rivera (Fig. 9.11), who, though best
known as a painter, had been publishing articles on architecture since 1924.[41] Dur-

ing the late 1920s Rivera's tastes were distinctly Corbusian, as O'Gorman's house for him in San Angel indicates (see Fig. 9.1).[42] By 1944, however, he and O'Gorman began working together on a new project: the Anahuacalli Museum in Mexico City's San Pablo Tepetlapa district, at the eastern reaches of the rocky and still undeveloped Pedregal. Finally completed in 1966, Anahuacalli is a massive, stepped pyramid made of local volcanic stone (Fig. 9.12). From a broad, rock-walled plaza, the visitor passes beneath corbeled arches and projecting forked-tongued stone serpents into a dimly lit warren of stairways and galleries. These galleries are filled with Rivera's personal collection of pre-Columbian art and artifacts, a collection that he later gave to the Mexican nation. Evoking an ancient tomb or temple, Anahuacalli bears a still, oppressive atmosphere, like that of a place of violent events long past. In this, the building stands in perfect keeping with the relics it houses and the volcanic landscape it surmounts.

The landscape of the Pedregal had long fascinated Rivera. With its swirling eddies and crests of lava, and its peculiar native flora, such as the *palos bobos,* or "crazy trees," the Pedregal was a desolate and dramatic place. A visual admixture of violence and serenity, it stands like a turbulent body of water quite suddenly frozen. Prior to the eruption that gave it its name as the "stony place," the region had been home to some of Mexico's earliest human settlements, Copilco and Cuicuilco, whose remains were unearthed beginning in the late nineteenth century. Because of these ancient ruins and the distinctive landscape and vegetation, the Pedregal by the 1920s was regarded by many as a place of particular scientific and cultural significance.[43] At the same time, these very features—the rugged badland topography and the enigmatic ruins—led others to view it as a setting for danger and mystery. One history published in 1913 reported that, "according to the Indians, the Pedregal is full of monstrous spirits and terrible witches, so much so that rare is the Indian who will walk through the place at night. . . . They call the Pedregal de San Angel the 'primary school' of witchcraft."[44] Elsewhere it was reported that the region was crawling with snakes, scorpions, and criminals.[45] Such stories helped forestall development and attracted a number of romantically inclined writers and artists. Rivera was one of these.[46]

By the early 1940s Barragán was also making forays into the Pedregal, often accompanied by his photographer, Armando Salas Portugal, and the elderly revolutionary and nationalist landscape painter Dr. Atl (born Gerardo Murillo). Barragán soon began buying property there—it was still quite inexpensive if purchased in large tracts—and working on a group of gardens that gave rise to his 865-acre subdivision El Pedregal, which opened to brisk sales and international critical acclaim around 1950 (see Figs. 9.5, 9.13, and 9.14). Later, Barragán would speak of this development, with its elegant minimalist houses, stark plazas, fountains, winding lanes, and rocky gardens, as "my most important and interesting work."[47] Henry-Russell Hitchcock, Richard Neutra, Esther McCoy, Gio Ponti, Damián Bayón, Kenneth Frampton, and many others would place it among the central achievements of Latin American modern architecture: a turning point in Barragán's career, a major revision of the International Style, an icon of Mexican cultural identity, yet still intensely personal, poetic, and mysterious.[48]

El Pedregal's is also an architecture that, with Rivera's encouragement, made distinct references to Wright. About the time he began work on Anahuacalli, Rivera wrote a short, unpublished essay in which he pointed to Wright as one of "the greatest architects of our time." In doing so he singled out the "ejemplo insuperable [para] terreno rocoso" of Fallingwater—the "insuperable example" that house provided for any architect engaged in planning for "rocky ground." Written about 1945 and titled "Requisitos para la organización de El Pedregal," Rivera's essay appears to have been produced at the request of Luis Barragán, who was then beginning work on the new subdivision.[49]

Although Barragán's specific reasons for seeking Rivera's advice are unclear, he may well have been intrigued by the work then under way at Anahuacalli. The museum's Aztec-revival form differed markedly from the cubic minimalism of Barragán's later Pedregal houses, yet like them it sought harmony with its rocky site.[50] Rivera's advice was predicated on the need to build in such a way as to preserve and accentuate this landscape. The development, he wrote, must be carefully managed in order "to assure conservation of the site's geographic character. . . . Nothing would be gained if the structures destroyed the natural beauty of the place." Consequently, Rivera demanded that strict conditions be imposed on builders and property owners: as a "*condición primordial* . . . the best possible use [must be made] of the stone of the Pedregal." The lava and the native vegetation must be protected, for these gave the area its unique character; roads must follow the natural contours of the land; and structures should be clad in the local stone, for this would keep down costs and further link built form with its setting.[51]

As originally planned and constructed (it has been altered much in forty-five years), El Pedregal provided clear-cut evidence of Rivera's influence on Barragán. In accordance with Rivera's advice, walls at El Pedregal were typically built of local stone, while its gently curving and rolling streets followed the swelling terrain. In a 1951 lecture in Coronado, California, Barragán described his efforts at El Pedregal "to build gardens and houses which enhance the beauty of the rocks . . . [and] to preserve the harmony of the architectural development and the landscape."[52] Gardens were designed to showcase native rocks and plants, while "modern" houses were planned so as "not to harm and spoil . . . [or] compete with" the landscape; these houses, said Barragán, "must be of such simplicity— abstract in quality, preferably straight lines, flat surfaces, and primary geometric forms."[53]

Rivera's essay was written near the end of what for Barragán was a period of professional stasis and frustration. Between 1940 and 1944 Barragán built little and struggled, with sometimes awkward results, to move beyond the Corbusian-inspired character of his work of the late 1930s.[54] With El Pedregal a mature artistic vision came into focus, one that he would refine and reformulate over the duration of his career. Rivera's allusion to Fallingwater suggests that Wright's example had a role in revitalizing Barragán's thinking at this time, helping him to step away from the International Style toward the site-specific regionalism for which he ultimately became famous. At El Pedregal, Rivera advocated and Barragán accepted the "ejemplo insuperable" of Wright's organicism. And like O'Gorman, Barragán concentrated on a single feature of that organicism—that of the necessary integration between building and site.

In Barragán's case, the political implications of this integration were never so openly stated as they were with O'Gorman. While O'Gorman linked Mexico's "Abstractionistic" International Style architecture with "colonial submission" and international capitalism, demanding instead a "Realistic architecture [that] tries to establish harmony between man and the land he inhabits,"[55] Barragán, characteristically, spoke in more subdued and ambiguous terms. "In the design of my houses," he said in 1951, "I have attempted to state new relationships between modern materials and the popular house of the villages and farms of my country, while in my gardens I have suggested new relationships between rocks and vegetation."[56] Although their views differed considerably on many points,[57] after the war both men clearly turned from the international toward the indigenous. In this, their work may be seen as part of what Mexican cultural anthropologist Roger Bartra has called "an extraordinary boom," during the 1940s and 1950s, in "speculations about Mexicanness."[58] And as it had for O'Gorman, Wright's organic American architecture provided an important model in the search for a Mexican one.

Although Wright's influence on Barragán has been almost universally ignored, on at least one occasion Barragán himself pointed to it. In his 1951 California lecture he cited the "fine and valuable influence" in Mexico of Richard Neutra and Frank Lloyd Wright. Yet like O'Gorman, he emphasized that it was "principles," not forms, that he and his colleagues were importing.

> When I speak of these influences I do not wish to say that Mexican architects copy the works of the architects that I have mentioned, or of other prominent architects in this country [the U.S.], but they have tried to study the principles that have guided the solution of such problems in the United States, and to use them in solving our problems in Mexico, in the various regions. We are trying to have the gardens and the houses that we design and build show that they are modern works, realized in accordance with the site, the program, and the building materials required in each case.[59]

In light of these remarks, it is of interest to view Neutra's Kahn House (1939–40, on which Max Cetto worked)[60] and Wright's Fallingwater beside the 1950 house at 140 Fuentes in El Pedregal (Fig. 9.13)—one of the two neighboring demonstration homes Barragán and Cetto designed to advertise the district's potential and provide appropriate models for building there. Like the Neutra and Wright buildings, 140 Fuentes is flat-roofed, cubic, and wedded to the rocks beneath it, like a cut and polished crystal emerging from misshapen, ig-

Figure 9.14
Advertisement for El Pedregal,
possibly designed by Luis Barragán.
From *Excélsior*, 8 July 1951.

neous stones at its base. In both Fallingwater and 140 Fuentes, some of the rough substructure was originally allowed to enter the more refined space of the superstructure: the living rooms of each once featured large chunks of unpolished natural stone rising up through the floor, elements that remain at Fallingwater, but which have long since been removed from 140 Fuentes. While the cubic forms of all three houses are organically bonded to rocky and uneven sites, Cetto and Barragán, like Wright, used far less glass, and placed far more emphasis on mass and the thickness and solidity of walls, than did Neutra. In so doing, their house took on a greater density, a greater sense of rootedness to place—the very quality that Barragán and Cetto, along with O'Gorman and Rivera, admired most in Wright's work.

There is still more direct evidence for linking Barragán's work to Wright's. On 8 July 1951, the Mexico City daily *Excélsior* carried a two-page advertisement offering property and listing the many advantages of home ownership in what it called "El Lugar Ideal Para Vivir"—"the ideal place to live"—the Jardines del Pedregal (Fig. 9.14).[61] A large drawing, captioned "vista parcial del Boulevard 'Paseo del Pedregal,'" showed a modern, flat-roofed house with cantilevered balconies and vertical accents of rough-hewn stone. The building was set behind a rock wall, with a late-model North American sedan parked out front and a median strip planted with rocks and flowers and *colorín* trees (a characteristic plant of the Pedregal) in the foreground. In a 1962 interview, Barragán claimed full responsibility for El Pedregal's publicity and advertising through 1953, so this ad was probably designed and almost certainly approved by him.[62] In fact, no such house was ever built at El Pedregal: the view is entirely imaginary. It is nothing but an advertisement suggesting the possibilities of the site and the developer's— that is, Barragán's—vision of the ideal building for it. What the drawing shows, of course, is Fallingwater. The perspective is identical to that found in William Hedrich's famous photograph, published in both *Architectural Forum* and *Time* in 1938, and clearly known to Barragán by 1951 (see Fig. 9.8).

Recipient of the Pritzker Prize in 1980, Barragán is without question the best-known, most admired, and most influential of Mexican architects. His work, which came to maturity with El Pedregal, has been cited as inspirational by respected designers both inside and outside Mexico.[63] Yet although the purported sources of his deceptively simple architecture have been often noted, they have rarely received sustained critical examination. A writer for *Artes de México* recently listed "Islamic art, the ziggurats, classical Greece, the metaphysical paintings of Giorgio de Chirico, the writings of St. Teresa of Avila, the work of Chucho Reyes, African art, the *poètes maudits* (especially Baudelaire), and finally the swimming pools painted by David Hockney" as elements entering into Barragán's work.[64] Wright's inclusion on any such a list seems long overdue. In pointing to Wright's impact on Barragán, and on Cetto, O'Gorman, and Rivera, it bears repeating that, however direct, his influence was much more the result of an idea than of a repertoire of forms. Specifically, Barragán and his colleagues were intrigued by Wright's notions regarding the integration of building and site, and the possibilities this suggested for creating a localized, culturally and geographically particularized modern architecture. However circumscribed it may have been, Wright's influence in this regard was profound, and because of the prominence of the designers involved, it touched a wide circle of modern architects in Mexico and abroad.

TEN: WRIGHT'S BAGHDAD

Mina Marefat

In May 1958 Wright's designs for Baghdad, hot off the drawing boards, were published in a multipage spread of the *Architectural Forum*.[1] "For Frank Lloyd Wright, here was a chance to demonstrate what he had tried to teach in Japan and to preach in the United States—that a great culture deserves not only an architecture of its time, but of its own."[2] For the nonagenarian architect, the Baghdad project was one of his last and most important commissions, and in his typically bombastic manner Wright dedicated his plans to Sumeria, Isin, Larsa, and Babylon—the ancient birthplaces of human civilization.[3]

As with the Imperial Hotel, the project provided Wright with a unique opportunity for grand planning beyond North America and Europe. His urban and architectural dreams were embodied in the master plan for an ancient city coming into modern times. Wright wanted his plan for Greater Baghdad to do for Iraq what the Imperial Hotel had accomplished in Japan, albeit on an even grander scale. He envisioned a Middle Eastern Broadacre City complete with opera house, civic auditorium, museums, shops, a terraced parking garage, botanical gardens, and a university campus (Fig. 10.1).

Contrary to recent interpretation, Wright's Baghdad project encompassed much more than a flight of fantasy into the architect's boyhood realm of *The Arabian Nights' Entertainments*.[4] Such assessment trivializes what might have been the crowning project of Wright's career, and overlooks the seriousness of the cultural message implicit in his Baghdad oeuvre. Wright's Middle Eastern involvement was a confirmation of the stature of the architect on a global scale, accented by his desire to build in a region that represented the birthplace of civilization. The project reaffirmed the continued presence of Wright among the giants of modernism, Le Corbusier and Walter Gropius, both of whom were also invited to build in Baghdad. One cannot help but conjecture that had Wright's project been

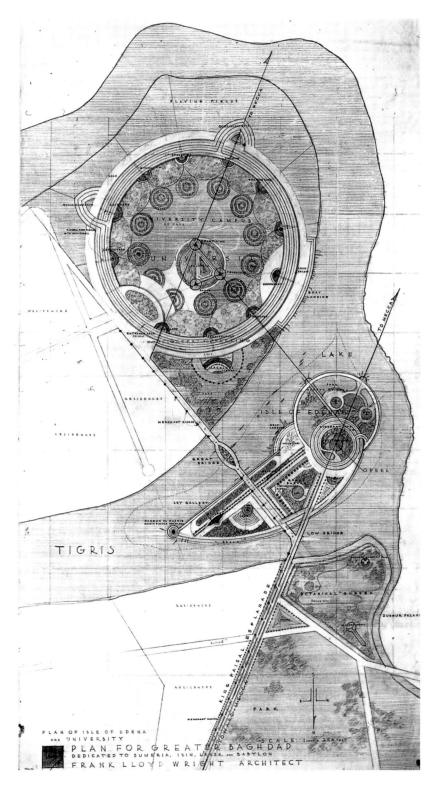

Figure 10.1
Plan for Greater Baghdad, 1957.
FLW, architect. (FLWA 5733.033)

built, it might have set an uncommon trend, softening the callous exchange between the West and the Middle East in the ensuing decades. Instead, Walter
Gropius's (and TAC's)[5] ultra-Western Baghdad University became the dominant
paradigm for the newly oil-rich Middle East.

Indirectly, the Baghdad enterprise also resulted in another unbuilt design in
another Middle Eastern capital city: Tehran, Iran. Little known and little published, Wright's 1958 design for a house in Tehran was one of the architect's last
residential projects. It offers another tangible example of the architect's desire to
build in an ancient and symbolic part of the world. While Wright's Middle Eastern projects remained confined to paper, they nevertheless paved the way for the
twenty-year relationship his successor firm, Taliesin Associated Architects (TAA),
enjoyed with Iran.[6]

IRAQ

Iraq came into existence as an emerging Middle Eastern state shortly after the
British declared it a nation in 1924. Its boundaries corresponded to no cultural
or historic heritage, but were determined by rivaling European powers.[7] Until
1932 the new country was politically dependent on the British, who had occupied the country since World War I, declared a mandate to the League of Nations, and installed Faisal I of the Hashemite family as king. Even once the mandate was terminated, making Iraq an independent sovereign nation, the British
continued to exert considerable influence in Iraq until the 1958 revolution.

The discovery of oil in the region, first in Iran (1908) and then in Iraq (1927),
transformed the destiny of the Middle East. After World War II, Iran and Iraq na-
tionalized their oil production, and the nations' governments began taking as much
as 50 percent of the revenues from increased production. To deal with these vastly
increased economic resources, Iraq created in 1950 a new administrative body
called the Development Board, which was responsible for allocating the 70 percent of all oil revenue targeted for development. The board's broad goal was to
raise the standard of living in Iraq.[8]

The Development Board embarked on its first program between 1951 and 1956
and initiated its second five-year program in 1955–59. The first program was primarily concerned with controlling and alleviating such fundamental infrastruc-
ture basics as irrigation, flood control, swamp drainage, construction of roads,
low-cost housing, and improvement of villages and rural conditions. By the end
of the first phase, hospitals, schools, factories, the royal palace, the house of parliament, and the Iraqi museum were also under construction.[9] By March 1957,
on the occasion of the second Development Week (the first having occurred a
year earlier), the board published a well-illustrated pamphlet summarizing the
progress of the first phase and outlining the goals for the second.[10] The second-
phase projects were to be designed largely by well-known Western architects, including Wright and several others. The pamphlet did not, however, mention these

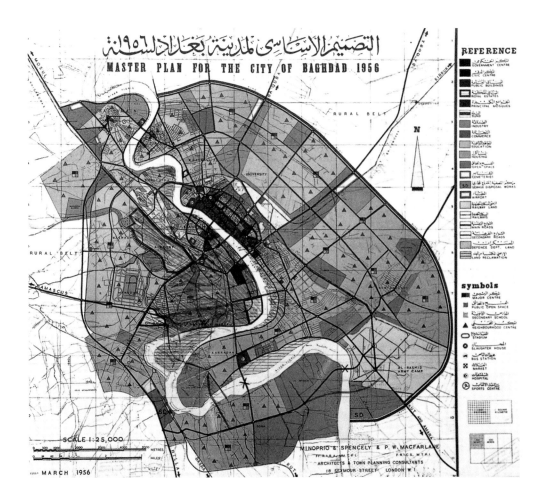

architects by name, an odd fact considering that most had already been commissioned by spring 1957, when the pamphlet was released.[11]

Another surprising omission in both reports was any reference to the first master plan for Baghdad, prepared by the British firm of Minoprio, Spencely, and Macfarlane, the text of which had been published in March 1956 (probably in time for the first Development Week).[12] The plan made specific recommendations for comprehensive urban expansion, including slum clearance, creation of a rural belt around the city, a comprehensive road system, five new bridges, and new bus, air, and railway terminals. Although many specific building projects and sites were mentioned, an opera house was not among them. That probably came from one of the executive members of the Development Board.[13] Wright would later use the large colored plan that Minoprio, Spencely, and Macfarlane produced (Fig. 10.2) as the base map of his own schemes for Baghdad. Perhaps he also had a copy of the written text, which in all likelihood accompanied the plan.

Figure 10.2
Baghdad Master Plan, 1954–56. Minoprio, Spencely, and Macfarlane, designers. With pencil additions by Wright. (FLWA 5733.001)

Figure 10.3
Ellen and Nizar Jawdat, n.d.
Photograph by Rifat Chadirji.

The budget for the Development Board's second-phase five-year plan for modernizing the country was $1.4 billion, so it is not surprising that the Iraqis cast their nets among the very best architects available. The international search may have also been an attempt to break the long-held British monopoly on foreign involvement in Iraq. The list of architects chosen to help build the modern Baghdad included Walter Gropius to design the university, Le Corbusier to design the stadium, Alvar Aalto to design a museum, and Gio Ponti to design the office building headquarters of the Development Board. Initially, Wright was not among the nominated architects. All of the architects the board approached were willing to work in Iraq except Oscar Niemeyer, who said he "would not work for oppressive regimes."[14]

While no official Iraqi documentation exists to confirm the process by which the selection was made, it seems plausible that a young couple who had recently graduated from Harvard University's Graduate School of Design, Nizar and Ellen Jawdat (Fig. 10.3), were instrumental.[15] The couple had set up their practice in Iraq and, being related to the prime minister, were clearly in a position to influence the Development Board's decisions in the choice of architects. In fact, they are directly credited by TAC as being instrumental in recommending Walter Gropius.[16] While modestly confirming their "informal" role in this matter—the Jawdats were avid enthusiasts of Gropius's work, both having been his students at Harvard—neither takes credit for suggesting Frank Lloyd Wright. Indeed, Ellen Jawdat recollects that she was skeptical about Wright, even though her sister, Frances Nimton (née Bovie), was at the time (and still remains) a member of Taliesin.[17] According to the Jawdats, it was an executive board member and a music aficionado, Abdul Jabbar Chalabi, who "pushed for Wright," recommending him specifically for a new opera house for Baghdad.[18] The Development Board secretary at that time, Fakri Bakr, confirmed the advisory role of the Jawdats, and affirmed the resolution of the Development Board to counter the control of the British by inviting international figures.

WESTERN ARCHITECTS

A brief examination of the other Western architects' designs for Baghdad will show Wright's unique sensitivity to the opportunities presented. In 1957 the contract for Baghdad University was awarded to Gropius; his firm was to create the master plan as well as the preliminary design for the new campus.[19] Gropius's design epitomized the International Style architecture in vogue in the 1950s and 1960s, and the structures looked remarkably similar to other projects completed in America at that time. Gropius's plan took as its main concern Baghdad's extreme climate.[20] The result was a system of "horizontal cantilevers and vertical baffles" on every facade. Ironically, the same cantilevers and baffles were used by TAC in other countries and other climates as well.

Except for the shading devices proposed for the roof, Alvar Aalto's project for an art museum also had little to do with the geographical or architectural particularities of Baghdad, but rather focused on allowing freedom of access for visitors.[21] His proposal was similar to a museum he was designing that same year for Aalborg, Denmark, and both those designs were refinements of his earlier museum in Revel, Estonia, created in 1934; the same concept was later applied to an unrealized museum in Shiraz, Iran (1970), as well.[22] It was a good design in the modernist tradition of the International Style and may well have been exactly what the Iraqi Development Board wanted, but ultimately Aalto's museum was never built.

Le Corbusier was asked to design an Olympic-caliber sports facility.[23] The French had recently completed a stadium in Beirut of which the Iraqis were envious, and they wanted their own. Like his colleagues, Le Corbusier did not attempt to create a design sensitive to the unique characteristics of Baghdad, but based his proposal on a previous scheme for a similar facility outside Paris. The final plan included a swimming pool with high dive, an air-conditioned gymnasium for basketball and volleyball, an enclosed facility accommodating five thousand spectators, and an open-air arena seating three thousand.[24]

Ponti was charged with the design of the headquarters of the Development Board itself—a building block of government offices. Working with "the Pirelli Team" (Studio Fornatelli-Rosselli and Studio Valtolina-Dell'Orto),[25] he produced a modified version of the Pirelli Building, the main difference being that whereas the parking space for the Pirelli was on top of the building, in Baghdad, "for reasons of climate," it was placed underneath a giant portico.[26] Ponti's description of his project provides a pointed contrast to the rhetoric that Wright would produce to accompany his plans for Baghdad:

> Architecture does not linger on local stylistic motives, that if interpreted by foreigners, are often ingenuous and not valid. It has been the architect's intention to contribute to Irak's development a perfect building which as far as climatic reasons are concerned fits in the local architecture, an architecture [of] which history has not preserved genuin [*sic*] realizations the architects could have referred to[.] Baghdad, this important city, destroyed by terrible historic events and associated in one imagination to "Aladdin and the tails of Thousand one night" [*sic*] now demands modern and technically perfect buildings.[27]

Ponti categorically rejected any notion that the building tradition of the Middle East should be considered in his plans. Wright, in contrast, was very concerned about the context of Baghdad, far more so than his celebrated contemporaries invited from around the world. Baghdad's historic context and Wright's own interpretation of the region form the basis for his design ideas.

When Wright received the commission for an opera house in Baghdad in January 1957, he knew that he was "expected to come to help 'modernize' Baghdad," but his speech to the engineers and architects of Baghdad, a diatribe against the blind expansion of Western commercialism, showed that he had a different approach to this "modernization" than the other architects involved in the process. He introduced himself as "one of the 'subjects' of Harun Al-Rashid by the way of the tales of 'The Arabian Nights,'" and stated explicitly that he was going "to do something useful not only to develop but to preserve the characteristic beauty that I have always felt to be due Harun Al-Rashid of the Middle East." Wright warned Baghdad not to follow in the footsteps of Western development, or the same problems of overpopulation and automobile congestion would overtake the city. He urged his audience to "preserve your own spiritual integrity according to great oriental philosophies, the spirit which has inspired East and West." Juxtaposing the materialism of the West with the spiritualism of the East, Wright championed the superiority of the latter and aligned himself with the East by way of oriental philosophy, claiming that "the greatest inspiration in my life was Laotze of Tibet."[28]

In today's "global village," Wright's statements seem far from radical, but in the late 1950s the culturally conscious ideas espoused by Wright were practically revolutionary. Contextualism was the last thing on the minds of his Iraqi clients. Nor can we dismiss his approach to "Orientalism" in the way Edward Said has condemned Western interventions in the Orient.[29] Wright's experience in Japan and his appreciation for non-Western cultures in general had resulted in an insight that was rare for his generation, and even more rare for his profession. But was Iraq in 1957 ready for and receptive to Wright's grand vision?

BAGHDAD

Baghdad, the capital and largest city of Iraq, was situated on two banks of the Tigris River about twenty-five miles north of the Euphrates River. Historically, the area had long been the center of imperial power, with Sumerians, Chaldeans, and Persians each leaving their mark. Built by the Abbasid caliph al-Mansur between 762 and 766, the city's plan was a perfect circle with progressive concentric walls. Four main roads radiated from the center, where the caliph's palace and the congregational mosque were located.[30] The city's mounting fame paralleled the rapid spread of Islam and reached its apex during the reign of Harun al-Rashid (786–809), who figures in many of the *Arabian Nights* fables. Throughout the medieval period the city's reputation in the West was somewhat intertwined with myth and legend, in part because it was often confused with the ancient kingdom of Babylon.[31]

The *Arabian Nights* tales were immensely popular during Wright's youth, and he was personally so fond of them that he embellished his children's playhouse in Oak Park with a mural depicting "The Fisherman and the Genii." Perhaps it was because of these stories that Wright erroneously credited Harun al-Rashid with the founding of the city instead of al-Mansur.

Wright also associated the history of Baghdad with its pre-Islamic Persian heritage, as seen in his response to the first letter inviting him to design the opera house. He would repeat this faux pas several times during his visit to Baghdad, even on the occasion of an audience with the king. As his son-in-law, William Wesley Peters, later recalled: "He [Wright] told him [King Faisal] how much he admired Persian architecture, which didn't go over very well with them at that time, but actually [the king] was taking the narrow view of it. Of course back in historic times [Baghdad] was part of the Persian empire and in fact it was at one time under the Shah of Persia."[32]

Wright was an enthusiast of Persian art, and in his 1953 book *The Future of Architecture* he wrote several pages in appreciation of Persian architecture:

[The Persian's] sense of scale was lofty, and he preserved it by never exaggerating the scale of his exquisite details. So these edifices stood out upon the plains, blue-domed against the sky among the rank and file of Persian cities as complete in themselves as the cypress trees around them were complete. . . . What a romantic of the race was this Persian, what mystic romance this Persia! Aladdin with the wonderful lamp? The wonderful lamp was Persian imagination.

By contrast, Wright offered little description of or insight into Arab architecture. He simply stated, "The opulent Arabian wandered, striking his splendid, gorgeous tents to roam elsewhere. He learnt much from the Persian." To Wright, Persian architecture was superior by comparison to even Hindu architecture, which he said "rivaled the Persian in exuberance but seemed to lack the pure and simple synthesis of form and clear pattern and color achieved by the Persian."[33]

Wright's impassioned portrait of Persian sensibility goes beyond descriptions he would have read in the popular and contemporary press. Underlying his ardent poetic fervor is an appreciation perhaps not just of the architecture of the Persian Empire, but of more rarefied manifestations of its rich cultural heritage.[34] Wright identified with what he saw as the Persians' quest for poetic and spiritual expression:

> Perhaps Persian architecture was the end of a quality of the spirit, a feeling for the abstract as form in architecture. Probably it was gradually lost, never to be surpassed unless the ideal of architecture as organic now reaches logical but passionate expression in years to come. These simple masses of noble mind and the exquisite tracery of fine human sensibilities remain in our grand vista to remind us of this phase of human architecture, called Persian. It is the natural home among the more self-conscious roofs of the world of architecture.[35]

Thus Wright interpreted Persian architecture as the natural precursor to his own "organic architecture." The homage to Persian architecture, written just a few years before his Baghdad commission arrived, can be interpreted as a basis for Wright's designs in the Iraqi capital, with Wright himself impersonating "Aladdin with his wonderful lamp, that was Persian imagination." Even if he ill-advisedly referred to Persia in addressing his Arab Iraqi clients, in his designs for Baghdad the reference to Persian architecture was deliberate.

The commission for the Baghdad opera house offered Wright the opportunity to leave a twentieth-century legacy in the land of ancient Persia. He responded to the letter of invitation from the Development Board enthusiastically:

> The commission from Baghdad to build an Opera House is an agreeable surprise and I am pleased to join IRAQ in a Twentieth Century enterprise. . . .To me this opportunity to assist Persia is like a story to a boy fascinated by the Arabian Nights Entertainment as I was. . . . I cannot tell you how pleased I am to serve my feeling for the Orient again. . . . With my sincere appreciation of the great opportunity held out to me by Baghdad IRAQ.[36]

The commission was for a single building in the densely built urban fabric of the old city. The Development Board had specified an opera house with services, on a site some nine thousand square meters in size, and serving a population of six hundred thousand.[37] There was no further elaboration of the scope of the project beyond the fact that Wright was to provide architectural and engineering services, including the supervision of the construction.

Within a few days of receiving this first communication Wright had accepted the commission, and within a few months, even before his visit to Iraq, he had reinterpreted the scope of the project. Not satisfied with the size of the site, for example, he started eyeing the "southern tip of Iraq." Evidently Wright obtained a copy of the master plan prepared by Minoprio, Spencely, and Macfarlane, which he used for his own base map, and he may also have had a copy of the accompanying written report;[38] in statements made before his trip to Baghdad, he makes reference to the Development Board's "one billion four hundred million dollar" budget, a figure he would have gleaned from these publications.[39] With the lofty aim of carrying forward the Persian "quality of spirit," Wright would soon transform his simple commission for an opera house into an elaborate plan for a Greater Baghdad cultural center.

A TRIP TO BAGHDAD

Wright traveled to Iraq in the last week of May 1957, accompanied by his wife and William Wesley Peters. He was met at the Baghdad airport by a former apprentice, Nezam Amery, and by Nizar and Ellen Jawdat.[40] Wright had already asked Amery, a young Persian architect educated at Kent State University and now living in Iran, to supervise the Baghdad project. Both Mr. and Mrs. Wright were very fond of Amery, and he in turn, Peters later recalled, "was very, very loyal to Mr. Wright."[41] After a year of apprenticeship with Wright in the early 1950s, Amery had returned to Iran and established his own office, promising Wright that he could count on him as his Middle Eastern representative.

It was by all accounts a successful trip, during which Wright visited the city, met with his clients, secured a site that he deemed acceptable, and expanded his commission. He was greeted by ministers and had two audiences with the king, he was shown around by his friends, and he delivered a speech to a gathering of architects and engineers. The *Iraq Times* newspaper, reporting on Wright's visit to the city, published a photograph of Dhia Jafar's visit with Wright at the Omar Khayyam Hotel, "for consultations with the Development Ministry on the designs for the projected Baghdad Opera House and General Post Office buildings, which Mr. Wright will supervise as consultant."[42] This was the first time the post office building was mentioned, confirming that Wright's commission expanded during his visit to Baghdad.

Amery and Peters accompanied Wright to see the site allotted for the opera, with which he had already declared himself dissatisfied. Determined to find a more appropriate site, one suitably grand and worthy of his building, Wright personally secured permission from the king to build on an island in the Tigris River. He also apparently expanded the scope of the project in his discussions with the king.

Because Peters had already left Baghdad before Wright's final meeting with the king, the only source of information about this meeting is Wright himself, who described it on several occasions both in print and to his apprentices upon his return to Taliesin.[43] According to his account, it was the flight over the city as they arrived that helped him identify the island on which the opera house should be built.[44] Of course, Wright also had the master plan, where the island was prominently visible and where he would have discerned the proposed university on the opposite peninsula. Although he was informed that the island belonged to the imperial household and could not be developed, Wright pursued it anyway, describing his plans to King Faisal. He must have been persuasive, for he recounts a positive response: "Well, he put his hand on this island place on the map and looked at me with an ingratiating smile and he said, 'Mr. Wright, it is yours.' Now that converted me to the monarchy right then."[45]

Known as Pig Island, the patch of land was uninhabited, in part because of frequent flooding, though the recent completion of the Thartar Dam now made it attractive for development. Wright, never one to be restrained by nature, reshaped the island to conform to a grand master plan of his own devising. By the time he was through he had created—on paper, at least—an area several times larger than the existing island, chiefly by annexing the peninsula reserved for the university. Instead of a simple opera house, as the commission had stipulated, Wright offered Baghdad a cultural complex worthy of a king.[46]

With the new site in mind, Wright expanded the commission for the opera house into a master plan for a "Greater Baghdad Cultural Center" (see Fig. 10.1), with the opera house doubling as a civic auditorium, a landscaped park with fountains and cascading waterfalls, a three-tiered parking ziggurat, museums for both monumental ancient sculpture and contemporary art, a grand bazaar, the King Faisal Esplanade, various bridges, big and small, lined with shops, a monument to Harun al-Rashid, a botanical garden and zoological park, a casino and amphitheater, a university complex, and several radio and television towers. In addition, outside this cultural complex, Wright designed a new Post and Telegraph Building to be located in the old city.[47]

On his way back to the United States Wright stopped in Cairo (Fig. 10.4), where he spent a few days with another former apprentice, Kamal Amin,[48] and then again in Paris and London. Upon his return to Taliesin Wright was already voicing some skepticism about the project, telling his apprentices:

Well, anyhow, I do not know that there is very much hope for the Baghdad project. This is really my proposition to them. The King gave me the island

Figure 10.4
Wright in Cairo, 1957, with Dr. Mohamad Amin *(left),* Olgivanna Wright, Mrs. Mohamad Amin *(right),* and Mawal Amin *(far right).*

that I asked for, but I do not have the slightest idea in the world what I'm going to do with it. And so, I am in a great haste to pull it all together and let them have it, before it's too late. . . . I sort of came in on the tail end of things, so what impression I can make now I do not know—but I am going to try.[49]

WRIGHT'S DESIGN

Despite possible doubts, Wright—having the apparent backing of the highest authority in the land, the king himself—set about confidently to prepare drawings for the new site, now with a totally new program relative to the original commission. Wright's own words remain the most detailed explanation of his intent and the scope of his proposal. He was very conscious of the unique opportunity the project offered him:

Well we've got it (the island site) and we've got a great opportunity there in the drafting room now to demonstrate that we are not destructive but constructive, where the original forces that built the civilization of the world are concerned and we are not there to slap them in the face but to do honor to them according to our abilities. That's the attitude I think that a modern architect should take toward the great life that's been his inheritance from the past to which he pays scant respect. You don't respect a thing as you know, boys, well enough by imitating it, and we are going to imitate nothing. But we're going to use the principles and the ideas that made that originality a great force in human thought and feeling, and do what we can to carry it alone. That I think is the duty of the modern architect.

He, Frank Lloyd Wright, would link the past with the present. As he put it, "It is rather interesting, isn't it, to have the—I think they call me the dean of the moderns or something like that—going back to the origin of civilization, to show what civilization amounts to now."[50]

Wright's proposal for a new civic center was intended to reinforce a cultural identity rooted in a rich historic past. To this end he mined both Islamic and pre-Islamic imagery, relying as much on myth and memory as on historical context. His circular plan was in fact reminiscent of al-Mansur's city of the eighth century, which was dominated by the green-domed great mosque. In Wright's plan, too, domed shapes and lofty spires conjured up Islamic religious edifices, and ziggurats and terraced forms went even further into the past, alluding to the ancient Assyrian and Mesopotamian heritage. But the image he evoked was also a city of memory, a city of imagination powerful enough to endure for centuries—as in the minds of those who read *The Arabian Nights' Entertainments,* even when the real city was long destroyed.

His stated intent was to "preserve the spirit and glory of the Eastern civilization that characterized the Iraq of Harun al Rashid," while simultaneously catering to modern "tourists" and creating a "place for people in general."[51] He combined historic tenets and modern principles to produce an unusual and complex plan that was simultaneously metaphoric and didactic, futuristic and practical, religious and profane. What Wright prepared in Baghdad was a rare mixture of respect for the past and for the technology of the future. It was neither "fantastic" nor unrealistic. Even if Wright was initially dazzled by the $1.4 billion budget, he was nevertheless both pragmatic and cost-conscious, taking cultural, social, and economic issues into serious consideration. What he offered overall was a "scientific modern principle" for Baghdad's urbanization, one that emphasized in particular "decentralization . . . because it is now inevitable to the survival of all great cities either West or East. In the Western World the cities themselves through acceleration are being destroyed by traffic congestion caused by the senseless greed of the high-building. To avoid calamitous traffic-jam is the basic consideration seen throughout this design for a *greater* (not just a *bigger*) Baghdad."[52]

Wright started by renaming Pig Island the Isle of Edena, "name of the ancient city where the Garden of Eden was historically located." He justified his selection of the island, calling it "a sensible . . . economical and convenient site for building well within city limits, costing Baghdad comparatively nothing for the site of a 'Greater Baghdad' Cultural Center." Using aerial photography to support his decision, Wright proposed to cut back the size of the island and raise it up to make the base for a ziggurat, "slightly armoring the off-shores of the Tigris

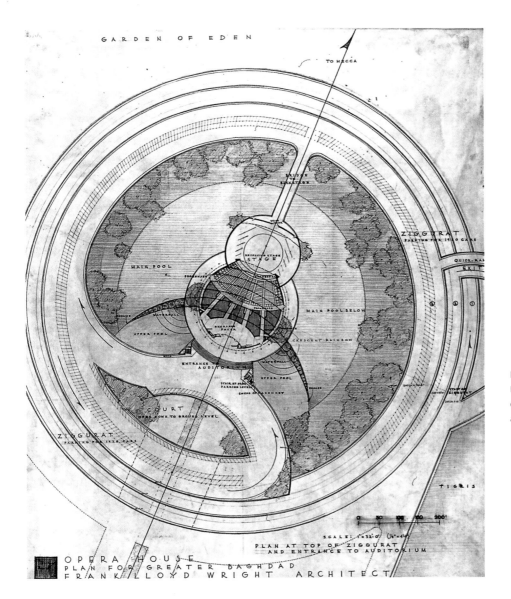

GARDEN OF EDEN

TO MECCA

Figure 10.5
Plan, opera house on the Isle
of Edena, Baghdad, 1957. FLW,
architect. (FLWA 5733.028)

by an inexpensive thin gunnite plating to take the force of the flow of the streams."[53] By proposing reinforcement, Wright was using modern engineering to offer a practical solution that might lead to annexation of the island for urban development.

His main organizational principle for the site was the ziggurat (Fig. 10.5), an ancient form that Wright had used before as a modern means of affording motor access and parking in such projects as Crystal Heights.[54] Besides solving traffic congestion, which he repeatedly identified as the city's most critical problem,[55] the ziggurat was a conscious means of blending architecture and landscape: "*All*

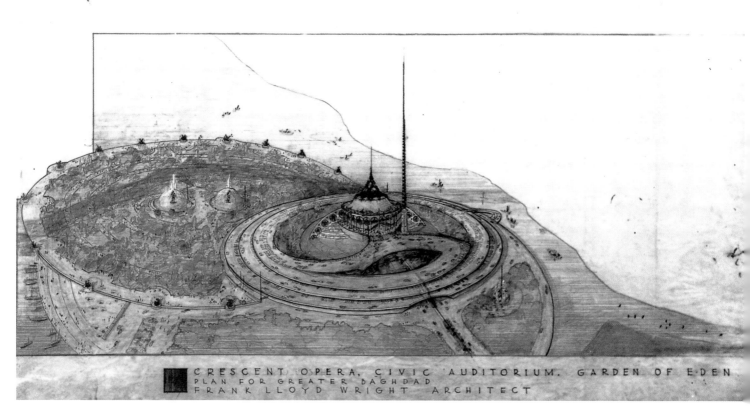

CRESCENT OPERA, CIVIC AUDITORIUM, GARDEN OF EDEN
PLAN FOR GREATER BAGHDAD
FRANK LLOYD WRIGHT ARCHITECT

Figure 10.6
Perspective view, Isle of Edena, showing the statues of Adam and Eve at left and the Crescent Opera House and Civic Auditorium at center, 1957. FLW, architect. (FLWA 5733.007)

public buildings whatever their nature, or masonry bridges here become integral parts of this general landscape of river, of the architecture. All features are here seen together as one. Includes greenery of parks, great wide highways and bridges: the great historical river is celebrated."[56]

The holistic vision of architecture as integral to the landscape was complemented by a realistic mercantile approach that targeted tourists, foreshadowing, in a sense, late-twentieth-century theme parks: "Lakes, forest-parks, botanical gardens, great fountains, sculpture, bridle paths, and country-clubs [are] to become appropriate to mercantile interests and all interwoven to preserve overall beauty and make Baghdad citizens' daily-life better worth living." His scheme promised "a new convenience and lively interest for tourists. Though a seeming extravagance—this would turn out to be a most profitable investment." Wright was ahead of the Development Board in recognizing the economic viability of tourism, which in that part of the world was not yet considered a source of revenues for economic development. His animatedly landscaped Garden of Edena, also called the Memorial Garden of Adam and Eve (Fig. 10.6), was to include "man, woman, and child of all races, and fruit trees of all climes."[57] It was a vision not unlike that of Walt Disney or other Hollywood moghuls, but the basis was a popular appeal that came intuitively to Wright. He knew that tourists would be less inclined to visit modern International Style structures and more likely to embrace his exotic landscapes. The "Wrightland" he imagined would be as entertaining for tourists as Disneyland was for children.

Long before Walt Disney's imaginings, Wright had acknowledged the significance of "fantasy" in his various projects (mostly unrealized) for resort communities. As early as 1895, his project for Wolf Lake Amusement Park anticipated present-day waterworlds and festive waterfronts. In Chicago's Midway Gardens (1913) he finally realized an architectural ambience of leisure, though Prohibition created financial strain that eventually brought an end to it. His later resort concepts included the Lake Tahoe Summer Colony (1922), which offered vacation accommodations in the form of floating barges, and with his plans for the Gordon Strong Planetarium in Maryland (1925), the Pittsburgh Point Park Civic Center (1947), and the Monona Terrace Civic Center in Madison, Wisconsin (1938, 1955), he hoped to define a new type of drive-in urban pleasure palace. In Baghdad, many ideas from these earlier experiments would reemerge to fit the new context. Thus, while Wright may have intended to create an *Arabian Nights*–style entertainment fantasy, it was nevertheless grounded in a comprehensive civic plan aimed at solving traffic, site, and even social problems.

THE ESPLANADE AND BRIDGES

Wright's analytical sketches, based directly on the Minoprio, Spencely, and Macfarlane master plan, showed that the island was a logical choice for any urban design intervention of substantial scope, being somewhat removed from the old city center but well situated next to the proposed university. Wright proposed a low masonry bridge to connect the island to the mainland, topped by a broad avenue that Wright directed toward Mecca and entitled King Faisal Esplanade. This grand thoroughfare, or "boulevard," formed the principal access both to the island with the opera house and to the peninsula with the university. Why he would choose the holy orientation—a requirement for religious edifices such as mosques, shrines, and madrasas—for a "wide traffic carrier . . . with commercial value of various sorts, by way of commerce kiosks along the way," remains somewhat of a mystery, since there was no precedent for public thoroughfares facing Mecca.[58] He may have been trying to raise the significance of the thoroughfare, or perhaps he was merely extrapolating inappropriately from the historic culture.[59]

In any event, he clearly recognized the necessity of commercial activity if the cultural center were to be viable. Islam in principle honors the merchant, and in cities throughout the Islamic world the bazaar—the principal commercial zone—has always been in close proximity to the mosque. Wright thus proposed a centrally located grand bazaar on the island itself.

As the continuation of the multilane King Faisal Esplanade, the boulevard spanned the Tigris River on a low bridge that forked just short of the island, one branch continuing to the opera and oriented toward Mecca, the other heading southeast across the island and over a "great bridge" to the university campus, passing the art gallery and sculpture museum. "The wide ferro-concrete bridge is low over the narrow branch of the Tigris, only a few feet above the high-water mark—enough to let a row boat pass beneath," while "over the wide branch of the Tigris was another bridge allowing passage of high craft." This great bridge was split with a lozenge-shaped median landscaped as a park. "Merchant kiosks" were to be located at equidistant intervals along the entire length of the esplanade, all the way to the university campus, and numerous underpasses and entrance and exit ramps would be provided. Even "the bridges [would] become broad malls with kiosks mounted on them at intervals on land as over the water."[60] Wright emphasized the great practicality of this bridge scheme, noting that not only would it be cheap and easy to build, but it would also generate income because the kiosks would be rented out by the city to the merchants. He insisted, moreover, that the bridge would require no maintenance.[61] Wright was confident in his statements because of his recent experience with several bridge designs, including the similar Wisconsin River Bridge (1947) and San Francisco Bay Bridge (1949), neither of which was actually built.

THE OPERA HOUSE

The centerpiece of the project was the opera house, which, "set in a natural water garden surrounded by the motor ziggurat," was conceived simultaneously as a civic auditorium (Fig. 10.7). Its main feature was a ceiling shaped "like a great horn" that "extends outward." Citing the Chicago Auditorium by Adler and Sullivan as "the most successful room for opera and large audiences in existence," Wright used a similar crescent shape over the proscenium "to carry sound as hands would be cupped above the mouth."[62] On the arch were circular openings, each containing a bronze sculpture representing a character from the *Arabian Nights*.

The crescent was tilted to one side and thus divided the structure into two asymmetrical sections. The auditorium offered flexible seating, with the possibility of additional seating to accommodate functions ranging from musical performances to civic demonstrations.[63] Inside there was a series of arches beginning at the proscenium. The highest arch projected out of the building over the roof and extended over a series of cascading pools. The opera house, like the esplanade, was oriented to Mecca, and had a revolving stage and a tunnel (also on the axis to Mecca) leading to a planetarium below the auditorium. On the ground level was an oval lozenge-shaped courtyard marking the main entrance, with ramps extending from the parking ziggurat. A circular pool surrounded the main auditorium.

The building was meant to be as inspiring "as any religious edifice." The crescent shape itself is a familiar Islamic symbol, referring to the lunar calendar and

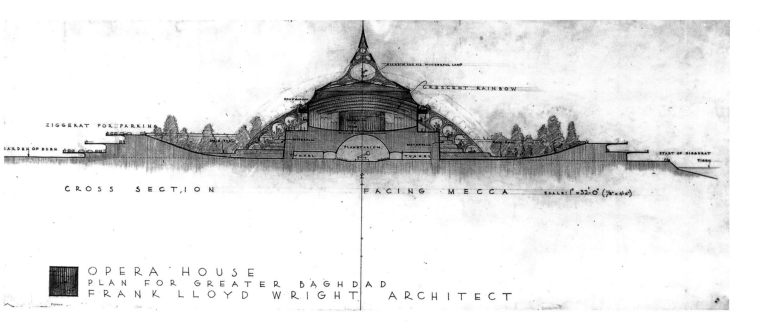

Within the figure:
ALLADIN AND HIS WONDERFUL LAMP
CRESCENT RAINBOW
ZIGGERAT FOR PARKING
GARDEN OF EDEN
MORTORC
AUDITORIUM
MATERIAL
START OF ZIGGURAT
TUNNEL   PLANTARIUM   TUNNEL   Tiaris

CROSS SECTION   FACING MECCA   SCALE: 1"=32'-0" (⅛"=4'-0")

OPERA HOUSE
PLAN FOR GREATER BAGHDAD
FRANK LLOYD WRIGHT   ARCHITECT

appearing on the flags of several Islamic countries. The domed roof with a single spire is also an archetypal image, characteristic of many mosques.[64] Wright does not describe or specify the function of the slim spire next to the auditorium, but one assumes it is a television antenna, since it is similar in proportion and size to the radio and television antennas he placed at the center of the university campus and is also very much like the two spires in the Arizona State Capital (Oasis) designed by Wright in 1956–57. It appears to be a metal and concrete structure similar to the crescent domed roof. In juxtaposition to the dome, the spire is reminiscent of the minarets that often flank mosques, especially in the Persian Islamic world. Wright's familiarity with Islamic architecture suggests that he selected this imagery deliberately, though ironically, it may not have been appreciated by his Iraqi clientele, most of whom were overtly secular and westernized.

For the sculptural decoration on the grand crescent, Wright turned not to religion for inspiration but instead chose the "tales of the classical Thousand and One Nights to decorate the gardens with appropriate sculpture as seen set into the wings of the daring crescent . . . A golden figure of Aladdin holding his wonderful lamp (symbol of human imagination) stands overhead at the center of the crenelated canopy terminating the main edifice as seen against the sky."[65] Wright informed his client that the cost of the building was reasonable: "Be assured that notwithstanding appearances there is nothing difficult or expensive to construct in this opus if sculpture by native artists is available and local crafts stimulated." He further stated that "a structure such as this could be built in America—(most expensive place of all in which to build) for almost $35 per sq. foot, sculpture not included or almost 3.5 million dollars, exclusive of ziggurat."[66]

Figure 10.7
Cross section, opera house, Baghdad, 1957. FLW, architect. (FLWA 5733.039)

Figure 10.8
Monument to Harun al-Rashid, Baghdad,
1957. FLW, architect. (FLWA 5751.004)

Figure 10.9 *(opposite)*
Plan, elevation, and section, museum
for Mesopotamian sculpture, Baghdad,
1957. FLW, architect. (FLWA 5748.003)

HAROUN AL RASHID
FRANK LLOYD WRIGHT · ARCHITECT

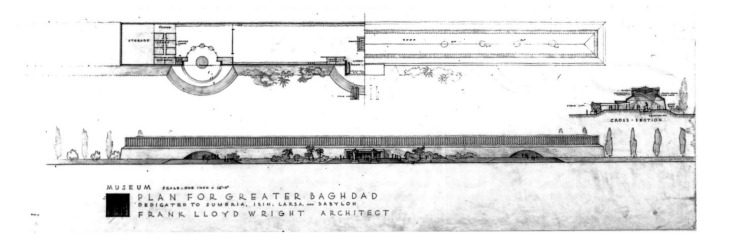

MUSEUM SCALE:ONE INCH = 16'-0"
PLAN FOR GREATER BAGHDAD
DEDICATED TO SUMERIA, ISIN, LARSA, AND BABYLON
FRANK LLOYD WRIGHT ARCHITECT

THE ISLAND

Landscaped with orchards, basins, fountains, and tree-lined allées, the island supported several other functions besides the opera house and civic auditorium. The circular Garden of Adam and Eve shaped the island's southern end into a public park, the Garden of Edena, with two monumental statues each under a water dome of fountain springs (see Figs. 10.1 and 10.6). Along the periphery were other statues commemorating various peoples and nations. The park was planted as a lush citrus orchard, attesting to Wright's belief that it was not an apple that Eve presented to Adam but an orange.[67]

The circular Garden of Edena was counterbalanced on the narrower northern tip by a three-hundred-foot-high ziggurat crowned by a statue of Harun al-Rashid raising his sword (Fig. 10.8). It was meant to be seen from a distance, a beacon for Baghdad like the Statue of Liberty in New York. The base was like a small tower of Babel and proportioned much like the minaret of the Mosque of Samarra, with a sculpted relief of a procession of mounted camels spiraling upward toward the feet of Wright's favorite caliph, all cast in concrete but to be covered with metal.

On the island Wright proposed two museums, one for large-scale archeological sculpture, the other for contemporary Iraqi art. Impressed with the Sumerian remains he had visited during his trip to Baghdad, Wright designed a monumental structure for Mesopotamian sculpture, the entrance to which he flanked with two huge winged Assyrian lions (Fig. 10.9).[68] The accompanying art gallery was to be an elongated lozenge-shaped building, from the center of which a

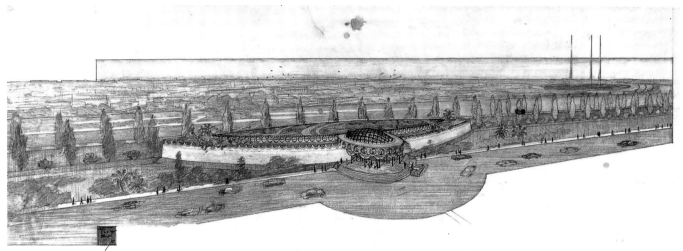

PRELIMINARY STUDY FOR ART GALLERY   ISLE OF EDENA
PLAN FOR GREATER BAGHDAD
DEDICATED TO SUMERIA, ISIN, LARSA, AND BABYLON
FRANK LLOYD WRIGHT ARCHITECT   · ARCHES BUM ·

BUILDING FOR THE ART DEPARTMENT
GALLERY ONLY (CLASS ROOM WING NOT INDICATED)
ARIZONA STATE UNIVERSITY
TEMPE, ARIZONA
FRANK LLOYD WRIGHT ARCHITECT

Figure 10.10 *(top)*
Perspective view, art gallery,
Baghdad, 1957. FLW, architect.
(FLWA 5749.005)

Figure 10.11 *(bottom)*
Perspective view, art gallery for
the art department, Arizona
State University, Tempe, 1959.
FLW, architect. (FLWA 5912.001)

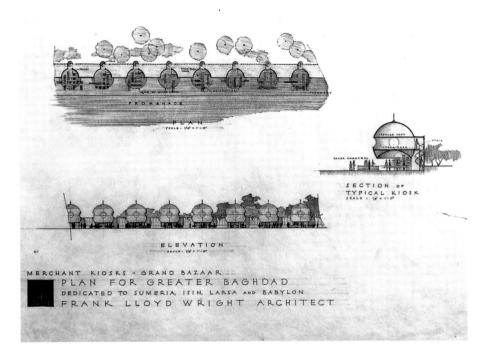

Figure 10.12

Elevation, plan, and section, merchant kiosks in the Grand Bazaar, Baghdad, 1957. FLW, architect. (FLWA 5750.003)

circle protruded, covered by a lattice dome of concrete and glass (Fig. 10.10). Under this dome was a sunken pool adorned by a sculpture, a theme repeated several times throughout the gallery. Both the museum and the art gallery had a ring of clerestory windows that allowed light to be reflected off the ceiling and then into the interior halls. The gallery design resurfaced in Wright's plan for Arizona State University (1959), this time as a gallery for the art department (Fig. 10.11).[69]

Not far from the art gallery Wright located a casino and outdoor amphitheater. On the other side of the esplanade, on the route to the university near the sculpture museum, was the grand bazaar, laid out in an L-shape around a landscaped court for pedestrian use only. The bazaar consisted of a series of domed structures similar to the kiosks lining the esplanade and bridge, made of concrete and supported by a continuous wall in the back, with stairs leading to a loft and storage room inside each dome (Fig. 10.12). During the day, when the bazaar was in operation, tables would be set under the dome and extended out as needed, making a quasi–outdoor market. At night, the merchandise would be stored in the lofts.

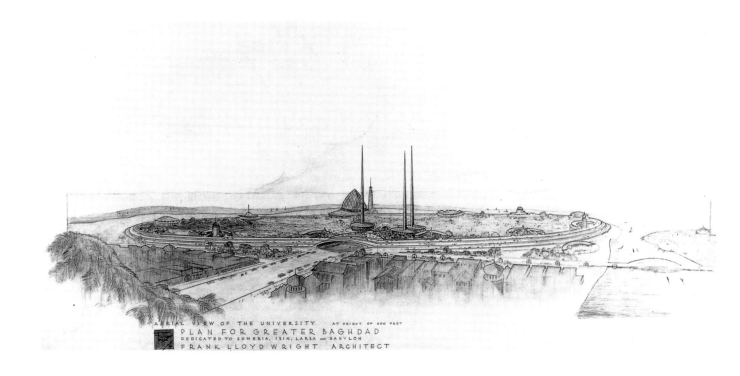

AERIAL VIEW OF THE UNIVERSITY   AT HEIGHT OF 300 FEET
PLAN FOR GREATER BAGHDAD
DEDICATED TO SUMERIA, ISIN, LARSA AND BABYLON
FRANK LLOYD WRIGHT   ARCHITECT

THE UNIVERSITY

In the preface to his design for the University of Baghdad, Wright wrote:

> This general design here proposed to the Development Board is an attempt
> to see beyond the materialistic structures called "modern" and barging in
> from the West upon the East, typical of capitalism but unqualified either
> by intelligence or by the poetic principle of architecture. . . . These draw-
> ings are voluntarily submitted for the purposes of this new freedom and
> are sent to the Development Board with this purpose in mind—prompted
> by respect and affection for the ancient East of the Middle East.[70]

Wright must have known that the university was already earmarked for Gropius,
but he designed it anyway, just as he knew that Aalto was charged with an art
museum but went ahead and designed two museums regardless. Both, after all,
were integral to the larger vision he had in mind.[71]

The university campus—another perfect circle—was raised on a three-tiered
parking ziggurat; it housed twelve faculties (or curricula) on the outer perimeter
and had a circular lake in the center with three television and radio transmission
towers that rose from a floating triangular base and dominated the surroundings
(Fig. 10.13). At the center of the lake was a jet fountain. In several of the sketches

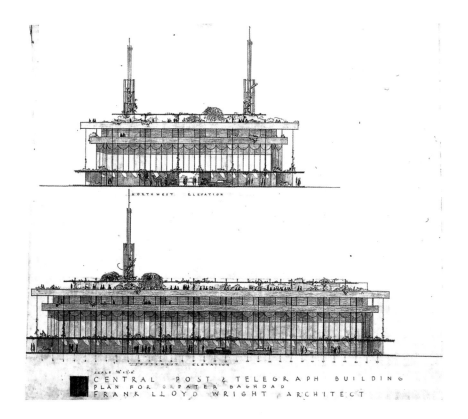

CENTRAL POST & TELEGRAPH BUILDING
PLAN FOR GREATER BAGHDAD
FRANK LLOYD WRIGHT ARCHITECT

Figure 10.13 *(opposite)*
Perspective view, university,
Baghdad, 1957. FLW, architect.
(FLWA 5759.007)

Figure 10.14
Elevations, Post and Telegraph
Building, Baghdad, 1957. FLW,
architect. (FLWA 5734.016)

Wright included a prominent mosque with a conical domed roof, but the mosque seems to have been whited out in the final drawing.

The campus was reserved for pedestrians only. Wright provided a boat landing on the waterfront and conceived of the drive to the university as a pleasurable activity. The main entrances for the university faced the highway, but student life focused inward.

His design premise for the circular campus was flexibility. Ziggurat parking was again Wright's solution to motor congestion, keeping the campus automobile-free and maintaining the campus's relationship with the riverfront. In discussing the plan's "flexibility," Wright noted that expansion of either the parking ziggurat or the faculties could be achieved by joining new buildings with additional rounds of the ziggurat.[72]

POST AND TELEGRAPH BUILDING

In contrast to the circular exuberance of the opera house and the university campus, the design for the Post and Telegraph Building—commissioned, as we saw, while Wright was in Baghdad—was simple and orthogonal (Fig. 10.14). The site, already occupied by an existing building, was in the old part of the city along

Rashid Street, not far from the river and close to the Omar Khayyam Hotel, where Wright had stayed.

Wright's "basic aim" was "to produce a building by extremely economic methods, greatly simplifying construction, one more suitable to IRAQ climate than any yet built."[73] The Central Post and Telegraph Building was to be a rectangular building with three main levels as well as two mezzanine levels of offices aboveground and a basement level for air-conditioning equipment, delivery docks, and garden courtyards. The skeletal structure would be made of steel tubes filled with concrete, forming a frame into which the largely glass walls would fit. A trellis made of steel tubing was to extend over the sidewalk and facade, forming a support for extensive plantings that would make a "wall" of greenery, shading the windows from the sun. The green insulation was also to be found on the roof, where there would be a fully planted garden, complete with sixteen inches of soil, and another trellis suspended overhead. A large sunken interior courtyard featured pools, fountains, and more greenery; it was sheltered by another overhead steel-tube trellis, and because the building was made of glass, the trees could be seen from the street.[74] In the last part of his written text for the Post and Telegraph Building, Wright defended his design with a postscript: "I respectfully suggest that the general character of the design of the structure is more suitable for most urban buildings in Baghdad because at the same time economic and flexible, it is suited to the extreme heat of the region, quiet in style and organic in character. Worthy to be called 'modern' architecture."[75]

THE COUP

A dramatic turn of events not unlike those told of in *A Thousand and One Nights* befell the Baghdad project. On 14 July 1958 a military coup led by General Abdul Karim Kassem put an abrupt end to the Hashemite monarchy; King Faisal and Crown Prince Abdul Ilah were assassinated, and the Development Board, among other governmental agencies, ceased to exist. Although some foreign architects continued to work under the new regime (including Ponti, Le Corbusier, and TAC, with the latter even expanding the scope of their work), Wright's project was rejected. The new leadership considered the project extravagant, and the imagery was probably too closely identified with the monarchy. For the young professional architects of Iraq, Wright's plan was not modern enough, and the opera house, in any case, was no longer relevant.[76]

When the revolution broke out, Amery was in Baghdad with Wright's drawings waiting for the delayed arrival of William Wesley Peters. Traveling as a dignitary, Amery carried no passport and narrowly escaped death himself when he was discovered with the drawings, which were considered government property. Only because a high-ranking military official recognized him as the son of a powerful Iranian sheikh did Amery finally manage to escape Iraq. He rescued the drawings he had with him, but those that had been submitted earlier to the king and the ministry were never recovered. Wright died less than a year later, in April 1959. In the ensuing years, Taliesin Associates tried several times to retrieve the drawings and claim their compensation, but each time another political change would deter their resolve.

AMERY HOUSE

As a direct result of Amery's involvement in Wright's Baghdad scheme came a project for a house for the Amery family in Tehran, conceived in the same year. Amery's father, the British-backed Sheikh Khazaal, had ruled over a vast domain in southern Iran, including parts of Iraq. When his rival, the new Persian monarch Reza Shah Pahlavi, had him assassinated, Amery—then a child—narrowly escaped a similar fate (as did his many brothers and sisters). Later, as a member of the privileged classes, he went abroad for his education and, through the advice of an acquaintance and compatriot, pursued architectural studies at Kent State University.

Once in the United States Amery became interested in the work of Frank Lloyd Wright and applied for an apprenticeship. Wright immediately liked Amery; Mrs. Wright was also fond of him. That Wright agreed to design a house for a former apprentice was atypical and a testament to his affection for Amery.

It was not unusual for Wright to start with an already designed project and adapt it as needed. In this case his client showed a predisposition to Wright's California concrete-block, or textile-block, houses, an appropriate style both because the warm weather in California is similar to the hot season in Tehran and because traditional craftsmanship in masonry has a long history in Iran.[77] The Amery House therefore took as its departure point the Millard House in Pasadena (La Minatura, 1923); both the plan and the size of the blocks were modified, however, to accord with the particular site and the conditions in Iran. Wright's perspective sketch shows the Alborz Mountains in the background and the cypress trees that are indigenous to Tehran (Fig. 10.15), and the pink hue of the concrete reflects the color of the Persian soil. In his preliminary sketches Wright studied the site, a rather irregular trapezoid (pinched at the center), noting the slopes, orientation, and street access. On the same sketch he listed the "materials available" in Iran: "bricks, stones, galvanized sheet metal, glaized [sic] tile, wood (untreated), no insulation material, waterproofing mostly tappen, burlap, steel beams (must order—[illegible]), used mostly for—[illegible], cement for plastering mostly."[78]

With Amery in his office working on the Baghdad project, Wright had direct access to information about traditional Persian homes, which he took into account in his design. Unlike the California houses, the house in Tehran is narrow to provide for cross-ventilation. The first floor is identified as an open loggia, the nomenclature often used for the *aivan* (a deeply recessed roofed space open on one side, often facing south) typical of traditional houses and buildings of Iran. Wright's loggia, like the aivan, functioned as an informal living space well suited to the hot and dry climate of Iran. Balconies on both the north and south al-

RESIDENCE FOR NEZAM AMER TEHERAN, IRAN
FRANK LLOYD WRIGHT ARCHITECT

Figure 10.15
Elevation, Amery House,
Tehran, 1957–58. FLW, architect.
(FLWA 5801.023)

lowed an extension to the outdoors, another common feature of Persian houses. Wright also provided upper-level terraces, to be used like the roofs of traditional homes for evening activities as well as for sleeping on summer nights. The living room was on the second level above the loggia, with access to a wide terrace on either side. With a high ceiling, it was a formal reception space not unlike the *talar* or formal reception rooms of traditional courtyard houses of Iran. Four bedrooms were arranged along a gallery, with one bath accessible to each set of two rooms. Access to the bedroom wing was through a small square transition space with a fountain in the center. The use of indoor pools and fountains was part of traditional architecture in Iran.

Detailed working drawings of the concrete blocks, the cabinetry (an elaborate workspace was planned for the kitchen), and even all the furniture, from coffee tables to beds, completed the preliminary designs. Like the buildings in Baghdad, however, the house was not built. When Amery returned to Iran he did not have the funds to build the house, and he then became immersed in his own practice. Years later, when he had just started to lay the foundation, the Iranian revolution took place, and like many of his compatriots Amery and his family fled Iran and settled in London.[79]

EPILOGUE

The story of Wright's Baghdad project continued in Iran, for Amery invited Taliesin Associated Architects to work with him on several projects contracted through his own office in Tehran. The first collaboration resulted from a villa that Amery had designed earlier for Princess Shams Pahlavi (sister of the shah) on the outskirts of Tehran. Having outgrown the first villa, the princess and her husband, Mehrdad Pahlbod (then the minister of culture), desired a larger residence— a palace. Amery asked Taliesin to participate in the design of Princess Shams's palace, which became known as "The Pearl Palace." It was a royal extravaganza worthy of Frank Lloyd Wright himself.[80]

That project led to a number of other designs by Taliesin, including a series of villas along the Caspian Sea (in Challus) and a university campus in Tehran (Damavand College). All of them were built, though none had been completed when the 1979 Islamic revolution broke out in Iran and the Pahlavi monarchy was overthrown. TAA was even involved in a resort project that bore a striking resemblance to the Baghdad concept, involving an island much larger than Wright's Isle of Edena, including some of the ziggurats and circular forms of the earlier plan, and even more ambitious in scope. But like its progenitor, the Minou Island Resort was not destined to be: the island was strategically too close to Iraq, and so the neighboring island of Kish was developed instead, though not by TAA.

In their book *Modern Architecture,* Manfredo Tafuri and Francesco Dal Co describe Wright's Baghdad oeuvre as

> a phantasmagoria of mountains, watercourses, and exotic objects culminating in a scintillating spire. The aggregation of the forms no longer shows the slightest necessity. The experience of the gratuitous aims to liberate the forms, at the ultimate to make them levitate, transforming them into nothing more nor less than improbable future-fiction flying objects.[81]

I have tried here to counter the attitude with which Tafuri and many eminent historians have categorically dismissed Wright's Baghdad project. Modernism had rejected history, which meant that Wright was definitely swimming against the tide with his historicizing images. Preceding the postmodern movement by more than a decade, Wright's designs appeared as a "fantasy," a fact that has clouded their interpretation even into the present time. Wright was futuristic in his vision, but he recognized the value of cultural identity and delved deeply into the historic context of Baghdad to conjure new and imaginative interpretations. His approach was contextually superior both to the eclectic colonial orientalist approach and to the tabula rasa International Style, in which climate was the only tangible element worth considering—resulting in the proliferation ad nauseam throughout the Middle East of the *brise soleil*. In his work, Wright pursued principles and methods that had withstood the test of time, and which certainly surpassed the formulaic postmodern imitations that later proliferated in Middle Eastern cities.

Near the end of the twentieth century the definition of cultural heritage has finally been expanded beyond physical objects and buildings, and now includes crafts, customs, social habits, and even collective memory. Wright seemed intuitively capable of recognizing all that half a century ago. His designs for Baghdad crystallized the historic city as it existed in the collective memory of both East and West, as a vibrant capital at the height of its glory. The circular plan, soaring spires, and lofty domes recalled the Abbasid city, and the cascading waters of lush gardens harked back to an even earlier era and one of the oldest myths of humankind: that of Adam and Eve. The functions of an opera house, a civic center, and a university were clearly modern ones, but Wright gave them forms that linked them to the past and imbued them with didactic cultural messages, collective images shared by both East and West. While meeting very modern needs, moreover, his design purposefully camouflaged the most dominant vestige of modernity: the automobile.

Norris Kelly Smith once claimed that Wright's last civic projects were lacking "of a historical dimension and a genuinely political dimension, [and that] Wright's architecture falls short of making manifest that system of philosophy and ethics he said we had the right to expect from an architect."[82] Smith was obviously not considering Wright's Baghdad oeuvre. I submit that the Baghdad project is a truly Wrightian invention, a "system of philosophy and ethics" for the Middle East that is rooted in the past, and not just the immediate past of the last thousand years, but going back to ancient times. It was also an invention that welded the East and West in a shared memory. But it stood against the values of the newly emerging Iraqi nation-state and, unfortunately, was dismissed as "anachronism" and "fantastic."

That Wright's Baghdad project was dismissed by his critics and admirers alike as science fiction is as unfortunate for Iraq as it would have been for America if Fallingwater, the Johnson Wax Building, or the Guggenheim Museum had remained merely a creation on paper. Based on drawings alone, Fallingwater appears as an architectural fiction, an unrealizable dream house, imaginative but un-buildable. The mushroom columns of Johnson Wax upon which the corporate ceiling floats seem as unstructural and exotic as the crescent arch of the Baghdad opera house; the inverted spiral of the Guggenheim appears as fanciful as the Baghdad ziggurat and the monument to Harun al-Rashid. Baghdad was not an exercise in science fiction; it was perhaps Wright's magnum opus.

The following abbreviations are used throughout the notes and in the figure captions.

*CW*1   *Frank Lloyd Wright: Collected Writings.* Edited by Bruce Brooks Pfeiffer, with an introduction by Kenneth Frampton. Vol. 1 (1894–1930). New York: Rizzoli International, 1992.

*CW*2   Ibid. Vol. 2 (1930–1932). 1992.

*CW*3   Ibid. Vol. 3 (1931–1939). 1993.

*CW*4   Ibid. Vol. 4 (1939–1949). 1994.

*CW*5   Ibid. Vol. 5 (1949–1959). 1995.

FLWA   Frank Lloyd Wright Archives, Frank Lloyd Wright Foundation, Scottsdale, Arizona

FLW   Frank Lloyd Wright

JSAH   *Journal of the Society of Architectural Historians*

NAI   Nederlands Architectuurinstitut, Rotterdam, The Netherlands

Sonderheft   Frank Lloyd Wright, *Frank Lloyd Wright: Ausgeführte Bauten* (American edition); *Frank Lloyd Wright, Chicago: 8. Sonderheft der Architektur des XX. Jahrhunderts* (European edition). Berlin: Ernst Wasmuth A.G., 1911.

CHAPTER 1

1.   See, for example, Elizabeth Gordon, "One Man's House," *House Beautiful* 88 (December 1946): 186–96, 235, on Wright's home, Taliesin West, in Scottsdale, Arizona. Professional journals devoted entire issues to Wright's work, for example: *Architectural Forum* 68 (January 1938); ibid. 88 (January 1948); ibid. 94 (January 1951); *Architectural Record* 23 (March 1908); as did more popular publications: *House Beautiful* 98 (November 1955); ibid. 101 (October 1959). Many articles appeared in popular magazines as well, for example: "Frank Lloyd Wright," *Town and Country* 92 (July 1937): 56, 85; "Lots Are Circular in This 50-House Group," *House and Garden* 49 (February

1951): 52–55, 100, 111; "Journey to Taliesin West," *Look* 16 (1 January 1952): 28–31; "A New House by Frank Lloyd Wright Opens Up a New Way of Life on the Old Site," *House and Home* 4 (November 1953): 122–27; "Our Strongest Influence to Enrichment," *House Beautiful* 99 (January 1957): 40–47, 105–6; Edgar Kaufmann Jr., "The Tradition of Ornament in Modern Architecture," ibid., 76–77.

2. Bruce Brooks Pfeiffer and David Brooks, eds., *Frank Lloyd Wright: The Masterworks* (New York: Rizzoli, 1993), 8. Seventy-five of Wright's 484 executed buildings have been demolished.

3. See Anthony Alofsin, *Frank Lloyd Wright: The Lost Years, 1910–1922* (Chicago: University of Chicago Press, 1993). For the traditional view, see Henry-Russell Hitchcock, "American Influence Abroad," in Edgar Kaufmann Jr., ed., *The Rise of an American Architecture* (New York: Praeger, in association with the Metropolitan Museum of Art, 1970), 34–38. Although this view has been outmoded by new research, Hitchcock's general treatment of American architectural influence abroad sets the wider context for the issues discussed here in the following essays.

4. See Alofsin, *Lost Years,* 29–78, for an account of Wright's travels to Europe, his dealings with the Wasmuth Verlag, and how both played into creating a previously unrecognized phase in his work.

5. "Architektura v Americe: z dopisu," *Volné Směry* 4 (1900): 177–80. C. Donald Cook kindly drew my attention to this publication in 1988. Collateral evidence indicates that the author was Miloš Jiránek. A painter, graphic artist, critic, and author, Jiránek (1875–1911) wrote for *Volné Směry* as of 1899 and would write subsequently on impressionism, Rodin, and French modern art. See *Nová encyklopedie českého výtvarného umění* (Prague: Academia Praha, 1995): 324. My thanks to Christopher Long for uncovering Jiránek as the author of the review.

6. Alceste [Max Dvořák], "Kunst aus der Welt, XVIII: Nachlese von Wiener Ausstellungen," reprinted in Roman Prahl and Lenka Bydžovská, *Freie Richtungen: Die Zeitschrift der Prager Secession und Moderne* (Prague: Torst, 1993), 150. Not only is Wright's early recognition by Dvořák surprising, but the reference to American architecture exhibited in Prague remains an intriguing topic for further study.

7. The Dutch publications were *Architectura* 12 (23 March 1912): 91–94; ibid. 13 (30 March 1912): 93–94, 98, 100; ibid. 14 (6 April 1912): 106, ill. 107. The German-language version was H. P. Berlage, "Neuere amerikanische Architektur," *Schweizerische Bauzeitung* 60 (14, 21, 28 September 1912): 148–50, 165–67, 178; also issued as an offprint.

8. See Thomas A. P. van Leeuwen, "The Method of Ariadne: Tracing the Lines of Influence between Some American Sources and Their Dutch Recipients," in *Bouwen in Nederland: Leids kunsthistorisch jaarboek,* vol. 3, 1984 (Delft: DUP, 1985), 239–64. My thanks to Dr. Herman van Bergeijk for drawing my attention to van Leeuwen's essay.

9. See Antonin Raymond, *An Autobiography* (Rutland, Vt.: Charles E. Tuttle, 1973), 46–53, 65–77.

10. See August Sarnitz, *R. M. Schindler, Architect, 1887–1953* (New York: Rizzoli, 1988), 16–17.

11. Robert L. Sweeney, "Frank Lloyd Wright Chronology, 1922–1932," in David G. De Long, *Frank Lloyd Wright: Designs for an American Landscape* (New York: Harry N. Abrams, in association with the Canadian Centre for Architecture, Library of Congress, and Frank Lloyd Wright Foundation, 1996), 190.

12. Neutra contacted Wright in 1921, arrived in America in 1923, and met Wright at the funeral of Louis Sullivan in April 1924. The Neutras would remain at Taliesin until early February 1925.

13. *Erich Mendelsohn: Letters of an Architect,* ed. Oskar Beyer (London: Abelard-Schumann, 1967), 73, 71. Neither Kuno Francke, who was living in the United States, nor Bruno Möhring or the

Dutch architect H. P. Berlage, who both traveled to the States and saw Wright's buildings, had been able to meet Wright. On his travels in October 1924, Mendelsohn visited the Larkin Building, then proceeded to Ann Arbor, Michigan, on the twenty-eighth to see Emil Lorch, Eliel Saarinen, and Karl Lonberg-Holm. After meeting Wright in Spring Green, Mendelsohn went to Oak Park and saw the Coonley House, in Riverside, with Barry Byrne, Wright's former apprentice, and the Midway Gardens in Chicago. Mendelsohn's letters indicate that he and Wright liked each other (*Mendelsohn Letters*, 16–18).

14. For Mendelsohn's text, see Hendricus Theodorus Wijdeveld, ed., *The Life-Work of the American Architect Frank Lloyd Wright* (Santpoort, Neth.: C. A. Mees, 1925), 96–100. This book was reprinted as *The Work of Frank Lloyd Wright: The Life Work of the American Architect Frank Lloyd Wright—The Wendingen Edition* (New York: Horizon Press, 1965; Bramhall House, [1965]); cited hereafter as *Wendingen*.

15. See Mendelsohn's tribute, "Frank Lloyd Wright," *Wasmuth's Monatshefte* 10, no. 6 (1926): 244–46, which was attacked by Leo Adler in the next issue of the journal, no. 7 (1926): 308–9. For further discussion, see Erich Mendelsohn, "Das Schiff," *Architectura* (Santpoort) 29 (18 April 1925): 145–46; idem, "Frank Lloyd Wright," *Architectura* (Santpoort) 29 (25 April 1925): 153–57. Both articles were reprinted from the *Berliner Tageblatt*, for which Mendelsohn was a correspondent as well as the architect of the newspaper's building.

Debate about the pros and cons of Wright's work continued. Citing the organicism of nature and unified living as the goal of housing, Adolf Rading included illustrations of Wright's Coonley House and Taliesin II, rebuilt after the fire of 1914, in his essay "Die Typenbildung und ihre städtebaulichen Folgerungen," in *Probleme des Bauens,* ed. Fritz Block (Potsdam: Müller & Kiepenheuer, 1928), 80. These illustrations were previously published in Heinrich de Fries, *Frank Lloyd Wright: Aus dem Lebenswerke eines Architekten* (Berlin: Ernst Pollak, 1926).

Werner Hegemann furthered the debate about the appropriateness of Wright's architecture as a German model and challenged Mendelsohn's accusation of Le Corbusier as merely "literary" in approach by saying the epithet applied to Wright as well; see Hegemann, "Bemerkungen, Baumeister, I, Frank Lloyd Wright," in *Die Weltbühne* 25, no. 26 (25 June 1929): 982 (my thanks to Christiane Crasemann Collins for calling my attention to this essay). Mendelsohn responded with "Frank Lloyd Wright und seine historische Beudeutung," *Das Neue Berlin* 4 (September 1929): 180–81.

16. For Wright's appreciation of the book, see Olgivanna Lloyd Wright's introduction to *Wendingen,* reprint ed., n.p.

17. J. J. P. Oud, "The Influence of Frank Lloyd Wright on the Architecture of Europe," in *Wendingen,* 87, 88.

18. J. J. P. Oud, in *De Stijl* 2, no. 10 (1919), quoted by Theo van Doesburg in *On European Architecture: Complete Essays from "Het Bouwbedrijf," 1924–1931* (Basel: Birkhäuser, 1990), 79.

19. Van Doesburg, *On European Architecture,* 62, 63. Van Doesburg's comments appear in a series of perceptive and provocative essays that he wrote from 1924 to 1931 for the Dutch periodical *Het Bouwbedrijf.* Founded in October 1924, the periodical was intended for a broad spectrum of individuals and companies involved in the construction industry.

20. Ibid., 68, 15.

21. Ibid., 158. Van Doesburg extends Wright's lack of influence to American architects generally: "America's influence on the new architecture in Europe did not reach beyond the material-technical aspect, and even there only to a slight degree; composition-wise, America could not teach us anything. The reverse is the case." The Stuttgart Werkbund exhibition to which van Doesburg

referred surveyed and epitomized the various strands of international modern architecture at a crucial point in the evolution of the Modern Movement.

22.   Sweeney, "Chronology," 197.

23.   Van Doesburg, *On European Architecture,* 263.

24.   See Alofsin, *Lost Years,* 29–260, for Wright's contact with the Secession as the catalyst for the primitivist phase of his work.

25.   De Fries, *Aus dem Lebenswerke,* 34.

26.   Grete Dexel, *Frankfurter Zeitung,* 12 December 1926, reprinted in Walter Dexel, *Der Bauhausstil—Ein Mythos: Texte 1921–1965* (Starnberg, Ger.: Joseph Keller, 1976), 91–92, 175.

27.   Adolf Behne, *The Modern Functional Building,* trans. Michael Robinson, with an introduction by Rosemarie Haag Bletter (Santa Monica, Calif.: Getty Research Institute for the History of Art and the Humanities, 1996), 98–100.

28.   See Bletter's perceptive remarks on Behne's interpretation of Wright in ibid., 37, 41.

29.   See Alofsin, "The *Call* Building: Frank Lloyd Wright's Skyscraper for San Francisco," in *Das Bauwerk und die Stadt/The Building and the Town: Essays for Eduard F. Sekler,* ed. Wolfgang Böhm (Vienna: Böhlau, 1994), 17–27.

30.   The scrapbook is in the collection of FLWA.

31.   The award was signed on 29 January 1932 by Max Liebermann, the academy's president (FLWA).

32.   Robert Scholz, "Der Poelzig Amerikas," Wijdeveld Scrapbook, FLWA.

33.   The exhibition catalog was by Alfred Barr, Henry-Russell Hitchcock Jr., and Philip Johnson, *Modern Architects* (New York: Museum of Modern Art, 1932). For a view behind the scenes and Wright's positioning as an elder statesman of the Modern Movement, see Terence Riley, "The Landscapes of Frank Lloyd Wright," in *Frank Lloyd Wright, Architect,* ed. Terence Riley (New York: Museum of Modern Art, 1994), 96–108. The slight to Wright was partly corrected when the Museum of Modern Art held an exhibition exclusively on Wright in 1940, his largest to that date. It received mixed critical response.

34.   Franz Schulze, *Mies van der Rohe: A Critical Biography* (Chicago: University of Chicago Press, 1985), 210–11, 236–38.

35.   For a brief discussion on Wright and Gropius, see my review of *The Architecture of Frank Lloyd Wright* by Neil Levine, *Harvard Design Magazine,* summer 1997: 76–77.

36.   Heidi Kief-Niederwöhrmeier, *Frank Lloyd Wright und Europa: Architekturelemente, Naturverhältnis, Publikationen, Einflüsse* (Stuttgart: Karl Krämer, 1983). This work appeared in an earlier edition (1978) as Heidemarie Kief, *Der Einfluß Frank Lloyd Wrights auf die mitteleuropäische Einzelhausarchitektur.* For the division of German critics into warring camps on the subject of Wright in the 1930s (de Fries vs. Gropius, Hegemann vs. Rading, Mendelsohn vs. Adler), see pp. 165–68; for Ernst Neufert's visit to Wright in 1936, see p. 171.

37.   My thanks to Nina Nedeljkov for her insights and her participation in our symposium, on 27 April 1994, during which she pointed out that German-language publications on Wright were limited to Werner Moser's *Frank Lloyd Wright: Sechzig Jahre lebendige Architektur/Sixty Years of Living Architecture* (1952) and translations of Vincent Scully Jr., *Frank Lloyd Wright* (1960); Peter Blake, *The Master Builders: Le Corbusier, Mies van der Rohe, Frank Lloyd Wright* (1960); and Bruno Zevi, *Frank Lloyd Wright* (1980; French and German editions). The appearance of the English-German-

French edition of Bruce Brooks Pfeiffer's *Frank Lloyd Wright,* ed. Peter Gössel and Gabriele Leuthäuser (Cologne: Benedikt Taschen Verlag, 1991), has rectified this situation to some degree.

38.   Kief-Niederwöhrmeier, *Wright und Europa,* 323–39.

39.   Eduard F. Sekler, *Josef Hoffmann: The Architectural Work* (Princeton: Princeton University Press, 1985), 236. I have supplied the year of Wright's visit to Russia.

40.   Ernst A. Plischke, *Ein Leben mit Architektur* (Vienna: Löcker, 1989), 114. A recent graduate of Behrens's master class, Plischke began his career in New York City. When the *New York Times* announced that Wright would be visiting the city in the late 1920s, Plischke and a friend invited the architect to a luncheon, where, according to Plischke, he appeared modest, warm, and friendly.

41.   Behne, *Modern Functional Building,* 99.

42.   Wright's lectures were published as *Modern Architecture: Being the Kahn Lectures for 1930* (Princeton: Princeton University Press, for the Department of Art and Archaeology of Princeton University, 1931). The Czech translation appeared as "O městu budoucnosti," *Styl* 16, no. 6 (1931): 93–95, 98.

43.   A contemporary review of the exhibition can be found in "Architect F. L. Wright," *Art Digest* 25 (15 February 1951): 16.

44.   Oskar Stonorov (1905–70) bridged Europe and America, which made him an ideal choice for organizer of Wright's huge exhibition. Born in Frankfurt, he had studied in Italy and in Zurich at the ETH before immigrating to the United States in 1929. He worked solo and in partnerships with Alfred Kastner, George Howe, and Louis Kahn, focusing his energies on the provision of low-cost housing and community planning. See *Macmillan Encyclopedia of Architects,* s.v. "Stonorov, Oskar."

45.   Werner Moser, *Frank Lloyd Wright: Sechzig Jahre lebendige Architektur/Sixty Years of Living Architecture* (Winterthur: Buchdruckerei Winterthur, 1952).

46.   FLW, *A Testament* (New York: Horizon Press, 1957). This work was eventually published in many countries and languages: British ed., 1959; Spanish ed., 1961; Italian ed., 1963; German ed., 1966; Japanese ed., 1966.

47.   See Riley, ed., *Frank Lloyd Wright, Architect.* An Italian edition has appeared: *Frank Lloyd Wright, architetto, 1867–1959* (Milan: Electa, 1994).

48.   Wijdeveld, "A Letter to Frank Lloyd Wright," 11 April 1931, FLWA.

49.   The opposition between Wright and Le Corbusier took many forms. Just as Wright and Joseph Maria Olbrich were frequently compared around 1910, in the 1920s Wright and Le Corbusier became paragons, in which comparison a broad European movement played against a singular American one. Some European modernists, looking at Wright's work in numerous new European publications, were revolted by what they considered his decadence. Included in that group was the young American architectural historian Henry-Russell Hitchcock, whose introduction to the first French monograph on Wright (*Frank Lloyd Wright* [Paris: Cahiers d'Art, 1928]) excoriated Wright's use of ornament.

For his own part, Wright was receptive to several of Le Corbusier's principles, such as the notion that the clean lines and surfaces of airplanes, ships, and certain machines constituted new models of modern beauty and that "styles" were dead. See Wright's review of the English translation of Le Corbusier's *Towards a New Architecture,* published in *World Unity,* Sept. 1928, 393–95 (reprinted in *CW*1, 317–18). Where Wright disagreed with Le Corbusier was in the area of interpretation and intention. Although both believed that the Machine Age demanded a distinct expression, Le Corbusier defined the house as a *machine à habiter,* whereas Wright rejected the notion that buildings should resemble machines. He believed buildings should have the efficiency of machines, but their appearance should reflect organic processes. When it came down to it, Wright saw Le Corbusier's creations as being derived directly from his own work: "The fact that all that Le Corbusier says or means was at home here in architecture in America in the work of Louis Sullivan and myself—more than twenty five years ago and is fully on record in both building and writing here and abroad has no meaning for him." Nevertheless, Wright ended his review with an accolade that he rarely bestowed on any architect, saying, "I wish everyone engaged in making or breaking these United States would read the Le Corbusier book." Wright may have been being ironic when he concluded: "So, welcome Holland, Germany, Austria, and France! What you take from us we receive from you gratefully" (ibid., 318). But not only irony was at work, for Wright truly believed that if American ideas—most notably his own—were to have an impact in the United States, they had to be recognized in Europe first, and then exported back.

50.   Wright departed for Rio de Janeiro in September 1931. He kept a scrapbook of the trip; see doc. 1044.002, FLWA. Although the impact of Wright's ideas in Brazil is still unestablished, at least one scholar, Adriana Irigoyen of São Paulo, is actively examining the subject. Further investigation also awaits in Argentina, where to date a single monograph has been published, Enrico Tedeschi, *Frank Lloyd Wright* (Buenos Aires: Editorial Nueva Visión, 1955).

51.   For Calico Mills, see Bruce Brooks Pfeiffer, ed., *Treasures of Taliesin: Seventy-six Unbuilt Designs* (Fresno: California State University Press; Carbondale: Southern Illinois University Press, 1985), pls. 35a and 35b.

CHAPTER 2

I would like to thank Anthony Alofsin, Bruce Brooks Pfeiffer, Prof. and Mrs. Masami Tanigawa, Shozo Uchii, Kiyoshi Sei Takayama, and Dan Watson for their support and assistance with this essay.

1.   Kevin Nute, *Frank Lloyd Wright and Japan* (New York: Van Nostrand Reinhold, 1993), 22, argues for an earlier introduction in the late 1880s, through Wright's first employer, Joseph Lyman Silsbee, a cousin of Japanese art scholar Ernest Fenollosa. In a 1917 manuscript, Wright himself names Fenollosa as a primary contact, dating the encounter, however, to about 1892: "When I first saw a fine print about twenty-five years ago, it was an intoxicating thing. . . . On one of his many journeys home, [Fenollosa] brought many beautiful prints. Those I made mine were the narrow tall decorative forms—*hashirakake*—." FLW, "The Print and the Renaissance," unpublished ms. (1917), in *CW*1, 149.

2.   Wright later claimed he had despised the fair, which he said he visited in but one afternoon and that he had not seen the Japanese pavilion. FLW, "Influence or Resemblance," unpublished ms. (1953), in *CW*5, 72.

3.   An album of photographs in the collection of the Frank Lloyd Wright Home and Studio Foundation in Oak Park, Illinois, and twenty-five negatives in the collection of the Frank Lloyd Wright Archives at Taliesin West in Scottsdale, Arizona, partially document this Japanese tour, Wright's first journey abroad. Arriving in Tokyo in early March, the Wrights eventually moved west through Nagoya, Kyoto, and Osaka to the castle towns of Okayama and Takamatsu on the Inland Sea, visiting Buddhist temples, Shinto shrines, and large landscaped estates, before returning to eastern Japan and departing for the States in late April. The photograph album was published recently as *Frank Lloyd Wright's Fifty Views of Japan* (San Francisco: Pomegranate Books, 1996).

4.   Not only did Wright not mention Japan before he made this first voyage, but he also rewrote sections of his earlier work in later essays to include Japan. This is especially noticeable in *The Japa-*

nese Print of 1912, where sections of his 1900 essay, "A Philosophy of Fine Art," reappear with Japanese references. Wright also claims in the Kahn lectures of 1932 to be repeating the manuscript of his 1901 lecture, "The Art and Craft of the Machine." In fact, the two lectures are quite different, with Japan being mentioned in the later, but not in the earlier, talk.

5. The appearance in Japanese waters in 1853 of the so-called Black Ships of the American commodore Matthew C. Perry marks an official end to Japanese isolationist policies. His demand that Japan open its ports was soon followed by similar demands from other countries. Unable both to repel the onslaught from the outside and to unify a divided country, the last shogun found himself overthrown in 1867. The imperial restoration saw the enthronement of the Meiji emperor in 1868 and the shift of the capital after nearly 1,100 years to Edo, now to be called Tokyo.

6. Following a fact-finding tour to Europe in 1872, the Japanese Ministry of Technology founded the Imperial College of Engineering. In 1877 Josiah Condor, a young British architect, became the first professor of architecture; he remained in Japan until his death in 1920. For a detailed discussion of this era, see chapters 1 and 2 in David Stewart, *The Making of a Modern Japanese Architecture* (Tokyo: Kodansha, 1987).

7. FLW, "The New Imperial Hotel," *Kagaku chishiki* (April 1922), reprinted in *CW*1, 164–65.

8. FLW, *An Autobiography* (New York: Longmans Green, 1932), reprinted in *CW*2, 252.

9. FLW, *Hiroshige* (Chicago: Art Institute of Chicago, 1906), reprinted in *CW*1, 80.

10. FLW, *The Japanese Print: An Interpretation* (Chicago: Ralph Fletcher Seymour, 1912), reprinted in *CW*1, 116–25.

11. Over the next several years Wright purchased thousands of prints for William Spaulding and his wife. In 1919 they bequeathed their collection to the Boston Museum of Fine Arts. It remains one of the finest print collections in the world.

12. According to a letter to Wright from Frederick Gookin, 16 October 1911, fiche G001C02, FLWA, Gookin had suggested Wright as a candidate for the Imperial Hotel commission to the manager, Aisaku Hayashi. Hayashi had previously been the manager of the fine art dealer Yamanaka's New York branch for many years before returning to Japan to become the hotel's manager in 1909. Although there is no documentary evidence, Wright and Hayashi may have known of each other before the latter's return to Japan.

13. The first aerial perspective of the hotel design was exhibited in April 1914 at the Art Institute of Chicago in the exhibit "Frank Lloyd Wright: Work since 1911."

14. Wright also amassed an impressive collection of scrolls, screens, textiles, ceramics, and lacquerware that he incorporated into the interiors of Taliesin. Many of these were lost in the fire of 1914. According to Nobu Tsuchiura, who along with her husband, Kameki, lived at Taliesin in the mid-1920s, many fine pieces, including at least one screen by the Rimpa school painter Ogata Korin, were also lost in the fire of 1925 (Nobu Tsuchiura to author, November 1993). The remains of this collection were featured in the recent exhibit "Frank Lloyd Wright and Japanese Art," which opened in Phoenix in 1995. A smaller version toured Japan in 1997. Recent scholarship in Japan, in conjunction with this exhibit, has documented the significance of several of the screens, even identifying one as a probable work of the seventeenth-century master painter Kano Eitoku. See Shinji Hata, *Furanku Roido Raito to Nihon* (Tokyo: Stichting Siebold Council, 1997), 134–39.

15. "If Japanese prints were to be deducted from my education," he stated, "I don't know what direction the whole might have taken. The gospel of elimination preached by the print came home to me in architecture. . . . Intrinsically it lies at the bottom of all this so-called 'modernisme.' Strangely unnoticed, unaccredited." *An Autobiography, CW*2, 250–51.

16. Ibid., 245.

17. "The truth is the Japanese dwelling . . . is in every bone and fiber of its structure honest." Ibid., 246–48.

18. C. R. Ashbee, *Frank Lloyd Wright: A Study and an Appreciation* (Berlin: Ernst Wasmuth, 1911), reprinted in Anthony Alofsin, *Frank Lloyd Wright: The Lost Years, 1910–1922* (Chicago: University of Chicago Press, 1993), 313.

19. Alan Crawford, "Ten Letters from Frank Lloyd Wright to Charles Robert Ashbee," *Architectural History* 13 (1970): 69. Wright edited out Ashbee's statement in the English edition of the monograph after Ashbee refused to change it.

20. FLW, *A Testament* (New York: Horizon Press, 1957), 205. The phrase "Lieber Meister" refers to Louis H. Sullivan.

21. While Wright's assertion of his creative independence places him squarely in the spirit of the twentieth century, his sense of humanity, mission, and destiny and his focused vision were very much in line with the nineteenth-century philosophy with which he was raised. Wright shared with the transcendentalists the belief that, through science and art, underlying principles of order could be discovered and the hidden unity of man and nature revealed. For further discussion of Wright and the transcendentalists, Emerson in particular, see William Cronon's "Inconstant Unity: The Passion of Frank Lloyd Wright," in *Frank Lloyd Wright, Architect*, ed. Terence Riley (New York: Museum of Modern Art, 1994), 8–31.

22. Wright defined in the very early years of his architectural practice principles for an "organic architecture" and consistently argued for them not only in his designs, but in his prolific writings and frequent lectures. Appropriate to time, place, and man, an organic architecture, he wrote, "proceeds, persists, creates, according to the nature of man and his circumstances as they both *change*. . . . Underneath forms in all ages were certain conditions which determined them. In them all was a human spirit in accord with which they came to be; and where the forms were true forms, they will be found to be organic forms—an outgrowth, in other words, of conditions of life and work they arose to express." FLW, *Ausgeführte Bauten und Entwürfe von Frank Lloyd Wright* (Berlin: Ernst Wasmuth, 1910), reprinted in *CW*1, 107.

23. Wright strongly believed Westerners should not copy Japanese lifestyles: "We of the West couldn't live in Japanese houses and shouldn't. But we could live in houses disciplined by an ideal at least as high and fine as this one of theirs if we went about it—for a century or two. I am sure the West needs sources of inspiration, for once, it can't copy. And the West can copy anything easier than it can 'copy' Japanese things for domestic uses." *An Autobiography, CW*2, 246–47. Wright further describes his buildings' contemporary character: "I know well that my buildings see clearly not only the color, drift and inclination of my own day but feed its spirit. All of them seek to provide forms adequate to integrate and harmonize our new materials, tools and shapes with the democratic life-ideal of my own day and time. Thus do I know work that is for all time." FLW, "Influence or Resemblance," *CW*5, 71–72.

24. Of these eleven projects, five were built, and two still stand. The built structures include three houses and a school building: the Fukuhara House in Hakone (1918), a summer villa in the Prairie style for the founder of the Shiseido cosmetic company, destroyed in the earthquake of 1923; a house in Tokyo (1917), only a single room of which remains, built for Aisaku Hayashi, the manager of the Imperial Hotel (1909–22); a house in Ashiya, near Osaka (1918), built for sake magnate Tazaemon Yamamura (now the guest house of the Yodogawa Steel Company, it was damaged in the 1994 earthquake); and the Myonichikan, of the Jiyu Gakuen (School of the Free Spirit), in

Tokyo (1921). Both the Yamamura House and the Myonichikan have been accorded the prestigious status of Important Cultural Properties.

25.   Respected author, translator, and longtime Tokyo resident Edward Seidensticker wrote that the hotel "gave repose in the noisy heart of the city" and that its demolition was "the greatest loss that postwar Tokyo has had to endure." *Low City, High City* (New York: Alfred A. Knopf, 1983), 276.

26.   *An Autobiography, CW2,* 267.

27.   The great Kanto earthquake struck at 11:58, 1 September 1923, just two minutes before the scheduled noonday celebration to mark the official opening of the hotel. Although the quake caused inestimable damage, the greatest loss, particularly of human life, was the direct result of the fires that ensued. The survival of the Imperial Hotel was a testament not only to the design and structural ingenuity of the building, but also to the dedicated staff, who used the water of the pools to prevent the hotel from catching fire as they watched the city burn around them.

28.   *Japan Advertiser,* 7 July 1922, from scrapbook, FLWA 1702.002.

29.   *Christian Science Monitor,* 28 August 1922, from scrapbook, FLWA 1702.004.

30.   "The new Imperial Hotel is not a Japanese building nor intended to be an Oriental building. It is an architect's sincere tribute to a unique nation, a building that respects Oriental tradition, at the same time that it keeps its own individuality as a sympathetic friend on Japanese soil." FLW, "The New Imperial Hotel, Tokio," *Western Architect* 32 (April 1923): 39–46, reprinted in *CW1,* 179.

31.   As quoted in the *San Francisco Chronicle,* 1922, from scrapbook, FLWA 1702.005.

32.   Louis Sullivan, "Concerning the Imperial Hotel, Tokyo, Japan," *Architectural Record* 53 (April 1923): 334.

33.   Antonin Raymond, *An Autobiography* (Rutland, Vt.: Charles E. Tuttle, 1973), 71–76.

34.   "I cannot name a single reason why I should like it. I departed . . . still considering it to be . . . like a person who has every characteristic which should make loathing him a pleasure, but whom I cannot dislike in spite of myself." J. Malcolm Morris, *The Wise Bamboo* (Philadelphia: J. B. Lippincott, 1953), 14, 20 (quotation above).

35.   The heavily ornamented Toshogu, the Tokugawa mausoleum at Nikko, which Wright is known to have visited in 1905, is often suggested as a possible Japanese precedent, although the ornament is applied, not structural.

36.   Peter Blake, *The Master Builders: Le Corbusier, Mies van der Rohe, Frank Lloyd Wright* (New York: Norton, [1960] 1996), 353.

37.   For a discussion of the possible influences of primitive and exotic architectures on Wright, see Alofsin, *Lost Years,* 201–60.

38.   Ibid., 254.

39.   Wright paraphrased a quote from Okakura Kakuzo, *The Book of Tea* (Rutland, Vt.: Charles E. Tuttle, 1956), 45: "The reality of a room was to be found in the vacant space enclosed by the roof and walls, not in the roof and walls themselves." The book was originally published in New York in 1912; Wright says he received a copy sometime in the 1920s. Doc. 1014.153, 8, FLWA.

40.   The concept of *ma* is very important in any discussion of Japanese space. It is a word with many levels of nuance, as discussed by Gunther Nitschke in "'Ma': The Japanese Sense of 'Place' in Old and New Architecture and Planning," *Architectural Design* 36 (March 1966): 116–55, and in *From Shinto to Ando* (London: Academy Editions, 1993).

41.   As quoted in Arata Isozaki, "Frank Lloyd Wright: Johnson and Son, Administration Building," *Global Architecture 1* (Tokyo: A.D.A. Edita, 1970), 2.

42. In the same article Isozaki goes on: "Any attempt to discuss Wright's space in terms of its multifarious historical and cultural antecedents is doomed to failure, for their vestiges, exemplified by Wright's reworking of Lao-tzu's fundamental principle, are rephrased and irretrievably buried in every aspect of his work. In order to understand Frank Lloyd Wright there seems very little need to examine the numerous currents of twentieth century architecture or the development of the concept of space since the Renaissance. . . . The incomparably individual process of Wright's work is the unprejudiced incorporation of the legacy of every civilization, of Whitman and Lao-tzu, of Aztec and Momoyama Japanese." Ibid., 2.

43. At the time of Wright's death in 1959, a tribute written by Tokyo architect Gunpei Matsuda and published in *Architectural Forum* stated that "Wright was one of the first to combine successfully the oriental and Western concepts to create a new art form. . . . While there is deep respect and admiration for his initiative, few Japanese architects have taken to his style, with the result that his influence on Japanese architecture is negligible." Others concluded that although Japanese architects respected Wright's originality, they did not attempt to follow his example. "Tributes to Frank Lloyd Wright, 1869–1959," *Architectural Forum* 110 (June 1959): 238–39.

44. Quoted in Hiroyasu Fujioka, "The Japanese View of Frank Lloyd Wright," in *Frank Lloyd Wright Retrospective* (Tokyo: Mainichi Newspapers, 1991), 70.

45. David Stewart, in *The Making of a Modern Japanese Architecture,* devotes two long chapters to a discussion of Wright, but concludes he had no lasting impact in Japan. Botund Bognar likewise suggests that "Wright's influence on the development of modern Japanese architecture, apart from drawing the attention of the Japanese to their own traditions in the midst of wholesale Westernization, was rather limited." Botund Bognar, *Contemporary Japanese Architecture* (New York: Van Nostrand Reinhold, 1985), 82.

46. Quoted in Kisho Kurokawa, *Rediscovering Japanese Space* (New York: Weatherhill, 1988), viii.

47. By contrast, Kameki Tsuchiura, a draftsman who also met Wright in Japan and who later came to the United States to work with him, disappointed Wright when he embraced the International Style. An incomplete letter in the FLWA records Wright chastising Tsuchiura for having "gone over—with Neutra—to the gas-pipe rail and dampfer style. . . . I am sorry to see this poverty of imagination in you." Undated letter, ca. 1931, fiche T002E10, FLWA.

48. Endo traveled to the United States to work on drawings for the Imperial Hotel at Taliesin in 1917–18.

49. FLW, *Experimenting with Human Lives* (Chicago: Ralph Fletcher Seymour, 1923), reprinted in *CW*1, 171.

50. See Fujioka, "Japanese View of Frank Lloyd Wright," 69.

51. Bognar, *Contemporary Japanese Architecture,* 123–25. Kurokawa's Nakagin Capsule building (Tokyo, 1972) is one of the best examples of the Metabolist style: the building consisted of 144 prefabricated capsules, which could be bolted onto the central core and then plugged into the utilities system.

52. Kisho Kurokawa, *The Architecture of Symbiosis* (New York: Rizzoli, 1987), 12–15.

53. Kiyoshi Sei Takayama, "Tadao Ando: Heir to a Tradition," in *Perspecta 20: The Yale Architectural Journal* (Cambridge, Mass.: MIT Press, 1983), 163–80.

54. Kisho Kurokawa, *New Wave Japanese Architecture* (London: Academy Editions, 1993), 18.

55. Ibid., 10.

56. Shozo Uchii, "Wright's Architecture and Its Background," in *Frank Lloyd Wright Retrospective,* 238.

57. Because most of these elements were also present in traditional Japanese architecture, this emulation of Wrightian architecture might also be viewed as a return to traditional design elements via the Prairie Style of Frank Lloyd Wright.

58. It is not uncommon to see in Uchii's buildings visual references to specific features of Wright's architecture. In the Setagaya Art Museum, for example, one might note the trusses of the pergola and their strong visual resemblance to the interior roof supports of the Hillside studio at Taliesin near Spring Green, Wisconsin. See Yukio Futagawa, *Frank Lloyd Wright Selected Houses 2: Taliesin* (Tokyo: A.D.A. Edita, 1990), 164–65.

59. Mitsui Norin and Mitsui Homes use the name "Frank Lloyd Wright" with the permission of, and under a licensing agreement with, the Frank Lloyd Wright Foundation.

60. The Japanese tendency was to import whole cloth systems and institutions they needed to keep abreast of "civilization." Once imported, they would selectively assimilate and modify the components to make them more compatible with their own sensibilities and patterns of behavior. The predilection for acceptance, accommodation, and the synthesis of outside influences over the centuries allowed a cultural continuity that is responsible even now for the continued existence of many traditional values.

61. "Modern Architecture, established under the dogma that Modernization equals Westernization . . . presented the International Style, which was to be spread to every corner of the world. . . . The history of Modern Architecture in Japan is due witness to that power." Kurokawa, *Architecture of Symbiosis,* 33.

62. FLW, *An Organic Architecture: An Architecture of Democracy* (London: Lund, Humphries, 1939), reprinted in *CW*3, 331.

CHAPTER 3

Translated from the Dutch, with funding from the Cultural Committee of the Netherland-America Foundation in New York. Thanks to Kathryn E. Holliday for her editing of this essay.

1. Although much has been said about Wright's influence in Holland, the commentary has often consisted of unsupported assertions of stylistic influence based on exterior formal similarities. It has been assumed, for instance, that the country house De Bark (1918), designed by Jan Frederick Staal in the Park Meerwijk villa district in Bergen, was based on an American concept because the plan creates a continuous space between the hall, dining room, and sitting room. (See Auke van der Woud, "Variaties op een thema: 20 jaar belangstelling voor het werk van Wright," in *Nederlandse architectuur, 1880–1930: Americana,* ed. Fons Asselbergs [Otterlo: Rijksmuseum Kröller-Müller, 1975], the catalog for the "Americana" exhibition held at the Rijksmuseum Kröller-Müller, 24–26 August 1975; hereafter cited as *Americana.*) Wright had indeed perfected the open interior, but there is no evidence to suggest that Staal was in fact influenced by Wright; see Mariëtte van Stralen, ed., "J. F. Staal," *Forum (Holland)* 36 (August 1993). Van der Woud also claims that the plan of 't Reigersnest (1921), a country house in Oostvoorne designed by Pieter Vorkink and Jac. Ph. Wormser, was inspired by Wright. The house is arranged along two axes, with the hub of family life, the living and dining room, at the center, creating an organic, comfortable interior space that harmonizes with the building's immediate surroundings. Although the plan is similar to Wrightian designs, again the assumption of influence is speculative and unsupported.

2. Berlage wrote, "Ik zeg dat dit vanzelf spreekt, ook al weer, omdat de Europeaan tegenover den Amerikaan zoo graag het recht opeischt van uitsluitend begrip en gevoel voor kunst te hebben" (I'm saying that this is taken for granted, once again, that Europeans, with regard to the Americans, assume exclusive right to the understanding of and the feeling for art). H. P. Berlage, *Amerikaansche reisherinneringen* (Rotterdam: W. L. & J. Brusse, 1913), 11. Cf. K. van Berkel, "Amerika als spiegel van de Europese cultuurgeschiedenis," in *Amerika in Europese ogen: Facetten van de Europese beeldvorming van het moderne Amerika,* ed. K. van Berkel (The Hague: SDU, 1990), 23–24.

3. Berlage, *Amerikaansche reisherinneringen,* 11. Wright's influence, though minimal, is visible in Berlage's design for the Gemeentemuseum in The Hague (1927–35). Between the facades on the lakeside, a low, central, protruding bay with loggia and projecting roof clearly stems from Wright's formal world. The same is true of the museum's entrance hall: "The proportions, the angularity, and the sense of vibrancy directly reflect the impact of Frank Lloyd Wright's room in the parish hall of the Unity Temple of 1906–8 in Oak Park." Pieter Singelenberg, *Het Haags Gemeentemuseum van H. P. Berlage* (The Hague: Haags Gemeentemuseum, 1996), 37, 48.

4. Berlage, "Frank Lloyd Wright," *Wendingen* 4 (November 1921): 3. Nicholas Pevsner used this phrase in his well-known article "Frank Lloyd Wright's Peaceful Penetration of Europe," *Architect's Journal* (May 1939), reprinted in *The Rationalists: Theory and Design in the Modern Movement,* ed. Dennis Sharp (London: Architectural Press, 1978), 35–41.

5. For a detailed discussion of Berlage's role in the dissemination of information about Wright and America, see Thomas A. P. van Leeuwen, "The Method of Ariadne: Tracing the Lines of Influence between Some American Sources and Their Dutch Recipients," in *Bouwen in Nederland: Leids kunsthistorisch jaarboek,* vol. 3 (Delft: DUP, 1985), 239–64. See also Van Stralen, "J. F. Staal."

6. Van der Woud, "De nieuwe wereld," in *Americana,* 10.

7. See Wim de Wit, "The Amsterdam School: Definition and Delineation," in *The Amsterdam School: Dutch Expressionist Architecture, 1915–1930,* ed. Wim de Wit (Cambridge, Mass.: MIT Press, 1983), 28–66.

8. Ibid., 32–33.

9. In 1921 Berlage wrote that although many Dutch architects viewed Wright as an industrial architect, he, Berlage, saw him as a romantic—a remark undoubtedly meant as criticism of the interpretation of Wright's work by De Stijl members. Berlage, "Wright," 3–4. Wright, in a letter to Berlage, corroborated the "romantic" characterization: "Yes, you are right. I have been romancing—engaged upon the great Oriental Symphony. . . . " FLW to Berlage, 30 November 1922, in Bruce Brooks Pfeiffer, ed., *Letters to Architects: Frank Lloyd Wright* (Fresno: California State University Press, 1987), 54–55.

10. Frits Bless, *Rietveld, 1888–1964: Een biografie* (Amsterdam: Bakker, 1982), 25. Bless wrote that Rietveld's contact with Wright helped shape the former's ideas of industrial, machine-made reproduction and of the function of furniture as a spatial interior element.

11. Kenneth Frampton, "Neo-plasticisme en architectuur: Formatie en transformatie," in M. Friedman et al., *De Stijl, 1917–1931* (New York: Libris Boekhandels, 1988), 113.

12. Van 't Hoff traveled to the United States in June 1913 and returned to Holland in July 1914. Carsten-Peter Warncke, *The Ideal as Art: De Stijl, 1917–1931* (Cologne: Benedikt Taschen Verlag, 1991), 208.

13. Only a sketch was made for the museum; the sketch no longer exists. Eveline Vermeulen, "Robert van 't Hoff," in Carel Blotkamp et al., *De beginjaren van De Stijl, 1917–1922* (Utrecht: Reflex, 1982), 215.

14.   Ibid., 209.

15.   One exception to the decline of Wright's influence on van 't Hoff is a residence design for four families of 1918–19 (Robert van 't Hoff Archive, NAI); his perspective drawing bears a strong resemblance to Wright's Larkin Building.

16.   Vermeulen, "Van 't Hoff," 215.

17.   The importance of Oud's correspondence with other modernists has been overemphasized. My investigation of the J. J. P. Oud Archive, Netherlands Architecture Institute, Rotterdam, shows that although he did correspond with many internationally famous architects and authors, including Philip Johnson, Walter Gropius, Bruno Taut, and Bruno Zevi, in general his letters were relatively businesslike; he was not on friendly terms with any of them. And although nearly every article published about the 1952 exhibition of Wright's work mounted in Rotterdam describes Oud as a friend of Wright's (see File F.A.D. 22, Oud Archive), this assertion is probably based on press releases that Oud himself issued for the exhibition; in reality, the contact between the two was too slight to be termed a real friendship.

18.   Oud to Olgivanna Wright, 4 May 1959, Oud Archive. In this letter Oud begins by referring to a meeting in Paris between himself and his wife and Wright and his wife. He continues: "Then there must be some misunderstanding: I never again heard from you. Why? Did I do something Frank did not like? I can only think of a little thing that disappointed me in a time as everything did not march as well as I hoped it would do. It had nothing to do with my affection but I always saw Frank as a father and I thought he would understand. I did not see a reason why there could not be some discussion between a good father and a good son."

19.   Oud's "The Influence of Frank Lloyd Wright on the Architecture of Europe" appeared in *Wendingen* 7 (1925) and in the book form of the combined *Wendingen* issues edited by H. Th. Wijdeveld, *The Life-Work of the American Architect Frank Lloyd Wright* (Santpoort, Neth.: C. A. Mees, 1925). This book was reprinted several times in the United States as well: in 1948 by A. Kroch and Son; in 1965 by Horizon Press and by Bramhall House. The article was also published as "De invloed van Frank Lloyd Wright op de architectuur in Europa" in *Architectura* 30 (February 1926): 85–89; and as "Der Einfluß von Frank Lloyd Wright auf die Architektur Europas" in Oud, *Holländische Architektur* (Munich: Albert Langen, 1926)—this book was reprinted in Dutch as *Hollandse architectuur* (Nijmegen: Socialistiesse Uitgeverj Nijmegen, 1983).

20.   J. J. P. Oud, "Architectonische beschouwingen bij bijlage VIII: Woonhuis van Fred C. Robie door F. L. Wright," *De Stijl* 1 (1918): 64–65.

21.   Although Oud correctly seized on the interpenetration of space as central to Wright's innovations, Wright had a particular definition of the term "plasticity," referring to the integration of structure and ornament into a continuous whole. See Edgar Kaufmann Jr., "Frank Lloyd Wright: Plasticity, Continuity, and Ornament," *JSAH* 37 (March 1978): 34–39, reprinted in *Nine Commentaries on Frank Lloyd Wright* (Cambridge, Mass.: MIT Press, 1989), 123. Though never built, the Purmerend factory was to be a high point in Oud's oeuvre; as he wrote to historian Sigfried Giedion with an almost religious fervor, the factory "was and still is in essence . . . my architectural testament": "Der Entwurf hat mich damals Anfangs ganz zerrüttet (auch bevor ich den Mut hatte!); es kam aus meinem tiefsten Inneren hervor und war (und ist) im Grunde mein Glaubensbekenntnis im Bauen." Oud to Giedion, 8 June 1957, Oud Archive.

22.   Oud, "The Influence of Frank Lloyd Wright on the Architecture of Europe" (1925), in *FLW: The Complete 1925 "Wendingen" Series* (New York: Dover, 1992), 88.

23.   Oud's statement is from a letter to G. A. Platz, 7 July 1926, included in Paul Hefting, "Cor-

respondentie met Amerika," in *Americana,* 105. Oud continued to assert his stylistic independence from Wright. To Colin Rowe he wrote that Wright had not defined the principles later seen in the work of van Doesburg and Rietveld: "May I inform you that I initiated this kind of architecture in a design for a factory in Purmerend (1919) which was reproduced in *De Stijl* (1920)." He wrote to Giedion that it was incorrect to regard the Purmerend factory as part Wright, part Malevich, and part Oud; that design, he again stated, had emanated from his "deepest inner soul." Oud to Rowe, 16 January 1957; Oud to Giedion, 8 June 1957, Oud Archive.

24.   Wright's influence can be seen again in Oud's tower design for a congress building in The Hague (1956–63), which is similar to Wright's Research Laboratory Tower in Racine, Wisconsin (1943–50). Both have shiny, transparent facades with a nucleus in the center, and the tower is used as a vertical accent in each extended horizontal complex.

25.   Jan Wils, "De nieuwe bouwkunst—bij het werk van Frank Lloyd Wright," *Levende kunst* 1 (1918): 209–19.

26.   Wils believed that the house would evolve into one large space, a possibility he saw in Wright's country houses. Wils, "De hall in het woonhuis," *Levende kunst* 1 (1918): 154–60, 180–84, 193–200. He refers to Wright in the last installment.

27.   Examples of Wils's early style include the J. Senf House in Wassenaar (1916), a church in Nieuw Lekkerland (1916–22), and the J. de Lange House in Alkmaar (1916).

28.   See Victor Freijser, "De stijl van Jan Wils," in *De stijl van Jan Wils: Restauratie van de Papaverhof,* ed. Victor Freijser (The Hague: Afdeling Verkeer en Vervoer, Openbare Werken en Monumentenzorg, 1989), 22–23.

29.   Wils, "De nieuwe bouwkunst," 211–13.

30.   Wils's Daal en Berg complex of middle-class houses in The Hague (1919–22), for example, achieves a strong plasticity in a cubist manner by shifting masses and wall planes in horizontal and vertical directions; the effect is gently accentuated by concrete drainpipes on the parapets of the balconies and along the eaves. See Freijser, "Stijl van Jan Wils," 39.

31.   Wijdeveld once summed up his position to Wils: "Although you worked with Van Doesburg you were actually a link between *De Stijl* and *Wendingen* because you understood that the intellect could not operate without the heart." Ibid., 11.

32.   Ibid., 55–57. The Hague School reached its peak between 1920 and 1925 with occasional incursions into the 1930s. Other members of the group included J. J. Brandes, W. Verschoor, D. Roosenburg, R. C. Mauve, H. Wouda, B. Hoogstraten, J. Limburg, A. Schadée, A. Pet, and F. Lourijsen. The work of the majority of these architects has been insufficiently researched to allow for an accurate indication of Wright's influence. Nevertheless, several of their designs reveal striking similarities with Wright's architecture, such as Lourijsen's Herenhuis (Mauvestraat, The Hague, 1925) and Wouda's Villa De Luifel (1924), Villa Van Berkel (1929–30), and Villa Mees (1930), all three in Wassenaar. See Monique Teunissen and Albert Veldhuisen, *Hendrik Wouda: Architect en meubelontwerper, 1885–1946* (Rotterdam: Uitgeverij 10, 1989).

33.   For more on Duiker and Bijvoet, see Maristella Casciato, "The Dutch Reception of Frank Lloyd Wright: An Overview," in *The Education of the Architect: Historiography, Urbanism, and the Growth of Architectural Knowledge,* ed. Martha Pollak (Cambridge, Mass.: MIT Press, 1997), 139–62. Cf. also Giovanni Fanelli, *Moderne architectuur in Nederland, 1900–1940* (The Hague: Staatsuitgeverij, 1978), 148–50. Other little-known architects who were influenced by Wright include P. G. Buskens and H. Sutterland, who designed St. Franciscus College, Beukelsdijk, Rotterdam (1922–24). The de-

sign consists of seven horizontal rectangular volumes of unequal height and breadth arranged into a harmonious whole. The monumental power of the receding and protruding horizontals culminates in the single vertical, towerlike structure of the chimney. See Anne-Mie Devolder, "Schoolgebouw, City College, architecten P. G. Buskens, H. Sutterland, 1922–1924," in *Architectuur Rotterdam, 1890–1945* (Rotterdam: MFR, 1991). Other good examples include J. de Bie Leuveling Tjeenk's house that he designed for himself (Museumplein, Amsterdam, 1927) and his office design for F. W. Braat (Delft, 1932).

34.   Casciato succinctly expressed what Wright represented to Dudok: "This architecture offered him the justification for the use of an extremely personal creative language, which in the name of architecture moved eclectically between different tendencies of history and tradition. He was able to recover elements and fragments which he reassembled in buildings of great spatial and figurative effectiveness." Casciato, "Dutch Reception of Wright," 139–62.

35.   Van der Woud, in "Variaties op een thema," 35–36, acknowledges Wijdeveld's considerable affinity to Wright, but he never goes beyond generalities. The picture he presents is also incomplete because he focuses on the relatively brief period of Wright's influence, from Berlage's trip until 1930.

36.   Mumford to Wijdeveld, 2 April 1959, Files B.40.1–B.40.3, H. Th. Wijdeveld Archive, Netherlands Architecture Institute, Rotterdam.

37.   Meryle Secrest, *Frank Lloyd Wright* (London: Chatto & Windus, 1992), 376.

38.   Other examples of Wright's early influence include an undated design for a country mansion in Heemstede, and a design for a large hotel consisting of several buildings (1914). For more on Wijdeveld's country houses, see van Stralen, "De landhuizen van H. Th. Wijdeveld," *Forum (Holland)* 37 (1994): 3–4.

39.   See Donald Hoffmann, *Frank Lloyd Wright: Architecture and Nature* (New York: Dover, 1986), 41.

40.   Ibid., 17.

41.   In a later sketch, however, Wijdeveld noted a similarity between the visionary character of the two designs: he pictures the Mile High alongside his own Plan for the Impossible, adding, "Wright seeks high, Wijdeveld explores deep." This undated sketch is contained in File B.31.8, Wijdeveld Archive.

42.   Wijdeveld, *A Work in Progress* (n.p., n.d.), published on Wijdeveld's own initiative, probably in 1948.

43.   In *A Work in Progress,* 21, Wijdeveld describes the experience of his Hall as follows: "As I waited in nervous expectation, sounds came to me wafted, as it were, on the wings of the wind, like far-off harmony and the music of the spheres. . . . An azure haze of light enveloped the audience, which, as we watched, deepened into gold. The music of the spheres swelled to a deafening crescendo as though the gorgeous dome were raised, opened, and torn asunder. . . . Then, emanating from a fiery glow, trillions of atom-sperms are thrown off in radiation, Time and Space are merged."

44.   Although he does not understand the importance of the influence Wijdeveld had on Wright, Hoffman outlined the basics of their correspondence. Hoffman did not know, for example, that Wijdeveld's nickname, since the year he lived in London in 1906–7, was "Dutchy," and wrote, inaccurately: "Wright called his guest [Wijdeveld] 'Dutchy,' embarrassingly enough." Donald Hoffman, *Frank Lloyd Wright: The Complete 1925 "Wendingen" Series,* vii.

45.   Wijdeveld, "Naar een internationale werkgemeenschap" (Santpoort: C. A. Mees, 1931).

46. For information on this correspondence, see Hefting, "Correspondentie met Amerika," in *Americana,* 91–112. See also the correspondence in the Wijdeveld Archive and FLWA.

47. Ibid., 108; also FLW to Wijdeveld, 30 October 1925 and 25 April 1926, Files B.28.15 and B.28.16, Wijdeveld Archive.

48. Hefting, "Correspondentie met Amerika," 108; also Wijdeveld to FLW, telegram, 12 July 1930, File B.28.20, Wijdeveld Archive.

49. FLW to Wijdeveld, 13 August 1931, File B.28.21, Wijdeveld Archive.

50. Letter dated 1931, File B.28.21, Wijdeveld Archive.

51. Letter dated 3 December 1931, File B.38.8, Wijdeveld Archive.

52. Ibid.

53. FLW to Arthur B. Gallion, College of Architecture, University of Southern California, 5 June 1948, fiche G094C03, FLWA. Wright recorded his ideas for the Hillside Home School in the brochure "The Hillside Home School of Allied Arts" (1931), reprinted in *CW*3, 40–49. The brochure names Wijdeveld as the director, with "direct charge of Architecture" (*CW*3, 47). Pfeiffer also notes that Wright's ideas for the school changed between 1931 and 1932 (*CW*3, 39).

54. FLW to Wijdeveld, 13 February 1932, File B.28.22, Wijdeveld Archive; also in Hefting, "Correspondentie met Amerika," 112.

55. FLW to Wijdeveld, 10 March and 7 April 1933, File B.29.23, Wijdeveld Archive. See also Hefting, "Correspondentie met Amerika," n. 62.

56. Wijdeveld began publication of a journal, *Elckerlyc,* in 1939 and published *Elckerlyc, Laag Vuursche: Studie in architectuur en beeldende kunsten onder leiding van architect H. Th. Wijdeveld* in 1948.

57. Correspondence between Wright and Wijdeveld resumes in 1947. Wright wrote to Wijdeveld, "But you could not (nor any older man I fear) work with me. I am too far gone in place and time with my own technique to employ the technique of another. And my time is getting too short to think of doing so." FLW to Wijdeveld, 11 October 1947, File B.29.37, Wijdeveld Archive.

58. Information on Wijdeveld's teaching post can be found in his letters to Ellen, his wife, File B.39.5, Wijdeveld Archive.

59. FLW to Wijdeveld, 5 June 1948, File B.29.38, Wijdeveld Archive.

60. Mumford to Wijdeveld, 2 April 1959, Files B.40.1–B.40.3, Wijdeveld Archive.

61. The Wijdeveld Archive contains an album of photographs of the exhibition; see File C.30.

62. FLW, "De architect en de machine," "Techniek en verbeelding," and "De nieuwe wereld," *Bouwkundig weekblad architectura* 14 (4 April 1931). These three articles from the 1927 series *In the Cause of Architecture* were specially translated into Dutch for the exhibit issue.

63. See Wijdeveld, "Architect Frank Lloyd Wright naar Europa: Een tentoonstelling van zijn werk te Amsterdam," ibid., 117.

64. J. P. Mieras, "Fallingwater, een landhuis van Frank Lloyd Wright," *Bouwkundig weekblad architectura* 17 (23 April 1938): 137–38.

65. Anon., "Nieuw kantoorgebouw van Frank Lloyd Wright," *Bouw: Centraal weekblad van het bouwwezen* 8 (10 October 1953): 792.

66. Anon., "Woestijnhuis van Wright," ibid. (3 October 1953): 774–75.

67. Wijdeveld's isolation was due, at least in part, to his collaboration during World War II with pro-German factions in Holland. Although he later explained that this collaboration was to ensure the safety of his Jewish wife and mother-in-law (who actually fled Germany to live at Elckerlyc

during the war), his activities counted heavily against him, since the Dutch were, as a people, proud of their reputation for resistance to the German occupation.

68. Oud to FLW, 3 July 1952, Oud Archive. Oud only supervised the exhibition; he was not responsible for the exhibition concept.

69. For further information on this exhibition, on display from 2 July to 19 August 1952, see File F.A.D. 22, Oud Archive.

70. Anon., "Frank Lloyd Wright, architect van de democratie," *Algemeen dagblad* 3 (July 1952), n.p., File F.A.D. 22, Oud Archive.

71. Oud writes in a text entitled "Frank Lloyd Wright," File F.A.D. 22, Oud Archive: "Certain dogmatic architectonic elements maintain that Frank Lloyd Wright forms a potential risk for up-and-coming architects who lack his talent. They are afraid of the appealing exuberance of his work, but their real objection is that he is not dogmatic enough in his work. But what great artist is?" This was probably the text of the speech Oud delivered at the opening of the exhibition on Wright's work in Rotterdam.

72. Anon., no title, *Bouw: Centraal weekblad van het bouwwezen* 13 (12 April 1958): 361.

73. Ibid., 3 (8 May 1948): 148.

74. Wright had not, however, lost his significance for the architect Oud. As we have seen, this tower served as an inspiration when Oud began designing his congress building in The Hague.

To assess the influence Wright exercised on Dutch architecture in the postwar period until his death in 1959 I consulted two specialists, Hans Ibelings, employed at the Netherlands Architecture Institute in Rotterdam, and architectural historian Jeroen Schilt from Rotterdam, as well as the Amsterdam architect Hans Tupker, who is also an expert on Wright and Dutch architecture. All three concurred that to the best of their knowledge Wright exercised no influence on Dutch architecture during this period.

75. A. Buffinga, "De profeet Lloyd Wright," *Bouw: Centraal weekblad van het bouwwezen* 13 (8 March 1958): 246.

76. W. M. Dudok, "Bij het overlijden van Frank Lloyd Wright," *Bouwkundig weekblad architectura* 37 (November 1959): 533.

77. See Casciato, "Dutch Reception of Wright," 155–57; Bruno Fortier, "La Grande Ville," interview with Rem Koolhaas, *L'Architecture d'aujourd'hui* 262 (1989): 90–103.

78. Personal communication with Wiel Arets.

CHAPTER 5
Translated from the Italian.

Without doubt, the greatest contribution to the elaboration of this essay was given me by Francesco Ragghianti, son of Carlo Ludovico Ragghianti, and I thank him for his patience and generosity. Among the papers in his father's archive at the Archivio "seleArte" in Florence are unpublished letters and an exceptional series of photographs taken during the inauguration of the Florentine show. Equal gratitude goes to Antonio Cortese and Maria Letizia Montefusco, currently involved in organizing Giuseppe and Alberto Samonà's private archive. They generously drew my attention to autographed letters from Wright and his wife Olgivanna as well as to documents related to the Venetian sojourn of the American master. On various occasions I spoke about this essay with Francesco Passanti, Savina Rizzi Zentner, Egle Trincanato, Livia Toccafondi, and Bruno Zevi. Their remarks were most helpful to me. I am also indebted to Giorgio Ciucci, who allowed me to consult his library on Wright and his collection of twentieth-century Italian magazines. Finally, I wish to thank for their collaboration Laura Agnesi, Suleima Autore, Mirka Benes, Manuela Castagnara, Ferruccio Dilda, Giorgio Di Loreto, Franco Panzini, Pietro Veronese, the Board of Directors of the Banco Ambrosiano Veneto, the Museo di Arte Moderna e Contemporanea of Trento and Rovereto, and the Library of the Faculty of Architecture of the University of Rome La Sapienza. Maddalena Libertini, Nancy Stieber, and Guido Zucconi read a draft of this essay and made thoughtful comments. Last but not least, I am grateful to Anthony Alofsin for his invitation to contribute to this book.

1. For the definitive account of the Florentine year, which saw the completion of the drawings and of the introductory essay to the Wasmuth portfolio, see Anthony Alofsin, *Frank Lloyd Wright: The Lost Years, 1910–1922* (Chicago: University of Chicago Press, 1993), 29–62. For Wright's personal account, see FLW, *An Autobiography* (New York: Longmans Green, 1932), reprinted in *CW2*, 220–21.

2. *Drawings and Plans of Frank Lloyd Wright: The Early Period, 1893–1909* (New York: Dover, 1983), n.p.

3. g.a. [Giovanni Astengo], "Frank Lloyd Wright in Italia," *Urbanistica* 7 (1951): 57.

4. Captured by his memories and perhaps as a sign of affection toward the Tuscany that had so generously welcomed him in 1910, Wright selected the long essay he had previously written while under the influence of that same land as a fitting introduction for "Young Italy" to the principles and ideas that, in his opinion, had transformed not only modern architecture but society in general during the intervening years. Prefaced by a brief greeting, the essay, "La sovranità dell'individuo," was published as an elegant accompaniment to the exhibition at Palazzo Strozzi. The essay was also included in a special issue of *Metron* devoted to the exhibition. See *Metron*, nos. 41–42 (1951): 21–31; FLW to Zevi, 7 March 1951, in Bruce Brooks Pfeiffer, ed., *Letters to Architects: Frank Lloyd Wright* (Fresno: California State University Press, 1984), 187.

5. Cesare Pavese, "L'influsso degli eventi," in *La letteratura americana e altri saggi* (Turin: Einaudi, 1953), 245–48.

6. See Manfredo Tafuri, *History of Italian Architecture, 1944–1985* (Cambridge, Mass.: MIT Press, 1990); Francesco Dal Co and Giuseppe Mazzariol, eds., *Carlo Scarpa: Opera completa* (New York: Rizzoli, 1984); Francesco Dal Co, ed., *Storia dell'architettura italiana: Il secondo novecento* (Milan: Electa, 1997); Amedeo Belluzzi and Claudia Conforti, *Architettura italiana, 1944–1984* (Bari: Laterza, 1985); Guido Canella, "Quella 'terza generazione' di Giedion," *Zodiac* 16 (1997): 4–21.

7. This conclusion is supported by the sporadic survival of an "organic" mannerism expressed almost exclusively in one-family dwellings; see Fabrizio Brunetti, *L'architettura in Italia negli anni della ricostruzione* (Florence: Alinea, 1986), 139–42. However, the house "alla Wright" is by now a cliché with profound roots in the collective imagination, including that of many Italians; to expound a negative judgment tout court on the banality of his spatial model is therefore certainly reductive.

8. Ernesto Nathan Rogers, "The Tradition of Modern Architecture in Italy," in G. E. Kidder Smith, *Italy Builds* (London: Architectural Press, 1955), 9–14. Rogers's essay is followed by the reprint of the preface Wright wrote for *On Architecture* (1941).

9. For the complete chronology, see Italo Insolera's "Wright in Italia, 1921–1963," *Comunità* 118 (1964): 48–63.

10. Marcello Piacentini, "Il momento architettonico all'estero," *Architettura e Arti Decorative* 1 (1921): 48. For Oud's statements, see *De Stijl* 2, no. 10 (1919), quoted in Theo van Doesburg, *On*

European Architecture: Complete Essays from "Het Bouwbedrijf," 1924–1931 (Basel: Birkhäuser Verlag, 1990), 79. Regarding Wright's influence on Dutch architecture, see my essay "The Dutch Reception of Frank Lloyd Wright: An Overview," in *The Education of the Architect: Historiography, Urbanism, and the Growth of Architectural Knowledge,* ed. Martha Pollak (Cambridge, Mass.: MIT Press, 1997), 139–62, and the essay by Mariëtte van Stralen in this volume (chapter 3).

11.   Mario Universo, ed., *Casabella: Per l'evoluzione dell'architettura dall'arte alla scienza, 1928–1943* (Treviso: Canova, 1978). Besides tracing the history of the magazine, the book includes an anthology of its most significant articles. *Casabella* distinguished itself from the other official architectural periodicals of the Fascist regime (the most preeminent of which was *Architettura e Arti Decorative,* later *Architettura,* published in Rome) and from its Milanese rival, *Domus,* by focusing on current trends and by pitting architects against each other as "militant" critics who engaged in "battles," as clearly expressed in Pagano's editorials.

12.   This fact can be deduced by the comment he wrote after viewing a photograph of the Martin House, and which he extended to all of the houses that had been produced in Oak Park: "The houses are famous, which is so very disconcerting because of their prophetic anticipation." Giuseppe Pagano-Pogatschnig, "Le ville," *Casabella* 67 (1933), 2–3.

13.   Persico (1900–1936) was shaped as a historian in the liberal atmosphere of Naples. He moved to Turin in 1925, where he worked at the Fiat automobile factory while also writing occasionally for Gramsci's journal *L'Ordine Nuovo.* From his Catholic faith Persico derived a sense of order and moral idealism. In 1931 he decided to collaborate with *La Casa bella,* and shortly thereafter he took over the magazine's layout and content. Persico approached the theme of architecture with his customary fighting spirit. His relationship with Pagano, though one of friendship and mutual esteem, was not marked by unconditional agreement, given the diversity of the two men's political and aesthetic creeds. Persico committed suicide in January 1936.

14.   In placing impressionism at the center of his thesis, Persico emphasized Wright's connection in two ways: he connected the plein air aesthetic with Wright's love for nature and noted that Japanese influence was a common factor to both as well.

15.   The lecture was published in *Casabella* 102–3 (1936) and reprinted many times; see, for example, Riccardo Mariani, ed., *Edoardo Persico: Oltre architettura—Scritti scelti e lettere* (Milan: Feltrinelli, 1977), 226–35. According to Insolera, "Wright in Italia," 62, Heinrich de Fries's book *Frank Lloyd Wright* was essential to Persico for the preparation of his talk. In 1933 Persico had already noted that "the term 'precursor,' which does not intend to establish merely a chronological fact, belongs to an American: Frank Lloyd Wright." Quoted in Bruno Zevi, *Frank Lloyd Wright* (Bologna: Zanichelli, 1979), 8. Persico had previously written on Wright in an article that was paradoxically published in a literary journal rather than an architectural magazine; see "L'architettura mondiale," *Italia letteraria,* 2 July 1933, 5. See also Persico's article "Brinkmann e Van der Vlugt, architetti," *Casabella* 87 (1935): 12–27; in it Persico underlines Wright's worth as a teacher, because for him "architecture has returned, after romanticism, to be uniquely art, rising above the technical criteria and the social program."

16.   "Message from Frank Lloyd Wright," in *Atti ufficiali: XIII Congresso internazionale architetti, Roma, 22–28 Settembre 1935–XII* (Rome: Accademia Nazionale di San Luca, 1935), 735–36. I thank Bart Thurber for drawing my attention to this text.

17.   "The architect is not the propagandist . . . what counts is . . . his awareness of the work." Raffaello Giolli, "L'ultimo Wright," *Casabella-Costruzioni* 122 (1938): 4–5, 40, reprinted in *Raffaello Giolli: L'archittettura razionale,* ed. Cesare De Seta (Bari: Laterza, 1972), 308–16. The landmark 1938

Casabella edition was occasioned by the monumental January 1938 *Architectural Forum* that focused on Wright's work in the 1930s.

18. The concluding passages of Giolli's editorial, taken from Wright's "Hymn of Work" (1896), have the flavor of prophecy. If the epoch of debate had been over, the ideas expressed in these few lines would have served to reconstruct the conscience of a nation: "I live as I work and as I am. No work for fashion or for pretence. My work shall be worthy of a man. I work as I think and as I am. I will not be a slave of fortune, I will not serve money . . . I will not give up. I will act as I will die and as I am. My liberty must protect my life, whatever thing happens to me." Arrested in September 1944, Giolli was deported and died the next year in the concentration camp at Gusen.

19. In his study of the discovery of American writers, Agostino Lombardo observed that Italian writers' "conception of the American nineteenth century is true above all in terms of their *own* poetics, in how much it sustained their *own* research . . . of a representational literature that would incarnate the aspirations of a new society and a new liberty." Agostino Lombardo, "La scoperta della letteratura americana," in *Gli Americani e l'Italia,* ed. Sergio Romano (Milan: Schweiwiller, 1993), 90. Emilio Cecchi's *America amara* (1939; repr. Padua: Muzzio Editore, 1995) is a further example of this literary interest in America. With wonderful irony, Cecchi's book gathered together the impressions and meditations that were the result of his two long sojourns in the United States and Mexico. However, a critical vein ran throughout, as belied by the title, "Bitter America." Cecchi saw America as a species of barbarism, "mere violence, without a breath of happiness."

20. Italo Calvino, introduction to Pavese, *Letteratura americana,* xi–xxxiii. Elio Vittorini, in his *Diario in pubblico* (1957), typified the attitude of many Italian intellectuals toward America: "In this type of universal literature that is moving toward one language, there is the American literature of today, where one finds that person to be most American who does not have a particular American past . . . one who is, perhaps, newly arrived from the old world. . . . America will signify for him a stadium of human civilization and he will accept it as such, and in this sense he will be a pure and new American." Quoted in Lombardo, "Scoperta della letteratura americana," 90.

21. Pasquale Carbonara, *L'architettura in America: La civiltà nord-americana riflessa nei caratteri dei suoi edifici* (Bari: Laterza, 1939). Following the much-noted cliché among European historians of Wright, Carbonara also compared Broadacre City with the Ville Radieuse by Le Corbusier, concluding that the two projects were totally opposite.

22. Both books were published in Milan; *Architettura e democrazia* by Rosa & Ballo, *Architettura organica* by Muggiani.

23. Zevi had only recently returned to Italy after having obtained his degree from the Graduate School of Design at Harvard University, then headed by Walter Gropius. See Zevi's autobiography, *Zevi su Zevi* (Milan: Magma, 1977).

24. Giulia Veronesi, "L'ora di Wright e la voce di Le Corbusier," *Il Politecnico* 31–32 (1946): 76–77.

25. Taking advantage of the unifying climate of the Resistance movement, which linked Italians of diverse religious and political provenance, the magazine gathered into its editorial board protagonists of two conflicting schools of thought, Rome's empirical realism and Milan's rationalism. It was directed by two architects of the old school: Luigi Piccinato served as editor of urban planning and Mario Ridolfi as architectural editor. Piero Bottoni, Gino Calcaprina, Luigi Figini, Eugenio Gentili, Enrico Peressutti, Silvio Radiconcini, and Enrico Tedeschi served on the editorial board. Bruno Zevi, who substantially contributed to the magazine's birth and was one of its most active voices, formally joined the board in 1946. From issue 13 on, the young Turinese town plan-

ner Giovanni Astengo began his collaboration and soon was part of the editorial board; Zevi and Radiconcini were elevated to the editing staff.

26.   The *Metron* issues devoted to Wright were nos. 41–42 (1951) and 49–50 (1954). For a complete bibliography of *Metron*, see *L'Architettura: Cronache e Storia* 9–10 (1956): 215–18, 293–98. For an analysis of magazines published after the war, see Brunetti, *Architettura in Italia*, 65–71; and Marco Mulazzani, "Le riviste di architettura: Costruire con le parole," in Dal Co, ed., *Storia dell'architettura italiana*, 430–43.

27.   APAO was formed with the guidance of a committee that included Berletti, Calcaprina, Fiorentino, Marabotto, and Zevi. The initiative was also supported by the teachers of the "School of Organic Architecture" (headquartered at Palazzo del Drago in Rome), Piccinato (city planning), Della Rocca (economy), Nervi (structural engineering), and Ridolfi (technology); by some members of the 15A Group, an association of fifteen designers led by Marabotto and Petrilli; and by other architects, some of whom were members of the *Metron* editorial board.

28.   Following this line of thought, Alfonso Gatto attributed almost a cathartic value to the organic creed, writing that Wright was "superior to any particular ideological situation. For him the same concept of democracy is 'the affirmation of a right to the life to live,' a reality whose reasons are more instinctive than explicit. [His democracy is] fruit of an empirical colonization more than a political culture." Alfonso Gatto and Giulia Veronesi, *Architettura organica: L'architettura della democrazia* (Milan: Muggiani, 1945), 10–11. On Gatto's significance as a critic of architecture, see "Alfonso Gatto e l'architettura," in *L'Architettura: Cronache e Storia* 247 (1976).

29.   "La costituzione dell'Associazione per l'architettura organica a Roma," *Metron*, no. 2 (1945): 75–76. See the English translation in Joan Ockman, *Architecture Culture, 1943–1968: A Documentary Anthology* (New York: Rizzoli, 1993), 68–69. It was the intention of the founders that this declaration not "be so precise and restrictive that it bind the liberty of the associates," nor "so agnostic and vague" that it impeded the active character of the association. The objectives that the association intended to follow presented a clear analogy with those set forth in 1944 at the formation in Milan of the Movimento di Studi per l'Architettura (MSA). As Brunetti has noted, the presence of Eugenio Gentili Tedeschi in both groups testified to an affinity of purpose between them; *Architettura in Italia*, 56–65. See Manfredo Tafuri, *Ludovico Quaroni e lo sviluppo dell'architettura moderna in Italia* (Milan: Edizioni di Comunità, 1964); Sara Protassoni, "Per un 'comune orientamento': Le associazioni di architetti italiani," in Matilde Baffa et al., *Il Movimento di Studi per l'Architettura, 1945–1961* (Bari: Laterza, 1995), 115–48.

30.   Zevi has frequently asserted the importance of the linking role the association played during the fascist years among the many diverse factions in Italian architecture. Giuseppe Samonà, then the respected dean of the School of Architecture in Venice, also supported these concepts. Invited to join APAO in 1946, he recognized in that association "a living force with the capacity to give vitality to our architecture which has fallen so low." *Metron*, no. 12 (1946): 75.

31.   For analyses of APAO's political stance, see Tafuri, *History of Italian Architecture*, 9; and Ockman, *Architecture Culture*, 68.

32.   Leafing through the pages of the first volumes of *Metron*, one can easily track the establishment of new APAO chapters. In 1946, the formation of a chapter in Liguria was announced; in the following year new chapters formed in Rome, Venice, Genoa, Naples, and in the provinces of Piedmont and Sicily. In December 1947, at the first national congress of APAO in Rome, regional chapters were formed in Tuscany and Emilia Romagna.

33. Enrico Tedeschi, review of Zevi's book, *Metron*, no. 1 (1945): 59–64.

34. Zevi, *Towards an Organic Architecture* (London: Faber & Faber, 1950), 10, 72.

35. The objective of Zevi's *Frank Lloyd Wright* (Milan: Il Balcone, 1947) was to replace the prevalent understanding of Wright's work with a complete and visionary treatment of the subject. About one hundred illustrations accompanied the text; they were gathered initially with the intent of forming an album accompanied by critical comments. Edgar Kaufmann Jr. translated the introductory essay into English, in *Magazine of Art* 43 (May 1950): 186–91.

The following year Zevi returned to this tendency toward the organic and the ties between Wright and APAO in "L'architettura organica di fronte ai suoi critici" (Organic architecture face to face with its critics). This essay, published in *Metron*, nos. 23–24 (1948): 39–51, was the introductory report delivered by Zevi at the first national congress of APAO Italian chapters (Rome, 6 December 1947). On that occasion, Zevi attempted to specify the qualitative elements of organic architecture, in response to calls for a precise definition. Although he was at that time unable to do more than offer a recipe based on the ingredients of Wright and Aalto, Zevi announced the publication of his new book, *Saper vedere l'architettura* (1948), in which, he said, he had expressed his thoughts on the question. At the congress itself he limited himself to a restatement of the fact that the originality of organic architecture lay in its way of drafting the project in spatial terms.

The polemics finally exploded at the time of the seventh CIAM Congress in Bergamo. Zevi, who was actually not present in Bergamo, addressed a long and polemical note to his colleagues, and in particular to Giedion, the secretary of the CIAM. This was published in *Metron*, nos. 31–32 (1949), and in part, together with Giedion's answer, in *Comunità* 5 (1949) and 6 (1950). It is quite clear in Zevi's text that his real objective was to reopen the debate on "modern traditions" through direct discussion with the most charismatic historian of twentieth-century architecture. More specifically, Zevi aimed to vindicate Wright's importance as the designer who had most influenced the architectural works of recent generations. Quite apart from concepts such as "postrationalism" or the "organic" that Zevi used to introduce a new chapter in the history of modern architecture, his argument was that Giedion had confined himself in his famous *Space, Time, and Architecture* (1941) to only a half-hearted recognition of the role played by Wright. In his astute reply to those who congratulated him on *Verso un'architettura organica*, Zevi's comment was: "Giedion is the one who should take the credit, not me. I just translated *Space, Time, and Architecture*, making one single modification: I put the chapter on Frank Lloyd Wright after the one on Le Corbusier." The heart of the matter for Zevi was to see spaces within architecture. He interpreted space not just as a figurative category on a par with planes, lines, volumes, or surfaces, but also as the place for individual and social life, for which it was the true projection. Giedion made a curt reply to Zevi, without responding to the questions raised, merely correcting occasional terminological or chronological inexactitudes. The rather superficial answer from Giedion unleashed a pinpoint reply from Zevi, who took up the various subjects in his message one by one.

36. "Frank Lloyd Wright definisce la democrazia" and "La nostra cultura e Metron," *Metron*, no. 13 (1947): 2–6; "L'architettura organica guarda l'architettura moderna," *Metron*, no. 48 (1953): 7–10.

37. In regard to the climate of reform that existed in Italy, Zevi counted as an especially significant factor the *Manuale dell'architetto*, a handbook compiled under the auspices of the Consiglio Nazionale delle Ricerche (National Research Council) by a small group of architects, including Zevi, Ridolfi, and Nervi. The *Manuale* was published by the United States Information Service (USIS). The same spirit of reform, Zevi also recalled, is what led APAO, being an "association of antifascist architects," to launch the idea in Italy for the creation of the Ministry of Urban Planning.

38. Piero Bargellini, *Libello contro l'architettura organica* (Florence: Vallecchi, 1946), 152. Bargellini wrote, "If I have permitted myself to argue with him [Wright], I haven't done it for him. I said this to the American mother-in-law with the hope that the numerous Italian daughters-in-law, who are already gathering in little groups to whisper, would hear."

39. *La Nuova Città* was a monthly magazine on architecture, urban planning, and interior design, founded by Giovanni Michelucci in 1945 and irregularly published until 1954. For a two-year period (1950–51) the magazine assumed the name *Panorami della Nuova Città*. For debates on organic architecture and on Wright, see the following articles: "Questo avviene in America," 1–2 (1945–46); Giusta Nicco Fasola, "Architettura 'organica,'" ibid.; Renato Bonelli, "Principi e teoria dell'architettura organica," 4–5 (1946); Fasola, "La visibilità e l'architettura," 6–7 (1946); Fasola, "Wright a Firenze," 5 (1951). See also Brunetti, *Architettura in Italia,* 131–33.

40. Giulio Carlo Argan, "Introduzione a Wright," *Metron,* no. 18 (1947): 9–24. Argan's essay was illustrated with photographs of Wright's then little-known house-office at Taliesin West, an edifice that, the author said, was "strange" and "difficult" but that posed to "intelligent architects a problem of spatial investigation." Among various other themes discussed by Argan were Wright's relationship to history; the place of the "monumental" in society; city planning as an instance of civilization, from which Wright's protest against the Mumfordian "megalopolis" derived. The article concluded with Argan's explicit invitation to Italian architects to mature and thus allow modern architecture to grow as a living entity. The results of this last appeal would very shortly bear fruit in the works of Carlo Scarpa and in the acute essay by Enzo Paci, "Wright e lo 'spazio vissuto,'" published in the special issue of *Casabella-continuità* "L'ultimo incontro con F. L. Wright," 227 (1959): 9–10.

41. Foreword to "Introduzione a Wright," *Metron,* no. 18 (1947): 9.

42. This version of the events that preceded the exhibition and its organization in Italy is reported in Pfeiffer, ed., *Letters to Architects,* 174–91. According to Meryle Secrest, however, the proposition was initiated by a certain Italian academy of art (no better identification is available) and advanced in the United States by Frederick Gutheim, who then involved both Wright and the Philadelphia-based architect Oskar Stonorov in its organization. Subsequently, Stonorov's mediation brought the project to Arthur C. Kaufmann. See Meryle Secrest, *Frank Lloyd Wright* (New York: Knopf, 1992), 529.

43. Carlo Ludovico Ragghianti to Giuseppe Samonà, 21 December 1950, Giuseppe and Alberto Samonà Archive, Rome.

44. Samonà to Ragghianti, 9 March 1949, Ragghianti Archive, Archivio "seleArte," Florence.

45. Ragghianti to Samonà, 21 December 1950.

46. Once the exhibition closed in Florence it toured Europe for two years before returning to the United States. On the significance of this tour, see Giancarlo De Carlo, "Wright a l'Europa," *seleArte* 2 (1952): 17–24. De Carlo had been studying Wright's teaching and organic architecture since the mid-1940s, as evidenced, respectively, in his essays published in *Domus* (1946) and *Casabella-Costruzioni* (1946).

47. Already in November 1949, in a letter to Stonorov, Wright mentioned that Kaufmann had agreed to donate $5,000 to the Frank Lloyd Wright Foundation as a gesture of appreciation for the enthusiasm with which he, Wright, had taken up the idea of the exhibition. See Pfeiffer, ed., *Letters to Architects,* 178.

48. Ragghianti's friendship with Zevi, whom Wright wanted as "arbiter of the installation in Italy," dated from 1939 when the two of them had met in London in circumstances that were, though

perhaps not felicitous, at least productive in the long term. See Zevi, *Zevi su Zevi,* 38. During the London years Ragghianti and Zevi were both caught up in intense antifascist political activity, which continued even after the war and resulted in common adherence to the Partito d'Azione. In particular, Zevi remained at Ragghianti's side while the latter occupied a political position. Zevi was, in fact, nominated director of urban planning, an office created under the auspices of the undersecretary of the arts—Ragghianti's position. For a brief intellectual profile of Ragghianti, see *Carlo L. Ragghianti: Bibliografia degli scritti, 1928–1990* (Florence: Centro Editoriale Università Internazionale dell'Arte, 1990), 339–43.

49.   On that same occasion, Wright was awarded the Star of Solidarity, an honor given him by the City of Venice. Manlio Brusatin records certain instances that give a measure of the enthusiasm with which Wright responded to the warm welcome given him by the Venetians. Upon leaving the Palazzo Ducale, for example, he reportedly exclaimed, "This is the most beautiful house in the world!" See Manlio Brusatin, "Carlo Scarpa architetto veneziano," *Controspazio* 3–4 (1972): 9. See also Zevi's essay in this volume (chapter 4).

50.   "Messaggio all'Italia," in *Mostra di Frank Lloyd: Catalogo itinerario,* a sixteen-page pamphlet reprinted from the January 1951 issue of *Architectural Forum;* and in *Metron,* nos. 41–42 (1951): 19. The brochure was a partial translation, specifically adapted to the Florentine exhibition, of the thirty-two-page brochure distributed when the show was presented at Gimbel's in Philadelphia. See Wright to Stonorov, 30 April 1951, in Pfeiffer, ed., *Letters to Architects,* 188.

51.   "La grande mostra di Wright a Firenze," *Metron,* no. 40 (1951): 4.

52.   "Messaggio a Frank Lloyd Wright," *Metron,* nos. 41–42 (1951): 20. The fawning praise of Wright in relation to this retrospective show aroused anger in some quarters.

53.   A list of the exhibited works and a plan of the show itself were presented in the double issue of *Metron,* nos. 41–42 (1951).

54.   *Mostra di Frank Lloyd Wright: Dialogo—Broadacre City* (Florence: Palazzo Strozzi, 1951).

55.   Of such critical reactions to the subservient tone of *Metron*'s message, Piero Bottoni's is especially noteworthy. Bottoni, a fervent communist, was a Milanese architect noted for his sensitivity to the functionalist idiom and an original member of *Metron*'s editorial board. In a letter to the editors of *Metron* that was destined to cause controversy, he stated his strong disagreement with the decision to honor Wright rather than interpret him in light of the political and social reality of Italy. Among other things, he said that "Wright's genius is diminished by the servile hand-kissing, just as would be that of Le Corbusier or Gropius. His lesson of spatial and organic liberty must be interpreted within the temperamental and traditional limits of each of us, not in the formal manner with which Italy is making this ostentatious display." *Metron,* no. 43 (1951): 6. In response to criticism, the *Metron* editorial board also issued a statement to its readers: "As was inevitable, we also became embroiled in the fire. We were accused . . . of being indiscriminate advocates of a poetic sensibility, accepting it whole and without discussion. . . . With this special issue of *Metron* we have tried, therefore, to offer material to those who would like to see and understand." "Cari lettori," *Metron,* nos. 41–42 (1951): 20.

56.   Enrico Sisi, "L'urbanistica di F. L. Wright," *Bollettino tecnico* 10 (1951); Edoardo Detti, "Urbanistica," *seleArte* 6 (1953): 15–23.

57.   Nicco Fasola, in "Wright a Firenze," confronted two questions: the relationship between Wright and nature and the development of his architectural works. In regard to the former, Nicco Fasola took up Persico's thesis on impressionism, reading in it the construction of the everyday do-

mestic environment to which Wright's houses refer. The novelty in the case of Wright lay in the fact he did not limit himself to placing an individual person at the center of his architecture but instead had offered, with his works, a new interpretation of the relationship between humans and nature. No longer was nature seen as object; it was now a myth that had acquired almost a religious value. On Wright's architectural development, Nicco Fasola's judgment was essentially negative. She considered his path an involution from great creative liberty (which he had taught to many, including many European architects) to a comfortable formalism stuffed with pleasing aesthetics. Another Florentine, Giovanni Michelucci, who was interested in the relationship of humans and nature and its effects on society, agreed with Nicco Fasola on the first of these questions. In Michelucci's opinion, Wright's point of arrival remained the individual, and "individual problems do not exist outside of society." In the end, noted Michelucci, there was not only a myth of nature within Wright's mentality, but also a myth of the individual. Giovanni Michelucci, "Un colloquio mancato," *L.A.—Letteratura e Arte Contemporanea* 11 (1951): 7–19.

58.   Wright to Samonà, 20 March 1952, in Pfeiffer, ed., *Letters to Architects,* 191. The excellent translation of Samonà's essay was executed by Edgar Kaufmann Jr., who also proposed it to the *JSAH;* it was never published, however. See the correspondence concerning this matter in Giuseppe and Alberto Samonà Archive, Rome.

59.   Giuseppe Samonà, "Sull'architettura di Frank Lloyd Wright," *Metron,* nos. 41–42 (1951): 33–42. Samonà had already confronted the question "What is organic architecture?" in a passionate text, never published, possibly dated 1946, when he joined APAO. His view is unquestionably clear: "The adjective organic has been undoubtedly diffused through Wright's building and his human attitude . . . but we do have some reservations about Wright's role and his ideas, which we have even sharply opposed. For us Europeans, the adjective organic has to be considered the distinctive attribute of the new postwar architectural language." Unpublished ms. [1946], Samonà Archive.

60.   A brief biographical sketch of Giuseppe Samonà (1898–1983), one of the most acute interpreters of Italian intellectual history, is necessary at this point. Samonà took his degree in civil engineering in 1922. He was both an architect and a teacher, and for more than three decades he taught with great passion. In 1936 he was named professor at the Istituto Superiore di Architettura (after 1945, Istituto Universitario di Architettura), Venice. From 1943 to 1972 he served as dean. For more information, see *Giuseppe Samonà, 1923–1975: Cinquant'anni di architetture* (Rome: Officina Edizioni, 1975); Francesco Tentori, *I Samonà: Fusioni fra architettura e urbanistica* (Turin: Testo & Immagine, 1996). Concerning the Venetian School, see Brusatin, "Carlo Scarpa"; and Giorgio Ciucci, "La ricerca impaziente, 1945–1960," in *Giuseppe Samonà,* 57–63.

61.   Faculty meeting minutes, with handwritten corrections, Venice School of Architecture, 6 April 1951, Giuseppe and Alberto Samonà Archive, Rome.

62.   Giuseppe Mazzariol, "Tre progetti per Venezia rifiutati: Wright, Le Corbusier, Kahn," in Lionello Puppi and Giandomenico Romanelli, *Le Venezie possibili: Da Palladio a Le Corbusier* (Milano: Electa, 1985), 270–71; Luisa Querci della Rovere, "Il Masieri Memorial di Frank Lloyd Wright," in ibid., 272–75. Mazzariol indicated strong corporations of architects and engineers as being among Wright's most implacable adversaries. He therefore suggested that at the base of the project's rejection was a conflict of interests much stronger than any criticism directed toward its design, which, indeed, introduced Viennese motifs that married well with the elegance of a certain Venetian tradition.

63.   For more on Angelo Masieri, see *Metron,* nos. 49–50 (1954); and Massimo Bortolotti, ed., *Angelo Masieri, architetto, 1921–1952* (Udine: Edizioni Arti Grafiche Friulane), 1995.

64.	Savina Masieri to FLW, 19 December 1952, in *Frank Lloyd Wright: In His Renderings,* Bruce Brooks Pfeiffer and Yukio Futagawa (Tokyo: a.d.A. Edita, 1988).

65.	FLW to Savina Masieri, 30 December 1952, in ibid. The bibliography on the Masieri Memorial is very large; reference here is therefore made to the most recent reconstruction in Bortolotti, *Angelo Masieri,* 53–71; and in Neil Levine, *The Architecture of Frank Lloyd Wright* (Princeton: Princeton University Press, 1996), 374–83.

66.	FLW to Savina Masieri, telegram, 26 January 1953, fiche M227E05, FLWA.

67.	FLW to Savina Rizzi, 19 February 1953, fiche M228B08, FLWA. Wright was to return again and again to the "Spirit of Venice." For example, he defended modernity when it was used so as to allow the emergence of "what was best and noble in local tradition of the Great Tradition." Quoted in Levine, *Architecture of Wright,* 380.

68.	*Metron* published a penetrating critical study of the Masieri Memorial project by Sergio Bettini, "Venezia e Wright," *Metron,* nos. 49–50 (1954): 14–26. The editors of *Metron* wrote that Wright's project had opened the debate on a pressing problem and concluded their editorial by demanding: "This is the building: should we or should we not construct it?"

69.	Quoted in Bortolotti, *Angelo Masieri,* 62.

70.	"In the national view, and perhaps even in that of Venice, the problem of Wright's house, even though it is touching for the motives of its origins and the sentiments behind them—as it is with every art work—beyond its aesthetic terms, one may say that [the issue itself is] certainly secondary." Ernesto Nathan Rogers, "Polemica per una polemica," *Casabella-continuità* 201 (1954): 1–4.

71.	It is worthwhile to note the eventual outcome of the project. In 1968 the Masieri Foundation asked Carlo Scarpa to propose a definitive design for the building, which by that time was in need of structural repair, so that it could be used as a student residence. The commissioner added the provision that the facade fronting the Grand Canal could not be changed. Scarpa prepared three proposals; the third one was sent to the municipal building committee in 1969, where it was finally approved in May 1973. After Scarpa's death, the project was completed by G. Maschietto and F. Semi, without many parts of Scarpa's original plan. In the meantime, because of a shortage of funds, the Masieri Foundation decided that the building should be used solely as a research institute.

72.	Quoted in Brusatin, "Carlo Scarpa," 10.

73.	Some of Scarpa's best-known students are the Friulian Bruno Morassutti, Gino Valle, and, of course, Angelo Masieri. In his design for the building of the Banca Cattolica of Tarvisio (1947–48)—Masieri's first work, developed in close contact with Scarpa—Masieri offered a context in which Wright's organic theories could be tested in Italy. The bank became an important fixture of Friulian architecture in the years immediately following World War II. Much has been written about this "via friulana" of architecture that united an organic inclination with spontaneous motifs of the local building tradition. See Marco Pozzetto, "Note sull'architettura moderna in Friuli," *Parametro* 135–36 (1985): 12–23; Giorgio Contessi, "La via friulana," *Costruire* 89 (1990): 266–71; Francesco Tentori, "Friuli anni 50," in *Friuli Venezia Giulia: Guida critica all'architettura contemporanea,* ed. Sergio Polano and Luciano Semerani (Venice: Arsenale, 1992), 147–53.

74.	Dal Co illustrated his thesis with numerous projects of Scarpa's in which one can see fragments both of Wright and of the formal iconism that overflowed in Klee's paintings: a cinema in Valdobbiadene (1946), a high-rise house with offices in Padua (1947), a church in Torre di Mosto (1948), a four-story apartment building in Feltre (1949), the designs for the Guarnieri and Taddei houses in Venice (1950, 1957), and finally the Zoppas Villa at Conegliano (1953). Scarpa came under Klee's influence when he installed the exhibition of the Swiss painter's works at the Italian Pavilion for the Twenty-fourth Biennale (1948) in Venice. An analogous influence was registered on the occasion of the Mondrian exhibition held at the Galleria Nazionale d'Arte Moderna of Rome in 1956.

75. Dal Co, "The Architecture of Carlo Scarpa" in Dal Co and Mazzariol, eds., *Carlo Scarpa,* 46–49.

76. Tafuri, "Carlo Scarpa and Italian Architecture," ibid., 89–90.

77. Brusatin, "Carlo Scarpa," 8–9.

78. *Metron,* no. 45 (1952): n.p.

79. Brusatin, "Carlo Scarpa," 13–14. Concerning the Venezuelan Pavilion, see Tentori, "Un padiglione di Carlo Scarpa alla Biennale di Venezia," *Casabella-continuità,* no. 212 (1956): 19–30.

80. Marcello D'Olivo, *Discorso per un'altra architettura: Cronologia delle opere 1948–1971, da Santo Domingo a Libreville* (Udine: Casamassima Editore, 1972). See also Guido Zucconi, "La professione dell'architetto: Tra specialismo e generalismo," in Dal Co, ed., *Storia dell'architettura italiana,* 298; and Guido Zucconi, ed., *Marcello D'Olivo: Architetture e progetti 1947–1991* (Milan: Electa, 1998).

CHAPTER 6

Translated from the French by Mary Beth Mader.

1. Anthony Alofsin, *Frank Lloyd Wright: The Lost Years, 1910–1922* (Chicago: University of Chicago Press, 1993); Alofsin, "Frank Lloyd Wright and Modernism," in *Frank Lloyd Wright, Architect,* ed. Terence Riley (New York: Museum of Modern Art, 1994), 32–57. See also the incomplete and dated analysis by Heidi Kief-Niederwöhrmeier, *Frank Lloyd Wright und Europa: Architekturelemente, Naturverhältnis, Publikationen, Einflüsse* (Stuttgart: Karl Krämer, 1983).

2. Jean-Louis Cohen, *Scenes of the World to Come: European Architecture and the American Challenge, 1893–1960* (Paris: Flammarion, 1995).

3. F. Rudolf Vogel, *Das amerikanische Haus,* vol. 1: *Die Entwicklung der Baukunst und des amerikanischen Hauses* (Berlin: Wasmuth, 1910).

4. H. P. Berlage, *Amerikaansche reisherinneringen* (Rotterdam: W. L. & J. Brusse, 1913). Discoveries made during the trip are recounted by Berlage in "Neuere amerikanische Architektur," *Schweizerische Bauzeitung* 60 (14, 21, 28 September 1912): 148–50, 165–67, 178.

5. S. Frederick Starr, *Melnikov: Solo Architect in a Mass Society* (Princeton: Princeton University Press, 1978), 23.

6. El Lissitzky, "'Amerikanizm' v evropeiskoi arkhitekture," *Krasnaia niva,* no. 49 (1925).

7. El Lissitzky, "Arkhitektura zheleznoi i zhelezobetonnoi ramy," *Stroitelnaia promyshlennost,* no. 1 (1926): 59–63.

8. The project is published in Moisei Ginzburg, *Stil i epokha: Problemy sovremennoi arkhitektury* (Moscow: Gos Izdatelstvo, 1924); in English as *Style and Epoch* (Cambridge, Mass.: MIT Press, 1982). Selim Khan-Magomedov states that Ginzburg was in Crimea to oversee work on the house; *Moisei Ginzburg* (Moscow: Izd. Lit. po Stroitelstvu, 1972), 8–9.

9. Ginzburg had been able to see photographs of the Heurtley and Thomas houses in the *Sonderheft.*

10. *Sovremennaia arkhitektura,* 1926, no. 3.

11. "Frank Lloyd Wright," *Sovremennaia arkhitektura,* 1927, no. 2.

12. Moisei Ginzburg, *Zhilishche* (Moscow: Gosstroyizdat, 1933), 38–39.

13.   Richard Neutra, *Kak stroit Amerika?*, introduction by Alexei Shchusev (Moscow: MAKIZ, 1929).

14.   Mikhail Okhitovich, "K probleme goroda," *Sovremennaia arkhitektura,* 1929, no. 4: 131–33, and "Zametki po teorii rasselenia," *Sovremennaia arkhitektura,* 1930, nos. 1–2: 7–16.

15.   There is little likelihood that Wright would have had detailed knowledge of "de-urbanist" projects, although he had every reason to have discovered them in the press, as in Berthold Lubetkin in *Architectural Review,* 1932.

16.   The file on the film can be found at TsGALI (State Archives for Literature and Art) in Moscow, and selections from it have been published in *Iskusstvo kino,* no. 3 (March 1979). Jay Leyda reproduces the pasted image in *Eisenstein at Work* (New York: Pantheon Books/Museum of Modern Art, 1982). The best analysis of this project has been done by François Albéra: see Sergei Eisenstein, with discussion by François Albéra, "Glass House: Note pour un film," *Faces,* no. 24 (summer 1992): 42ff.

17.   "I view the USSR as a heroic endeavor to establish more genuine human values in a social state than any existing before. Its heroism and devotion move me deeply and with great hope. But I fear that machine worship to defeat capitalism may become inverted capitalism in Russia itself and so prostitute the man to the machine." FLW, "First Answers to Questions by *Pravda*" (1933), in *CW*3, 141–42.

18.   "In organic architecture, composition, as such, is dead. We no longer compose. We conceive the building as an entity. Proceeding from generals to particulars by way of some appropriate scheme of construction we try to find the equation of expression best suited, that is to say most natural, to all the factors involved." FLW, "Kak ia rabotaiu," *Arkhitektura SSSR* 2 (February 1934): 70–71; published in English as "Categorical Reply to Questions by 'Architecture of the USSR,'" in *CW*3, 145.

19.   "The only way classical or modern architectural monuments can be helpful to us is to study that quality in them which made them serviceable or beautiful in their day and be informed by that quality in them. As ready-made forms they can only be harmful to us today. What made them great in their day is the same as what would make great buildings in our own day. But the buildings we should make would be very different, necessarily." Ibid.

20.   *Arkhitektura sovremennogo Zapada* (Moscow: OGIZ-IZOGIZ, 1932). For the *Wendingen* article, Arkin in fact used the 1926 version published in Berlin: Frank Lloyd Wright, "Für die Sache der Baukunst: Die dritte Dimension," in Heinrich De Fries, *Frank Lloyd Wright: Aus dem Lebenswerke eines Architekten* (Berlin: Ernst Pollak, 1926).

21.   David Arkin, "Frank Lloyd Wright," in *Arkhitektura sovremennogo Zapada,* 88.

22.   David Arkin, *Iskusstvo bytovoi veshchi* (Moscow: OGIZ-IZOGIZ, 1932), 42–43.

23.   David Arkin, "Amerikanskaia arkhitektura i kniga Mumforda," preface to Lewis Mumford, *Ot brevenchatogo doma do neboskreba: Ocherk iz istorii amerikanskoi arkhitektury* (Moscow: Izd. Vses. Akademii Arkhitektury, 1936), 15–16. Translated from the German edition, *Vom Blockhaus zum Wolkenkratzer* (Berlin: Bruno Cassirer, 1926); originally titled *Sticks and Stones* (New York, 1927), 185–202.

24.   See Hugh D. Hudson Jr., *Blueprints and Blood: The Stalinization of Soviet Architecture* (Princeton: Princeton University Press, 1994).

25.   FLW, "Address to the Architect's World Congress—Soviet Russia 1937," in *An Autobiography* (New York: Horizon Press, 1977), 573. This passage from Wright's talk is reprinted neither in *Izvestia,* which published selections from it on 26 June 1937, nor in *Arkhitektura SSSR* 7–8 (1937): 49–50, which likewise presented extracts of his speech. See Donald Leslie Johnson's analyses of

these textual variants: "Frank Lloyd Wright in Moscow," *JSAH* 46 (March 1987): 65–79; and *Frank Lloyd Wright versus America: The 1930s* (Cambridge, Mass.: MIT Press, 1990), 179–230.

26.   "The USSR must now construct buildings on a scientific basis, guided by common sense and making the most efficient use of high quality building materials. The left wing of the so-called 'new' architecture also advocated the principles of creating an organic architecture but, to all intents and purposes, did not proceed beyond plain wall panels, flat roofs, and ornamental corner windows; and the right wing of said 'new' architecture turned the buildings into ornaments. Both tendencies are generated by decaying old cultures. The correct path to the creation of organic architecture consists of the scientific organization of building activity and animating it with a genuine spirit of humanity." FLW, in *Arkhitektura SSSR* 7–8 (1937): 49–50; translated in Johnson, *Wright versus America,* 229.

27.   Boris Iofan, "Materialy o sovremennoi arkhitekture SShA i Italii," *Akademia arkhitektury,* 1936, no. 4: 47.

28.   These remarks are reported by Simon Breines, a young American architect then present in Moscow; interview with the author, New York, 22 September 1997.

29.   FLW, "Architecture and Life in the USSR," *Soviet Russia Today,* October 1937, 14–19, and *Architectural Record* 82 (October 1937): 59–60.

30.   FLW to David Arkin and Karo Alabian, 20 January 1943, in Bruce Brooks Pfeiffer, ed., *Letters to Architects: Frank Lloyd Wright* (Fresno: California State University Press, 1984), 101–3.

31.   "When we shut our eyes and try to resurrect in memory the country in which we spent four months, we see before us not Washington with its gardens, columns, and a full collection of monuments, not New York with its skyscrapers, its poverty and its wealth, not San Francisco, with its steep streets and suspension bridges, not hills, not factories, not canyons, but the crossing of two roads and a petrol station against the background of telegraph wires and advertising bill-boards." Ilya Ilf (pseud.) and Eugene Petrov (pseud.), *Little Golden America* (London: G. Routledge & Sons, 1944), 65.

32.   Roman Khiger, *Planirovka poselkov v SShA* (Moscow: Gosudarstvennoe Arkhitekturnoe Izd-vo Akademii Arkhitektury, 1944); *Maloetazhnye doma v SShA* (Moscow: Gosudarstvennoe Arkhitekturnoe Izd-vo Akademii Arkhitektury, 1944).

33.   David Arkin to Harvey Wiley Corbett, Moscow, n.d. [1944], Lonberg-Holm Archive, New York.

34.   Architects' Committee, National Council of American-Soviet Friendship, *News Bulletin,* no. 11 (5 December 1945): n.p. and no. 14 (8 January 1947): n.p. See also "Architecture Exhibit Presented to Russia," *Architectural Record* 98 (December 1945): 134; "Exhibit for the USSR," *Architectural Forum* 81 (September 1944): 194.

35.   A portion of the following analyses have been published in Jean-Louis Cohen, "Wright et la France: Une découverte tardive," introduction to FLW, *Ausgeführte Bauten und Entwürfe von Frank Lloyd Wright* (Paris: Herscher, 1986).

36.   Lewis Mumford, "Frank Lloyd Wright and the New Pioneers," *Architectural Record* 65 (April 1929): 414.

37.   Jacques Gréber, *L'architecture aux Etats-Unis: Preuve de la force d'expansion du génie français* (Paris: Payot, 1920).

38.   "In laying out the ground plans for even the more insignificant of these buildings, a simple

axial law and order and the ordered spacing upon a system of certain structural units definitely established for each structure, in accord with its scheme of practical construction and aesthetic proportion, is practiced as an expedient to simplify the technical difficulties of execution, and, although the symmetry may not be obvious, always the balance is usually maintained. The plans are as a rule much more articulate than is the school product of the Beaux-Arts." FLW, "In the Cause of Architecture," *Architectural Record* (March 1908), reprinted in *CW*1, 94.

39. Le Corbusier, introduction to Willi Boesiger and Oskar Stonorov, *Le Corbusier et Pierre Jeanneret: Oeuvre complète, 1910–1929* (Zurich: Girsberger Verlag, 1930), 10.

40. Berlage, "Neuere amerikanische Architektur"; and FLW, *Sonderheft.*

41. "It is around 1914 or 1915 (?) that I saw for the first time reproductions of Wright's villas and of an office building. Since then, I've seen nothing else. . . . This does not prevent me from stating that the sight of those few villas in 1914 had greatly impressed me. I was totally unaware that there could have been in America so purified and so innovative an expression of architecture. With Wright's plans, one had the sense of 'learning the good lessons' of the Ecole des Beaux-Arts here, that is to say, a tendency toward order, toward organization, toward a creation that is of pure architecture. This was in great contrast at the time to the bouts of erratic regionalism, to that invasive and paradoxical malady of the modern mind to tend toward quaint or rotten old villages built in a haphazard fashion with rudimentary tools. Wright *ordered,* and he commanded respect as an architect. But, even further, his sections and his facades make prominent use of reinforced concrete. At that point in time, this was something of a distinction. Moreover, Wright—one of the first, to my knowledge—identified the architectural solutions of reinforced concrete. Others used reinforced concrete without discovering its essential rhythm; he asserted the horizontal—reinforced concrete's marvelous contribution, and an architectural value of the first order. I was unaware of nearly all of Wright's work, but I nonetheless vividly recall the impact produced on me by these spiritual villas, smiling . . . with a Japanese laugh." Le Corbusier to Hendricus Theodorus Wijdeveld, 5 August 1929, Netherlands Architecture Institute, Rotterdam; reprinted in Paul V. Turner, "Frank Lloyd Wright and the Young Le Corbusier," *JSAH* 42 (December 1983): 359.

42. Charles Jeanneret to Auguste Perret, 30 June 1915, cited by Alofsin, *Lost Years,* 334.

43. Turner has stressed that certain modes of grouping volumes, the overhang of the roofing, and the corner windows have their origins in the Prairie houses. See Turner, "Wright and the Young Le Corbusier."

44. Jean Badovici, "L'art de Frank Lloyd Wright," *Architecture vivante* 2 (winter 1924): 26–27 and pls. 34–35.

45. J. J. P. Oud, "The Influence of Frank Lloyd Wright on the Architecture of Europe," in Hendricus Theodorus Wijdeveld, ed., *The Life-Work of the American Architect Frank Lloyd Wright* (Santpoort, Neth.: C. A. Mees, 1925), 87.

46. "Wright, unknown yesterday still, even by professionals, will soon take up his place in the phalanx of the great creators. And his body of work will have an enormous influence, as will that, moreover, of his colleagues who 'see' as he does. Wright's architecture is human, it is true, and it will be understood and loved everywhere." Robert Mallet-Stevens, "Frank Lloyd Wright et l'architecture nouvelle," in Wijdeveld, ed., *Life-Work,* 92–93.

47. In the work of the Dutchman Piet Kramer, he identified, "in a different form, the same spirit, the same assertion of horizontals, the same calmness of undeniable grandeur." Mallet-Stevens, "Les raisons de l'architecture moderne dans tous les pays," lecture delivered at the Colosseum Hall in 1925, *Conferencia* (1 December 1928): 592–93.

48. On the work of this architect, see Jean-Louis Cohen, *André Lurçat (1904–1970): Autocritique d'un moderne* (Paris: Institut Français d'Architecture; Liège, Bel.: Pierre Mardaga, 1995).

49. "Among the most striking figures in the architectural renewal, one must recognize the American architect Frank Lloyd Wright, so poorly understood in his early years, and who today wields enormous influence. Along with Tony Garnier in France, Otto Wagner in Austria, Behrens in Germany, Berlage in Holland, and Van de Velde in Belgium, he is one of the great promoters of that architectural movement that, in seeking to match the modern spirit precisely, has recaptured the great principles that have governed the art of building for all time." [André Lurçat], "Frank Lloyd Wright," *Cahiers d'art* 2, no. 9 (1927): 322ff.

50. André Lurçat to FLW, Paris, 29 October 1927, FLWA; FLW to André Lurçat, n.d. [1927], Archives André Lurçat, Institut Français d'Architecture, Paris.

51. Peter Smith van der Meulen, a friend of Hitchcock's, was at that time a draftsman with Lurçat; Henry-Russell Hitchcock Jr., interview with the author, New York, 20 February 1985.

52. Willi Boesiger, interview with the author, Zurich, 22 October 1984.

53. The German captions from the *Ausgeführte Bauten und Entwürfe* are retained. Only the plans for the Millard House had been published in *Wendingen,* and Wright and Lurçat's correspondence bears in part on the subject of the shipment of photographs of its completion. See Alofsin, "Wright and Modernism."

54. "Wright is not only an architect, that is to say, an artist who draws and creates his constructions, who is perhaps greater than his contemporary European colleagues—who are not always devoid of that lack of restraint to which he occasionally abandons himself—but he is also a brilliant engineer and a brilliant technician." Henry-Russell Hitchcock Jr., *Frank Lloyd Wright* (Paris: Editions Cahiers d'Art, 1928), n.p.

55. "That there should be in his theory of a pure architecture a mixture of adoration of nature, of individualist and ecstatic expression in the manner of Whitman, and of an Orientalism whose serious influence upon his ornamentation we have indicated—rather than literary influences, which no longer would be acceptable to the contemporary mind—all this does nothing but augment the lyrical value of this theory as poetry. Nevertheless, this tendency can diminish the artist's intellectual and logical mastery and cultivate in him a positive taste for ornament that is as dangerous for his doctrine as for his architecture." Ibid.

56. Henry-Russell Hitchcock Jr., *Modern Architecture: Romanticism and Reintegration* (New York: Payson & Clarke, 1929).

57. André Lurçat, *Architecture* (Paris: Au Sans-Pareil, 1929), 21. Lurçat also published plates on Wright in *Terrasses et jardins* (Paris: Editions d'Art Charles Moreau, [1929]).

58. Louis Gillet, "L'art au Canada et aux Etats-Unis," in *Histoire de l'art depuis les premiers temps chrétiens jusqu'à nos jours,* ed. André Michel, vol. 8 (Paris: Armand Colin, 1929), 1168.

59. Myron Malkiel-Jirmounski, *Les tendances de l'architecture contemporaine* (Paris: Delagrave, 1930), 87–90. An art historian, Malkiel-Jirmounski pursued his career in Portugal beginning in 1940.

60. "Wright created works that are still fresh today because they carry the guarantee of universal laws. He saw beyond his time better than did Wagner, Berlage, or Peter Behrens. . . . Influenced by Asian temples, whose spirit he deepened without overly attaching himself to their formal appearance, he knew how to create empty masses, logical forms, devoid of ornamentation, volumes that proudly trace themselves out in light, architectures that respond in an absolute fashion to the laws laid down by the new means of construction. At first sight, Wright's works seem to us too re-

mote, too cold, too measured, and too logical. However, upon close examination one discovers in them an exquisite sensibility. The mathematical rigor conceals a moving lyricism and a freedom that seize one who attentively studies [his] plans." Jean Badovici, "Frank Lloyd Wright," *Cahiers d'art* 1, no. 2 (1926): 30–32.

61. "He had achieved wisdom at a time when in general madness and disorder equally formed the mind of architects who attacked the staunch and time-worn hierarchies of art. Thus, he was the leaven of hope for all those who did not let themselves be fooled by the turbulent studies of false prophets. And all those who distanced themselves from nebulous endeavors, from compromise and trickery, found in Wright the cherished guide to their artistic destinies.

"He led them to invention along the path of probity, of logic, and of that proud modesty that makes the past combine with yet unrealized possibilities within a work. Numbers of Wright's fellow students have surpassed his lesson. That is the best proof of his fecundity. This fecundity contained within it what his successors—I mean above all the young Dutch architects—would develop with admirable mastery." Ibid., 33.

62. "In a land without tradition, where he saw about him no form from which he could derive the elements of a new style, in a setting all of whose preoccupations were exclusively of a practical, industrial, and commercial order, Wright created an architecture of an entirely new spirit and expression, of extremely modern lines and, at the same time, of an altogether classical purity. . . . Whether under Chicago's heavy sky or beneath the cheerier sky of California, Wright created by modern means works that are like natural products of the climate in which they are born; they express its character and soul at the same time as they express their own end, the character and habits of those who must live in them. Europeans will perhaps find that he sometimes forgets that we are beings of flesh and blood, that he lacks a bit of that intimate sense to which we are accustomed. But Americans are different from us, and they rarely sense the need for those intimate nooks that we like to find in our homes." Jean Badovici, "Frank Lloyd Wright," *L'Architecture vivante,* spring–summer 1930, 50.

63. Eugène Beaudouin, "Urbanisme et architecture en USA," *L'Architecture d'aujourd'hui,* no. 9 (November–December 1933): 54–68.

64. The article to which Giedion was responding is Frank Lloyd Wright, "An meine Kritiker!" *Schweizerische Bauzeitung* (1931): 136ff.

65. "Like every great architect, Lloyd Wright [*sic*] had his imitators, especially in Holland, which, after 1910, provided the immediate impetus for subsequent development. . . . But only those who profited from his impulses by joining them more securely to our new technical possibilities and to our modern way of seeing truly learned from Wright. . . . Wright's ideas are extended in the work of Le Corbusier, but one can scarcely tell this from the outside. No architect of his time has like Wright from the outset situated the problem of dwelling at the very center of his work. He showed for the first time how to break with the traditional rigidity of the plan, to link the various levels of a house, to restore liberty to the elements of the cubic mass, to destroy the notion of the facade, and to orchestrate the passage from house to landscape. It is not by chance that Le Corbusier's efforts bear upon the same matters.

"Not having been able to see in reality the curious constructions of Lloyd Wright's in recent years, we will not risk taking any distinct position. Certainly, there is, in the way he respectfully takes into account the slightest fold in the terrain—with which his constructions sometimes meld—a sort of renunciation of the notion of architecture, a tendency to the cosmic that in the future will no doubt be called upon to play an important role. But it is equally possible that there be, in these houses that purposely avoid any pronounced structure, a flight into solitude and individuality with which we would be unable to align ourselves." Sigfried Giedion, "Les problèmes actuels de l'architecture: L'occasion d'un manifeste de Frank Lloyd Wright aux architectes et critiques d'Europe," *Cahiers d'art* 7, nos. 1–2 (1932): 70–72.

66. "His first years as an architect were happy and hard ones. Like Balzac, Wright fueled his ardor for work with debts. He attained originality; his houses, admired by some, mocked by others, occasionally frightened his clientele, who requested of him concessions to traditional taste. He explained to them, and he sometimes succeeded in realizing for them, his model for the Prairie House, his first original creation—a sort of new standard model, capable of being adapted depending on the site, and on the size of the family. No more traditional house in the form of a cube: there was no lack of ground; on the flat prairie, the slightest rise indeed makes effect enough. All the interior layouts are calculated on a human scale—five feet, eight inches, according to Wright. To within a half-inch, that is his own height. They said that if he had been two inches taller, his houses would have been different. 'Maybe,' he replied, good-naturedly." Jean Prévost, *Usonie: Esquisse de la civilisation américaine* (Paris: Gallimard, 1939), 154. Prévost (1901–44) was a celebrated essayist, author of such diverse works as *Plaisirs des sports* (1925) and *Eiffel* (1929), a monograph on Gustave Eiffel. He died a hero of the Resistance in the Vercors underground forces.

67. "Tiny masterpieces—*Fallingwater,* the Kaufmann House in Bear Run, Pennsylvania, which expresses the affinity between the house, the forest, and the waterfall that the house has laid hold of; *Wingspread,* or the Johnson Cottage, the new Prairie House, and *Honeycomb,* the Hanna House in Stanford, California, which speak of the intimate union of house and landscape, are of a human scale, are capable of instructing all minds. They teach a pride more intimate than the naive vanity of the skyscrapers: the sense of the present, the sense of leisure. Cruel enemies of all routine, they are little temples from man to purified man, to the new man." Ibid., 157.

68. Marcel Lods, "Visite à Neutra," *L'Architecture d'aujourd'hui,* no. 6 (May–June 1946): 4–5; Alexandre Persitz, "Un architecte d'aujourd'hui," ibid., 9.

69. André Remondet, "Transformations de l'architecture américaine," *Architecture française* 7, no. 54 (January 1946): 29–33.

70. "Frank Lloyd Wright," special issue of *Architecture française* 13, nos. 123–24 (1952).

71. Louis-Georges Noviant, "L'architecture organique regarde l'architecture moderne," ibid., 71–72.

72. FLW, "Massacre on the Marseilles Waterfront" (1952), in *CW*5, 59.

73. This is notably the case with Hervé Baley, who after 1968 taught at the Ecole Spéciale d'Architecture. Gilbert Cordier's courses, based on abundant visual documentation, would likewise contribute to the spread of images of Wright's houses.

74. Jean Castex, *Le printemps de la Prairie house* (Liège, Bel.: Mardaga, 1987). See also Daniel Treiber's short monograph *Frank Lloyd Wright* (Paris: Hazan, 1986).

75. The exhibit, which included Wright's drawings, was held from 23 January to 15 April 1997. See the catalog edited by Jean-Louis Cohen, *Les années 30: L'architecture et les arts de l'espace entre industrie et nostalgie* (Paris: Editions du Patrimoine, 1997).

CHAPTER 7

I should like to thank Alan Crawford for many discussions and unstinting help in relation to this paper, and Richard MacCormac, Alan Powers, John Sergeant, and Gavin Stamp for suggestions and stimulation. I have relied also on reminiscences from Roderick Gradidge, Tom Greeves, Birkin Haward, Colin Penn, Godfrey Rubens, and the late Sir John Summerson.

1. John Summerson, *The Unromantic Castle* (London: Thames & Hudson, 1990), 235–44; first published in *Acts of the Twentieth International Congress of the History of Art* (New York, 1963).

2. "Sir Edward Lutyens: The Memorial Volumes, Reviewed by Frank Lloyd Wright," *Building* 26 (July 1951): 260–62.

3. Summerson, *Unromantic Castle,* 244. For the Mary Ward Settlement, see Adrian Forty, "The Mary Ward Settlement," *Architects' Journal* 190 (2 August 1989): 28–49; and *The Studio* 16 (1899): 12.

4. David Gebhard, "C. F. A. Voysey—To and from America," *JSAH* 30 (1971): 304–7. Notable evidence for British interest in American architecture during the 1880s comes also in the unpublished diaries of Harold Peto's travels in the United States; kindly communicated by Hilary Grainger.

5. *American Architect and Building News* 38 (31 December 1892): 211, with heliochrome illustration.

6. Summerson, *Unromantic Castle,* 244; also Richard Oliver, *Bertram Grosvenor Goodhue* (New York: Architectural History Foundation; Cambridge, Mass.: MIT Press, 1993), 122ff.

7. Gavin Stamp, in *Architectural Design Profiles,* vol. 13: *London 1900* (1978): 363.

8. Alan Crawford, *C. R. Ashbee* (New Haven: Yale University Press, 1985), 96–99.

9. See especially Eileen Boris, *Art and Labor: Ruskin, Morris, and the Craftsman Ideal in America* (Philadelphia: Temple University Press, 1986), 45–52; Richard Guy Wilson, "Chicago and the International Arts and Crafts Movements: Progressive and Conservative Tendencies," in *Chicago Architecture, 1872–1922: Birth of a Metropolis,* ed. John Zukowsky (Munich: Prestel Verlag, 1987), 208–27. For an older view, see H. Allen Brooks, "Chicago Architecture: Its Debt to the Arts and Crafts," *JSAH* 30 (1971): 312–17.

10. FLW, "The Art and Craft of the Machine" (1901), in *CW*1, 58–69.

11. Ernest Crosby to Edith Lethaby, 1 March 1905; kindly communicated by Godfrey Rubens.

12. Forty, "Mary Ward Settlement," 40. Alan Crawford tells me also that Smith and Brewer were connected with Ashbee's first scheme for the *Survey of London* and intended in 1895 to write up Whitechapel, where Toynbee Hall is situated. They withdrew on receipt of a major commission, almost certainly the Mary Ward Settlement.

13. As remembered by Godfrey Rubens, though the remark is not in the published introduction to A. R. N. Roberts, *William Richard Lethaby* (London: Central School of Arts and Crafts, 1957). See also William Johnstone, *Points in Time* (London: Barrie & Jenkins, 1980), 242–44.

14. Wilson, "Chicago and the International Arts and Crafts Movements."

15. Nikolaus Pevsner, *Pioneers of the Modern Movement from William Morris to Walter Gropius* (London: Faber & Faber, 1936), 30.

16. See, for example, the *Alexander Thomson Newsletter,* no. 6 (January 1993): 3; no. 7 (June 1993): 6–7; no. 18 (February 1997): 6 and 11. The Thomson claim rests on the idea that his great villa of Holmwood at Cathcart, Glasgow, published in his *Villa and Cottage Architecture* (1868), may directly or indirectly have influenced Unity Temple: "The route from Cathcart to Oak Park may be even more direct than has often been supposed," proposes Gavin Stamp, *Alexander Thomson Newsletter,* no. 18 (February 1997): 11.

17. FLW, "The Architect and the Machine" (1894), in *CW*1, 25.

18. Boris, *Art and Labor;* also Wendy Kaplan, ed., *The Art That Is Life: The Arts and Crafts Movement in America, 1875–1920* (Boston: Museum of Fine Arts, 1987).

19. Undated entry, ca. December 1900, Ashbee Journals, King's College Library, Cambridge; kindly communicated by Alan Crawford.

20. FLW, "The Art and Craft of the Machine" (1901), in *CW*1, 59, 64.

21. FLW, "In the Cause of Architecture: The Third Dimension" (1925), in *CW*1, 209. Further embroideries of the Hull House occasion are given in "In the Cause of Architecture VIII" (1928), in *CW*1, 305–9; and in the Princeton "Modern Architecture" lectures of 1930, in *CW*2, 19–79, which influenced Pevsner's view.

22. Crawford, *Ashbee,* 154–55; Anthony Alofsin, *Frank Lloyd Wright: The Lost Years, 1910–1922* (Chicago: University of Chicago Press, 1993), 51–52, 61–62. See also Alan Crawford, "Ten Letters from Frank Lloyd Wright to Charles Robert Ashbee," *Architectural History* 13 (1970): 64–73.

23. Crawford, *Ashbee,* 151–52.

24. FLW to Ashbee, 31 March 1910, Ashbee Journals.

25. Crawford, *Ashbee,* 154–55.

26. "Lloyd Wright in Britain, Mr. R. Furneaux Jordan's Radio Talk," *The Builder* 179 (24 November 1950): 540. Also see Furneaux Jordan, "A Great Architect's Visit to Britain," *Listener* 44 (28 September 1950): 415–16.

27. Crawford, *Ashbee,* 143–48.

28. The quarrel is fully discussed by Crawford and by Alofsin, *Lost Years,* 340n.161. The text of Wright's letter of 26 September 1910 to Ashbee is published in full in Crawford, "Ten Letters," 69–70.

29. FLW to Ashbee, 9 February 1916, Ashbee Journals.

30. Crawford, *Ashbee,* 164; H. Allen Brooks, *Writings on Wright* (Cambridge, Mass.: MIT Press, 1981), 3–4; Ashbee to FLW, 8 May 1939, and reply by FLW (text in Crawford, "Ten Letters," 71).

31. Regarding the possible stopover, see *Journal of the Royal Institute of British Architects* 46 (9 May 1939): 643.

32. Andrew Saint, *Towards a Social Architecture* (London: Yale University Press, 1987), 14–16; John Allan, *Berthold Lubetkin* (London: RIBA Publications, 1992), 313–71.

33. John Summerson, "Bread and Butter and Architecture," *Horizon* 6 (October 1942): 242–43.

34. Miscellaneous Papers of the Sulgrave Manor Board, Sulgrave Manor, Northamptonshire.

35. When S. E. Rasmussen first visited London in 1927, he discovered that nobody who wrote about architecture knew any German. See Stein Eiler Rasmussen, "First Impressions of London," *AA Files* 20 (1990): 19; translation of an article from *Wasmuths Monatshefte für Baukunst* 12 (1928): 304–13.

36. C. H. Reilly, *Scaffolding in the Sky* (London: George Routledge, 1938), 216–19.

37. Andrew Saint, "Americans in London," *AA Files* 7 (1984): 30–43.

38. See, for example, Robert Wojtowicz, *Lewis Mumford and American Modernism* (Cambridge: Cambridge University Press, 1996), 84, 117, 119.

39. Alvin Rosenbaum, *Usonia: Frank Lloyd Wright's Design for America* (Washington, D.C.: Preservation Press, 1993), 68–75, 117–18.

40. Howard Robertson, *The Principles of Architectural Composition* (London: Architectural Press, 1924), 112, 119; and *Modern Architectural Design* (London: Architectural Press, 1932), vii, 65, 68–71, 73, 196. Midway Gardens is shown in *Architect and Building News,* 5 August 1927, 236, in one of many articles by Robertson on American and European architecture in that magazine, 1926–28.

41. Ashbee to FLW, 6 August 1934, FLWA.

42. *Architects' Journal* 84 (16 July 1936): 76–78; (23 July 1936): 111–12; (30 July 1936): 141–42; and (6 August 1936): 173–74. For the Dos Passos review, see *New Republic*, 3 June 1936, 94–95.

43. Pevsner, *Pioneers*, 177–81. Later editions of this book, retitled *Pioneers of Modern Design*, omit the oath and radically revise the account of Wright.

44. Nikolaus Pevsner, "Frank Lloyd Wright's Peaceful Penetration of Europe," *Architects' Journal* 89 (4 May 1939): 731–34.

45. *Journal of the Royal Institute of British Architects* 46 (9 May 1939): 643. The visit is also fully reported in *The Builder* 156 (28 April 1939): 789; (5 May 1939): 855; and (12 May 1939): 890, 909–10.

46. Crawford, "Ten Letters," 71; Minutes, May 1939, Art Workers' Guild, Queen Square, London.

47. Minutes of the Board, 12 July 1939, Sulgrave Manor, Northamptonshire.

48. *AA Journal* 66 (August–September 1950): 44–46. The lectures published in Britain as *An Organic Architecture* did not appear in the United States until 1953, as pp. 222–318 of Wright's *The Future of Architecture*. A précis of the texts with some questions and answers appeared in *The Builder* 156 (5 May 1939): 856; (12 May 1939): 907–9; (19 May 1939): 953–54.

49. Peter Blake, *No Place like Utopia* (New York: W. W. Norton, 1993), 11.

50. Ibid., 11–13; personal reminiscences of T. A. Greeves and Birkin Haward to author; review by Ernestine Carter in *Architectural Review* 87 (April 1940): 148. Reaction from an older architect, Percy Morley Horder, appears in *Journal of the Royal Institute of British Architects* 46 (22 May 1939): 743.

51. "Frank Lloyd Wright," *Journal of the Royal Institute of British Architects* 46 (8 May 1939): 643.

52. Ibid., 22 May 1939, 700.

53. Frank Lloyd Wright, *An Organic Architecture* (London: Lund Humphries, 1939), 35.

54. "An Organic Architecture: Mr. Wright's Third Watson Lecture," *The Builder* 156 (19 May 1939): 954; later reprinted in John Sergeant, *Frank Lloyd Wright's Usonian Houses* (New York: Whitney Library of Design, 1976), 197.

55. "To the Fifty-eighth: Mr. Frank Lloyd Wright Replies," *Journal of the Royal Institute of British Architects* 47 (16 October 1939): 1005–6.

56. Blake, *No Place like Utopia*, 12.

57. "Dinner to Mr. and Mrs. Frank Lloyd Wright," *Architectural Association Journal* 66 (August–September 1950): 44–46.

58. Ibid., 54 (May 1939): 268–69.

59. Personal reminiscence of Roderick Gradidge to author.

60. "Dinner to Mr. and Mrs. Wright," 44–46.

61. *The Builder* 179 (14 July 1950): 51.

62. "Lloyd Wright in Britain," 540; personal reminiscence of Peter Moro to author.

63. Personal reminiscences of the late Sir John Summerson and of Colin Penn to the author.

64. "Broadside from FLW," *The Builder* 191 (27 July 1956): 132; Clough Williams-Ellis, *Architect Errant* (London: Constable, 1971), 187–88, 209–10.

65. Kenneth J. Robinson in *Architects' Journal* 124 (26 July 1956): 109–11.

66. These paragraphs are based mainly on unpublished researches by Alan Powers on British private houses built between 1945 and 1970.

67. The White House, Hyver Hill: researches of David Atwell for the former Greater London Council and of Steven Brindle for English Heritage, London Region. House at Camberley ("Betterwords," 11 Crawley Hill); information supplied by Margaret Buntrock of Browns Estate Agents, Camberley, 1994.

68. Neil Jackson, *The Modern Steel House* (London: E. & F. N. Spon, 1996), 137–38; Reyner Banham, *Theory and Design in the First Machine Age* (London: Architectural Press, 1960), 145–47, 156–57.

69. Colin Rowe, "Chicago Frame," *Architectural Review* 120 (November 1956): 285–89.

70. John Sergeant, *Frank Lloyd Wright's Usonian Houses* (New York: Whitney Library of Design, 1976).

71. Richard MacCormac, "The Anatomy of Wright's Aesthetic," *Architectural Review* 143 (February 1968): 143–46, and "Froebel's Kindergarten Gifts and the Early Work of Frank Lloyd Wright," *Environment and Planning B,* 1974, no. 1: 29–50. For criticism, see Edgar Kaufmann Jr., *Nine Commentaries on Frank Lloyd Wright* (Cambridge, Mass.: MIT Press, 1989), 4–5.

72. Patrick Hodgkinson, review of *The Architecture of Frank Lloyd Wright* by Neil Levine, in *Times Higher Education Supplement,* 10 January 1997, 27.

CHAPTER 8

Translated from the Spanish.

1. José Luis Romero, *Latinoamérica: Las ciudades y las ideas* (Mexico City: Siglo XXI, 1996), 64.

2. Graziano Gasparín, in his essay "Colonial Architecture in Venezuela," described the interaction of native and European styles: "One should not forget that colonial Baroque art was a provincial art and, as such, had always to vary and modify the models of the mother country, either simplifying them or breaking the equilibrium via exaggeration, repetition, and exuberance." Graziano Gasparín, *La arquitectura colonial en Venezuela* (Caracas: Ediciones Armitano, 1965), 246.

3. See Francisco Stasty, *¿Un arte mestizo? América Latina en sus artes* (Mexico City: Siglo XXI, 1974), 150–60.

4. Mariano Arana and Lorenzo Garabelli, *Arquitectura renovadora en Montevideo, 1915–1940: Reflexiones sobre un período fecundo de la arquitectura en el Uruguay* (Montevideo: Fundación de Cultura Universitaria, 1991).

5. For more on Smith, see Mario Pérez de Arce A., *Josué Smith Solar: Un arquitecto chileno del 900* (Santiago: Editorial Pontificia Universidad Católica de Chile, 1993).

6. FLW, "Roots," in *Frank Lloyd Wright: Writings and Buildings,* ed. Edgar Kaufmann and Ben Raeburn (New York: Meridian, 1960), 28.

7. Henry-Russell Hitchcock, *In the Nature of Materials;* Spanish version titled *Frank Lloyd Wright Obras 1887–1941,* trans. Justo G. Beremendi (Barcelona: Editorial Gustavo Gili, 1978).

8. Roberto Dávila, "Técnica y creación," *Revista editada por la Facultad de Arquitectura y Urbanismo [Universidad de Chile]* 2 (n.d.): 84.

9. Quoted in ibid.

10. Also a student at the Catholic University, German Lamarca Subercaseaux was a young architect of great natural talent who went to the United States to study the work of Frank Lloyd Wright in Chicago and later in Wisconsin. He died young (in 1956, at thirty-five years of age), leaving us a small but interesting range of work that is to be found in groups in the residential neighborhood "Lo Castillo." His houses have a large amount of modeling and geometry learned from Wright;

some, though preserved in an excellent state, are threatened dangerously by demolition, owing to the appreciation in real estate prices in the area.

11.   Patricio Schmidt to author, personal communication.

12.   José Covacevich to author, personal communication.

13.   For more on Browne's domestic architecture, see *Enrique Browne: Casas y escritos* (Santiago: Taller America, 1989).

14.   New generations came, and with them new challenges; the city grew, and so began the problems inherent in its inorganic conformation. From this period are the Gallo House in the hills of Los Domínicos and my final project, the Pereyra Braz House, which in 1997 was in the construction stage in the Santa María de Manquehue hills between centennial *arrayanes* (Chilean myrtles) and *boldos* (Chilean jalap), underlining the magnificence of the metropolitan Santiago landscape.

15.   FLW, *Testamento* (Buenos Aires: Fabril, 1961), 189–209.

16.   In preparing this essay, I found several volumes especially helpful. On Frank Lloyd Wright: FLW, *El futuro de la arquitectura*, 2d ed. (Barcelona: Poseidón, 1978); FLW, *Testamento.* On Latin America and its colonization: Pedro Rojas, *Historia general del arte mexicano, época colonial* (Mexico City: Hermes, 1963); Gianni C. Sciolla, *Ville Medicee* (Novara, 1992); Romolo Trebbi del Trevigiano, *Arquitectura espontánea y vernácula en América Latina.* (Valparaiso: Ediciones Universitarias de Valparaíso, Universidad Católica de Valparaíso, 1985). For more on my philosophy and work, see Alberto Sartori, *Revista editada por la Facultad de Arquitectura y Urbanismo* 2 (n.d.), 5; Alberto Sartori, *Revista: 140 Años* (privately published), 618.

CHAPTER 9

1.   Near the end of his life, Wright remembered "how as a boy, primitive American architecture—Toltec, Aztec, Mayan, Inca—stirred my wonder, excited my wishful admiration. I wished I might someday have enough money to go to Mexico, Guatemala and Peru to join in excavating those long slumbering remains of lost cultures; mighty, primitive abstractions of man's nature." FLW, *A Testament* (New York: Horizon Press, 1957), 111. Wright also published a tribute to Mexico, "To Espacios," *Espacios,* no. 13 (1953): n.p. On Wright and pre-Columbian architecture, see Anthony Alofsin, *Frank Lloyd Wright: The Lost Years, 1910–1922* (Chicago: University of Chicago Press, 1993), 221–60; and Robert L. Sweeney, *Wright in Hollywood: Visions of a New Architecture* (New York: Architectural History Foundation; Cambridge, Mass.: MIT Press, 1994), 234.

2.   For more on these designers, see Carlos Altezor Fuentes, *Arquitectura urbana en Costa Rica: Exploración histórica, 1900–1950* (Cartago: Editorial Tecnológica de Costa Rica, 1986); Samuel Gutierrez, *Arquitectura actual de Panamá, 1930–1980* (Panama City: Gutierrez, 1980); Thomas Marvel, *Antonin Nechodoma, Architect 1877–1928: The Prairie School in the Caribbean* (Gainesville: University Press of Florida, 1994); and John Loomis, "Walter Betancourt's Quiet Revolution," *Progressive Architecture* 76 (April 1995): 41–44.

3.   Quoted in Clive Bamford Smith, *Builders in the Sun: Five Mexican Architects* (New York: Architectural Book Publishing, 1967), 18.

4.   On Villagrán and the early years of Mexican modernism, see Víctor Jiménez, ed., *José Villagrán* (Mexico City: Instituto Nacional de Bellas Artes, 1986); and Marisol Aja, "Juan O'Gorman," *Apuentes para la historia y crítica de la arquitectura mexicana del siglo XX,* vol. 2 (Mexico City: Instituto Nacional de Bellas Artes, 1982), 11–12.

5.   O'Gorman, for one, claimed to have read *Vers une architecture* four times during his nineteenth year, 1924–25; Smith, *Builders in the Sun,* 18.

6. Esther Born, "The New Architecture in Mexico," *Architectural Record* 81 (April 1937): 12, 18–19.

7. Quoted in Roberto Segre and Fernando Kusnetzoff, eds., *Latin America in Its Architecture,* trans. Edith Grossman Holmes (New York: Meier, 1981), 194.

8. On Cetto, see Suzanne Dussel Peter, "Investigación teórica sobre la vida y obra de Max Cetto y proyecto de administración del Hotel San Jose Purúa, Michoacán" (master's thesis, Universidad Nacional Autónoma de México, 1990), esp. 171–81; Lilia Gómez and Miguel Angel Quevedo, "Entrevista con el arquitecto Max Cetto," in *Testimonios vivos* (Mexico City: Instituto Nacional de Bellas Artes, 1981), 115–20; and Keith Eggener, "Expressionism and Emotional Architecture in Mexico: Luis Barragán's Collaborations with Max Cetto and Mathias Goeritz," *Architectura: Journal of the History of Architecture* 25 (1995): 77–94.

9. In 1932 Henry-Russell Hitchcock and Philip Johnson placed Wright among "the last representatives of Romanticism. . . . more akin to the men of a hundred years ago than to the generation which has come to the fore since the War." Henry-Russell Hitchcock Jr. and Philip Johnson, *The International Style* (New York: W. W. Norton, 1966), 27.

10. For Wright's views on the city at this time, see his *Modern Architecture, Being the Kahn Lectures for 1930* (Princeton: Princeton University Press for the Department of Art and Archaeology of Princeton University, 1931).

11. Quoted in Smith, *Builders in the Sun,* 176. For a contemporary overview of progressive Mexican architecture during the 1930s, see Esther Born, ed., *The New Architecture in Mexico* (New York: Architectural Record, 1937). This book, a slightly expanded version of the special "New Architecture of Mexico" issue of *Architectural Record* published in April 1937, included statements by Villagrán, Carlos Contreras, Justino Fernández, Beach Riley, and F. Sánchez Fogarty and illustrations and discussion of work by Barragán, O'Gorman, Villagrán, and many others.

12. Ann Binkley Horn, "Modern Mexico," *Architectural Record* 102 (July 1947): 71.

13. Max Cetto, *Modern Architecture in Mexico* (New York: Praeger, 1961), 22.

14. "Frank Lloyd Wright y México," *Arquitectura México,* June 1959, 119; "Número dedicado a Le Corbusier," *Arquitectura México,* December 1965. The notice of Wright's death, appearing in the magazine three months after the fact, consisted primarily of exaggerated claims for his borrowings from pre-Columbian architecture.

15. Smith, *Builders in the Sun,* 16. O'Gorman made related statements as early as 1951; see Esther McCoy, "Juan O'Gorman," *Arts and Architecture* 68 (August 1951): 26, 46.

16. Looking back in 1962, Barragán said, "I renounced the profession in 1940, and dedicated myself to real estate speculation. . . . So went the years forty to forty-five, [taken up] with this kind of speculation . . . [without] the freedom to do anything worth mentioning" ("Renuncié a la profesión en 1940. Me dediqué a especular con bienes raíces; dentro de esa especulación entró parte de construir en ellos para vender, entonces rodaron los años cuarenta a cuarenta y cinco, en ese tipo de especulación sin haber hecho algunos edificios o algunas residencias digamos ni en volumen, ni en libertad para algo que valiera la pena de mencionarse"); Alejandro Ramírez Ugarte, "Entrevista," in *Luis Barragán: Clásico del silencio,* ed. Enrique X. de Anda Alanís (Bogotá: Escala, 1989), 225.

17. This phenomenon was hardly unique to Mexico. Designers in many locales now paid increased attention to psychological factors, local materials, and traditions, and the integration of architecture and site. Even such early proselytizers of the International Style as Hitchcock and Sigfried Giedion called for a "regional approach" influenced by culture, climate, and vernacular building. See Henry-Russell Hitchcock, "Uniformity and Variety in Modern Architecture," *Arts,* no. 1 (1946):

41–47; and Sigfried Giedion, "The State of Contemporary Architecture: The Regional Approach," *Architectural Record* 115 (January 1954): 132–37.

18. Quoted in McCoy, "Juan O'Gorman," 26, 46.

19. In 1955 Hitchcock called the University City "the most spectacular extra-urban architectural entity of the North American continent," one that had "achieve[d] a peculiarly Mexican intensity in which references to the Indian heritage . . . play a positive role." Henry-Russell Hitchcock, *Latin American Architecture since 1945* (New York: Museum of Modern Art, 1955), 44. Meanwhile, the popular Mexico City daily *Hoy* hailed El Pedregal as "a coming together of modern construction and designed landscape, so perfectly resolved in point of *mexicanidad* that from any of its aspects it shouts to the visitor: you are in Mexico!" ("Lo esencial, desde el ángulo de nuestro comentario, es la realización, en México, de un conjunto de construcciones modernas y adaptación del paisaje, tan perfectamente resulto en punto a mexicanidad que, desde cualquiera de sus aspectos, le grite al visitante: estás en México"); Margarita Nelken, "El arquitecto y paisajista Luis Barragán," *Hoy,* 26 April 1952, 45. For Barragán's comments on El Pedregal, see his "Gardens for Environment: Jardines del Pedregal," *Journal of the AIA* 17 (April 1952): 167–72. Though absorbed by the idea of making a distinctly Mexican modern architecture, the aristocratic and elitist Barragán—speculative developer and builder of homes for the wealthy—expressed little interest in the progressive social agenda shared by such colleagues as O'Gorman and Villagrán.

20. Carlos González Lobo, "Luis Barragán," *Mimar,* June 1992, 59.

21. For example, *Architectural Forum* reported that "Mexico has turned for architectural ideas almost wholly to the French leader Le Corbusier rather than to the American Wright or other leaders." "Mexico's Architecture," *Architectural Forum* 97 (September 1952): 101. Somewhat contradictory, there appears on this same page one of the few contemporary references to Wright's influence in Mexico, made in relation to Barragán's "Pedregal Gardens" (portrayed on the cover): "In landscape architecture, too, there is a new ideal—hitherto preached systematically in modern times only by Frank Lloyd Wright—making the buildings part of the landscape the way the pyramids were, 'of it' instead of 'on it.'"

22. Cetto wrote to Wright from Los Angeles on 1 September 1938; Wright responded on 10 September from Spring Green. The Frank Lloyd Wright Archive, Getty Center for the History of Art and the Humanities, Santa Monica, Calif. (hereafter FLWA-Getty). In tracing the intellectual origins of regionalist architecture in Mexico, it is worth noting that even as Cetto worked with Neutra, Neutra was producing articles such as his "Regionalism in Architecture," *Architectural Forum* 70 (February 1939, "Plus 2" supp.): 22–23.

23. When I visited his office in 1989, Creixell still held original signed plans for buildings that he had worked on with Cetto and Barragán; interview with author, Mexico City, 27 January 1989.

24. See, for example, the special issue of *Architectural Forum* devoted to Wright, January 1938, and the issue of *Time* published that same month featuring Wright and Fallingwater on its cover (see Fig. 9.8), "Usonian Architect," *Time,* 17 January 1938, 29–32.

25. The Hotel San Jose Purúa is discussed and illustrated in Dussel, "Investigación teórica sobre Max Cetto," 226–68; and William Arthur Newman, "Glimpses of Architecture in Modern Mexico," *Architect and Engineer,* September 1945, 28–30, 46.

26. Antonio Luna Arroyo, ed., *Juan O'Gorman: Autobiografía, antología, juicios críticos y documentación exhaustivo sobre su obra* (Mexico City: Cuadernos Populares de Pintura Mexicana Moderna, 1973), 137–38.

27. Reportedly, this rejection was due to O'Gorman's "critical portrayal of US charities and set-tlement houses." James Norman, "The Ten-Story Picture," *Americas* 7 (March 1951): 26.

28. "El edificio es de una belleza magnífica, probablemente es uno de los más bellos que hay en el mundo. . . . Pensé que sería muy importante en México hacer una casa, un edificio, aplicando los principios generales de la arquitectura orgánica de Frank Lloyd Wright"; Luna Arroyo, *Juan O'Gorman: Autobiografía, antología,* 137–38, 154.

29. *Life* called the house a "mosaic-mad grotto near Mexico City . . . the most bizarre of all ar-chitect's homes." "Houses Architects Live In," *Life,* 19 January 1959, 52–53.

30. Quoted in Smith, *Builders in the Sun,* 33; and "Houses Architects Live In," 53.

31. In 1908 Wright had said that "a building should appear to grow easily from its site and be shaped to harmonize with its surroundings." He expressed the social dimension of this belief when he wrote in 1936 that "organic architecture must come from the ground up into the light by grad-ual growth. It will itself be the ground of a better way of life." In *Frank Lloyd Wright on Architecture,* ed. Frederick Gutheim (New York: Grosset & Dunlap, 1941), 34, 190.

32. See his comments regarding functionalism as quoted in McCoy, "Juan O'Gorman," 26, 46.

33. Luna Arroyo, ed., *Juan O'Gorman,* 154; and Juan O'Gorman, "Qué significa socialmente la arquitectura moderna en Mexico?" *Espacios,* May 1953, n.p. Also see O'Gorman's "An Intent of Realistic Architecture," *Espacios,* June 1955, 31.

34. O'Gorman, "Qué significa socialmente la arquitectura moderna en Mexico?" n.p.

35. Quoted in Smith, *Builders in the Sun,* 18.

36. Ibid. Though he does not specify, O'Gorman was probably referring to Taliesin West; Taliesin East contains no apparent Meso-American references.

37. FLW, *Testament,* 111.

38. FLW to Carlos Lazo, 15 March 1954, FLWA-Getty.

39. Lazo's invitation to Wright is dated 1 May 1952; Wright's acceptance and his description of the exhibition are found in a letter to Lazo dated 30 August 1952, FLWA-Getty.

40. FLW to Lazo, 15 November 1952, FLWA-Getty.

41. Rafael López Rangel, *Diego Rivera y la arquitectura mexicana* (Mexico City: SEP, 1986), 135. A 1952 photograph of the two men together in Mexico City, seated with Oskar Stonorov, appears in *Diego Rivera: A Retrospective* (New York: Founders Society, Detroit Institute of Arts, in associa-tion with W. W. Norton, 1986), 109.

42. Along these lines see "Diego Rivera on Architecture and Mural Painting," *Architectural Record* 75 (January 1934): 4–5. Adopting Corbusian language, the artist writes of "true mural painting" as "necessarily a functional part of . . . the machine which is the building."

43. See Manuel Gamio, "Las excavaciones del Pedregal de San Angel y la cultura arcaica," *Amer-ican Anthropologist,* no. 22 (1920): 127–43; and Byron Cummings, "Ruins of Cuicuilco May Rev-olutionize Our History of Ancient America," *National Geographic* 44 (August 1923): 202–20. In the nationalistic climate of the mid–twentieth century, this ancient heritage led to the region's be-ing upheld as the cradle of the Mexican nation. In 1952, for instance, one writer described it as the home of "el Hombre del Pedregal," the "most remote ancestor" of the Mexican nation, who "lived, loved, suffered, and died, leaving us his skeleton as a root of Mexico, jealously guarded by the fire made stone" (" . . . donde el más remoto antepasado de nosotros los mexicanos—el 'Hom-bre del Pedregal'—vivió, amó, sufrió y murió, dejándonos su esqueleto fosilizado como raíz de

México, celosamente guardada por el fuego hecho piedra"); Raúl Carranca Trujillo, "Valoración de la Ciudad Universitaria," in *México: Realización y esperanza* (Mexico City: Editorial Superación, 1952), 318. For further discussion along these lines, see Keith Eggener, "Luis Barragán's El Pedregal and the Making of Mexican Modernism: Architecture, Photography, and Critical Reception" (Ph.D. diss., Stanford University, 1995), 46–52.

44.   "Según los indios, el Pedregal está lleno de nahuales monstruosos y de terribles brujas, de modo que pocos son los indios que de noche se atreverían a caminar por esos lugares. . . . El Pedregal de San Angel se puede llamar como la escuela primaria de la brujería"; Francisco Fernández del Castillo, *Apuntes para la historia de San Angel y sus alrededores: Tradiciones, historia, leyendas,* 2d ed. (repr. Mexico City: Porrua, 1987), 149.

45.   On the snakes and criminals, see "Mexico's Pedregal Gardens," *House and Home,* October 1952, 127; on the artists and writers, see Clementina Díaz y de Ovando, *La Ciudad Universitaria de México: Reseña histórica, 1929–1955* (Mexico City: UNAM, 1979), 115–17.

46.   As early as 1936, the writer Joseph Henry Jackson told how Rivera took him, "through a pet road of his own . . . through one of the most desolate regions of the world, the area known as the *Pedregal*—the Stony Place." *Mexican Interlude* (New York: Macmillan, 1936), 165–66.

47.   Quoted in Andrea O. Dean, "Luis Barragán, Austere Architect of Silent Spaces," *Smithsonian* 11 (November 1980): 154.

48.   For discussion of El Pedregal's critical reception, see Eggener, "Luis Barragán's El Pedregal," 136–94.

49.   I found Rivera's document, "Requisitos para la organización de El Pedregal," sealed among Barragán's papers in the collection of the Fundación de Arquitectura Tapatía, Guadalajara, in January 1994. My thanks to Sergio Ortíz and Juan Palomár of the foundation for opening the collection to me at that time. Rivera's essay is discussed in more detail in Keith Eggener, "Diego Rivera's Proposal for El Pedregal," *Source: Notes in the History of Art* 14 (spring 1995): 1–8, and "Luis Barragán's El Pedregal," 102–9, 204–7. Not long before his death in 1957, Rivera would again refer to Wright as "the greatest plastic genius in the world today." Quoted in Selden Rodman, *Mexican Journal: The Conquerors Conquered* (Carbondale: Southern Illinois University Press, 1958), 61.

50.   Though separated by several kilometers, Anahuacalli and El Pedregal both stand within the larger Pedregal region.

51.   Rivera, "Requisitos," 1–4.

52.   Published as "Gardens for Environment," 168, 170. In places Barragán's language here is borrowed directly from Rivera's text; see Eggener, "Diego Rivera's Proposal for El Pedregal," 8n.19.

53.   Barragán, "Gardens for Environment," 171.

54.   See, for example, the modernist-revivalist hybrid Villaseñor House of 1940, located near O'Gorman's house for Rivera in San Angel.

55.   "This architecture that is called Modern . . . is the denial of what is Mexican, and its domineering characteristic lies in its imitative condition of what is foreign. . . . It is only possible to understand this architecture as a reflection of the interests of a National Class for whom the industrialization of Mexico means the alliance with the International Capitalistic Class." O'Gorman, "Qué significa socialmente la arquitectura moderna en México?" n.p.

56.   Quoted in Esther McCoy, "Jardines del Pedregal de San Angel," *Arts and Architecture* 68 (August 1951): 23.

57.   See my forthcoming "Remaking Modernism in Postwar Mexico: Luis Barragán and His Crit-

ics of the 1950s," in *The New Inside the New: Latin American Architecture and the Crisis of the International Style, 1937–1954,* ed. K. Michael Hayes (featuring papers adapted from a symposium of the same title, Graduate School of Design, Harvard University, 19–20 April 1996).

58.   Roger Bartra, *The Cage of Melancholy: Identity and Metamorphosis in the Mexican Character,* trans. Christopher J. Hall (New Brunswick, N.J.: Rutgers University Press, 1992), 5. Also see Eggener, "Luis Barragán's El Pedregal," 13–18, 137–42.

59.   Barragán, "Gardens for Environment," 171. Neutra's presence in Mexico was significant. He was a frequent and much-respected visitor there, and by the late 1940s Spanish translations of his writings were widely available, published in *Arquitectura México, Espacios,* and elsewhere. Although his writings rarely address garden or landscape design per se, he, like Wright, maintained that the forms of nature were best not altered too much, and that the house should be integrated with the preexisting landscape. See, for example, his 1951 *Mystery and Realities of the Site* (Scarsdale, N.Y.: Morgan & Morgan, 1951), of which Barragán owned two first-edition, English-language copies. (In one of these, pages describing "a house in the desert," followed by photos of the 1946 Kaufmann House in Palm Springs, California, are folded back and highlighted. As of 1994 these books were owned by the Fundación de Arquitectura Tapatía in Guadalajara.) With the widely publicized Kaufmann House, a minimized, cubic-form, glass and concrete pavilion open to the contrastingly rugged forms of its mountainous desert setting, Neutra provided an irresistible model for builders working at El Pedregal, especially Francisco Artigas, who built several Neutra-esque houses there. The Kaufmanns' Palm Springs house was first published in Mexico in Mauricio Gómez Mayorga, "Casa en el desierto, Richard Neutra, Arq.," *Arquitectura México,* February 1950, 276–80.

60.   The Kahn House is illustrated in Arthur Drexler and Thomas S. Hines, *The Architecture of Richard Neutra* (New York: Museum of Modern Art, 1982), 76–79.

61.   *Excélsior,* 8 July 1951, 22A–23A.

62.   Ramírez Ugarte, "Entrevista," 225.

63.   See, for example, the statements by Mark Mack in Diane Dorrans Saeks, "Big Mack: A Bay Area Architect's Major Museum Retrospective," *San Francisco Chronicle,* 6 October 1993, D-1; and by Ricardo Legorreta in James Steele, "Interview: Ricardo Legorreta," *Mimar,* June 1992, 62.

64.   "An Afternoon at the Home of Barragán," trans. Roberto Tejada, *Artes de México,* no. 23 (spring 1994): 110.

CHAPTER 10

The author would like to acknowledge and thank the following individuals: Brian Hunter, Anthony Alofsin, Margo Stipe, Bruce Brooks Pfeiffer, Tom Casey, Frances and Stephen Nimton, Indira Berndtsen, Nizam and Shelly Amery, Rifat Chadirji, Kamal Amin, Nizar and Ellen Jawdat, Nameer Jawdat, Fakri Bakr, and Mary Daniels.

1.   "Frank Lloyd Wright Designs for Baghdad," *Architectural Forum* (May 1958): 89–101. During Wright's lifetime and until shortly after his death there were a number of news articles, publications, and exhibitions on Wright's project: *New York Times,* 27 January 1957, 57; ibid., 28 January 1957, 22; "Wright to Design Baghdad Opera," *Architectural Forum,* March 1957, 97; "Exhibition in New York at the Iraq Consulate," *New York Times,* 3 May 1958; *Drawings for a Living Architecture* (New York: Horizon Press, 1959); "Frank Lloyd Wright," *Architecture aujourd'hui,* February 1960, 56–59; Arthur Drexler, ed., *The Drawings of Frank Lloyd Wright* (New York: Horizon Press, 1962). As with his other works, Wright never hesitated to use the public media to promote the project. More recently the Baghdad drawings have been published in Bruce Brooks Pfeiffer, *Treasures of*

Taliesin: Seventy-six Unbuilt Designs (Carbondale: Southern Illinois University Press, 1985); Terence Riley, ed., *Frank Lloyd Wright, Architect* (New York: Museum of Modern Art, 1994); and Bruce Brooks Pfeiffer, *Frank Lloyd Wright Drawings* (New York: Abradale Press, 1996), the catalog of a recent exhibition at the Phoenix Art Museum that included Baghdad drawings. Despite the proliferation of books on Wright and its similarities to other projects, relatively little has been published about the Baghdad project. See Stephen D. Helmer, "Grady Gamage Auditorium and the Baghdad Opera Project: Two Late Designs by Frank Lloyd Wright," *Frank Lloyd Wright Newsletter* 3 (1980): 10–17. I would like to thank Anthony Alofsin, Taliesin Archives, and the Taliesin Associated Architects for their help, without whom this research would not have been possible.

2.   FLW, "Designs for Baghdad," 89.

3.   The captions on the drawings identified the plans for Greater Baghdad and dedicated them to these ancient cities.

4.   Neil Levine's recent book *The Architecture of Frank Lloyd Wright* (Princeton: Princeton University Press, 1996) dedicates pages 383–404 to the Baghdad project, providing valuable information and new research by students in his 1992 Baghdad Seminar at Harvard, but in his final analysis he reduces the project to "architecture of fantasy."

5.   The Architects Collaborative (TAC) was the architectural firm founded by Gropius in 1945 in Cambridge, Massachusetts.

6.   Taliesin Associates Architects is the name of the professional firm that succeeded Frank Lloyd Wright. It was active in Iran until the 1979 Islamic revolution that toppled the monarchy. Taliesin Associates Architects now sponsors the Frank Lloyd Wright School of Architecture.

7.   For the history of Iraq in the twentieth century, see S. H. Longrigg, *Iraq 1900–1950: A Political, Social, and Economic History* (London: Oxford University Press, 1953); M. Khadduri, *Independent Iraq, 1932–1958: A Study in Iraqi Politics,* 2d ed. (London: Oxford University Press, 1960); E. Monroe, *Britain's Moment in the Middle East, 1914–1956* (London: Chatto & Windus, 1963); P. Marr, *The Modern History of Iraq* (London: Longman, 1985); H. Batatu, *The Old Social Classes and the Revolutionary Movements of Iraq* (Princeton: Princeton University Press, 1978); Lord Arthur Salter, *The Development of Iraq: A Plan of Action* (n.p., 1955). See also William Yale, *The Near East: A Modern History,* rev. ed. (Ann Arbor: University of Michigan Press, 1968).

8.   "The country's revenues became such that it was possible to embark on new works according to an order of priority." Development Board Pamphlet, "Development of Iraq," Government of Iraq Board of Development and Ministry of Development, 1956.

9.   "Development of Iraq," 24.

10.   Second pamphlet published by the government of Iraq's Board of Development and Ministry of Development in 1957 entitled "Development of Iraq." According to Secretary of the Development Board Fakri Bakr, the publication appeared separately in English and in Arabic. I am indebted to Nameer Jawdat for helping me locate Fakri Bakr, whom I interviewed on 21 October 1997.

11.   Ibid., 28. The only Western architects identified by name in the pamphlet were the Greek firm of Doxiadis Associates, under the "housing" section. The proposal by Constantinos Doxiadis included a year-long study of Iraq's housing problem.

12.   "The Master Plan for the City of Baghdad 1956," report prepared by Minoprio, Spencely, and Macfarlane, architects and town planning consultants, London, 1956. The firm received the commission both for the master plan and for redevelopment plans for the city's four older quarters in December 1954. Doxiadis Associates replaced Minoprio, Spencely, and Macfarlane in 1958 to produce a second master plan for Baghdad.

13.   This information is based on information obtained through my interviews with Nizar and Ellen Jawdat in Washington, D.C. (June 1997), and with Nameer Jawdat (1 October 1997), Fakri Bakr (11 October 1997), and Rifat Chadirji (18 October and 11 December 1997).

14.   The Jawdats were supported by other young Iraqi architects, among them Rifat Chadirji and Qahtan Awmi. Noting that most public buildings, including "some large projects like Baghdad, Central Station, the Parliament, and the Palace . . . were commissioned to British architects whose works were conventional and not modern," Chadirji said, "we decided to approach the authorities and state our concerns." They met with the minister of planning, Dr. Nadeem Pachachi, and submitted a list of international architects. According to Chadirji, the list included Wright, Le Corbusier, Gio Ponti, Alvar Aalto, and Oscar Niemeyer (Gropius had already been selected). Rifat Chadirji to author, 24 October 1997.

15.   When Nizar Jawdat, son of the Iraqi ambassador to the United States, graduated in 1946 he married a fellow classmate, Ellen Bovie. When he returned to Iraq with his wife, his father was the prime minister. The Jawdats were interviewed by the author in Washington, D.C., in June 1997.

16.   The origin for the university commission to Gropius was traced back and credited to Nizar and Ellen Jawdat in *The Walter Gropius Archive,* vol. 4: *1945–1969: The Work of the Architects Collaborative,* ed. John Harkness (New York: Garland, 1991), 189. I am grateful to Mary Daniel at the Harvard Graduate School of Design Loeb Library for her assistance.

17.   She now goes by the name Frances Nimton, and was previously Frances Lockhart. I am grateful to Frances Nimton for giving me the address of Ellen and Nizar Jawdat.

18.   Author's interview with Ellen and Nizar Jawdat, Washington, D.C., June 1997. Although it may have seemed odd for the stellar cast of Western architects to include German, French, Finnish, and Italian nationals but no Americans, the absence of British names was deliberate, a response to the British monopoly in Iraq.

19.   According to TAC principal Louis McMillen, Gropius "was involved from the beginning of 1957 until his death in 1969" and "took a very active role as a design critic during the master planning and preliminary design phases." Harkness, ed., *Gropius Archive: Work of the Architects Collaborative,* 190–91.

20.   Ibid., 190.

21.   *Alvar Aalto: Projects and Final Buildings,* ed. Elissa Aalto and Karl Fleig, 3 vols. (Zurich: Editions d'Architecture Artemis, 1990), 3:150.

22.   Ibid., 2:144–51.

23.   According to his own sketchbook, Le Corbusier was in Baghdad 8–13 November 1957. He stayed at the Omar Khayyam Hotel and met with Akram Fahmy, Iraq's minister of education and director of physical education. *Le Corbusier Sketchbooks,* vol. 3: *1954–57* (New York: Architectural History Foundation and Fondation Le Corbusier; Cambridge, Mass.: MIT Press, 1981), L50, 1056–73.

24.   Le Corbusier's design for the stadium was not completed until after his death. The site was changed and the project was built in reduced size by his associate Georges Presenti, with construction by the local Iraqi firm of Rifat Chadirji (1973–80). It was named Saddam Hussein Gymnasium.
      Rifat Chadirji has discussed his association with Le Corbusier and the design of the stadium in Baghdad in his book *Al-Ukhaidar and the Crystal Palace* (in Arabic). Chapter 8 is about Doxiadis and chapter 10 is about Le Corbusier's involvement in Baghdad. Chadirji was head of the Fifth Technical Section for Iraq from 1958 to 1959.

25. Lisa Licitra Ponti, *Gio Ponti: The Complete Work, 1923–1978* (Cambridge, Mass.: MIT Press, 1990). The date mentioned for this project in *The Complete Work* is 1955, but this is erroneous, as confirmed by the *Domus* article of September 1960 (no. 370), which mentioned that "it is more than three years [ago] that Gio Ponti, his associates Fornatelli and Rosselli, together with Valtolina and Dell'Orto, have been called to design the new Development Board Building to be erected in Baghdad."

26. G. Ponti, "Prima e dopo la Pirelli," *Domus*, no. 379 (1961): 31ff.

27. G. Ponti, "Progetto per l'edificio del Development Board in Baghdad," *Domus*, no. 370 (1960): 6 (English translation; errors in the original).

28. Speech delivered to the Engineers and Architects of Baghdad, FLWA ms., FLWA 2401.378.

29. Edward W. Said, *Orientalism* (New York: Vintage Books, 1979).

30. For early contemporary Arab accounts of Baghdad, see John Alden Williams, ed., *The Abbasid Revolution*, vol. 27 of *The History of al-Tabari* (Albany: State University of New York Press, 1985), 154–57; translation of Mohammed ibn Janr al-Tabari, "Tarikh al-rusul wa al-muluk."

31. Only eight buildings remain from the Abbasid period, which lasted five centuries before the area was sacked by the Mongols. Fewer than thirty-four historic monuments remain that predate 1869, when the Ottoman wali of Baghdad began his modernization program. For a description of contemporary Baghdad, see Ihsan Fethi, "Contemporary Architecture in Baghdad: Its Roots and Transition," *Process: Architecture* (Tokyo) 58 (May 1985): 112–32.

32. Roger Adebon interview with William Wesley Peters (who accompanied the Wrights to Baghdad), 3 April 1984, FLWA.

33. FLW, *The Future of Architecture* (New York: Horizon Press, 1953), 54–57.

34. He was aware of the Persian collections in the Oriental Institute in Chicago and in Philadelphia (the John Frederick Lewis Collection) and had a Persian tile collection of his own. One can only assume that he had read Omar Khayyam's *Rubaiyat* and was aware of the symbolism of the nightingale and that to the Persian, poetry represented the sublime and the most spiritual of the arts.

35. FLW, *Future of Architecture*, 56–57.

36. FLW to the Development Board, 24 January 1957, FLWA. He mentioned in the same letter his pleasure at the "building of opera especially since the building of opera was my early training and I am now building a new theater for Dallas, Texas." The comment about the Orient was a reference to his experience in Japan.

37. Development Board to FLW, 15 January 1957, signed by D. Jafar, Minister of Development, FLWA.

38. A copy of this report was deposited at the FLWA by Neil Levine in 1993 after it was given to him by his Harvard University student Thomas Doxiadis.

39. In his private correspondence he declared: "We are off to IRAQ, invited by King Faisal to help spend the one billion four hundred eighty million public improvement fund. Our assignment— opera on the Tigris and a world-resort in the Garden of Eden down at the tip of Iraq. The king is a good ruler—wants the oil-increment to go to the people." FLW to Bettina Ray, 7 May 1957, FLWA. And again, with an inflated description of the commission: "We are off to IRAQ—invited by King Faisal to help spend the one billion four hundred eighty million appropriation for public works. My share I believe is the opera—(probably meaning civic-center and a world resort in the Garden of Eden) at the Southern tip of Iraq." FLW to Fowler, May 1957, FLWA.

40. Wright spent the week of 21–27 May in Baghdad, having made arrangements to meet with Amery and the Jawdats through Frances Bovie (Nimton).

41. Transcript of a video interview conducted by Indira Berndtson and Greg Williams with William Wesley Peters, 13 February 1991, 3, FLWA.

42. "Mr. Lloyd Wright in Baghdad," *Iraq Times,* May 29, 1957.

43. Video interview with Peters, 3. Peters did not attend this final meeting between Wright and King Faisal. Instead Wright instructed Peters to go to Iran with Amery to "see why he couldn't get his palace built, that Mr. Wright had designed. It was largely a big house, but on the drawings it said, 'Palace for Nezam Amery.'" For more on the Amery House, see below. According to Amery, he had invited the Wrights and Peters to visit him in Iran, but Peters was the only one who could make the trip (from author's interview with Amery in London, March 1997).

44. While he had obviously thought about (and had mentioned in his personal correspondence) a Garden of Eden resort center prior to his visit to Baghdad, he attributed the selection of the island site to his flight over the city. Wright's account (see note 45) indicates that he saw the island on his flight into Baghdad, whereas Amery remembers that when Wright was displeased with the site originally proposed, he was given a plane to fly over the city to find a more appropriate site.

45. For the full account in Wright's words, see FLW, *His Living Voice* transcript, 16 June 1967, 51–52, FLWA.

46. Peters later recalled that Wright started the Baghdad drawings in Wisconsin, immediately upon return from his trip.

47. While the archival documents do not include the contract for the building, the drawings for the PTT project were advanced to a working drawing phase, confirming that the building was indeed a second commission. The *Architectural Forum* article "Wright Designs for Baghdad" mentioned this project, as did the *Iraq Times* (see note 42).

48. Kamal Amin accompanied the Wrights on their visit through Cairo. He eventually returned to Taliesin Associates, then later set up his own practice in Scottsdale, Arizona. The author is indebted to him for all his information and assistance.

49. Talk delivered to the Taliesin Fellowship, 23 June 1957, transcript, 6–7, FLWA. Wright did not exactly come at the tail end of things; his visit to Baghdad preceded Gropius's and Le Corbusier's visits by many months.

50. Talk delivered to the Taliesin Fellowship, 16 June 1957, transcript, 7, 8, FLWA.

51. FLW ms., FLWA 2401.378, 3.

52. FLW ms., FLWA 2401.379, EE, 3–4.

53. Ibid., 2.

54. Ibid., 5–7.

55. "Today instead of flood or invasion, Baghdad is threatened by the increasing thousands of motor cars. (The city now has 30,000 cars, six times as many as ten years ago. Most are American makes.) Thus Baghdad is in danger, and I have here hoped to see the Middle East put first things first. . . . Thus, fine buildings may be built with spirit and enjoyed without seeing them flooded by acres of antipathetic motor cars." *Architectural Forum,* May 1958, 91.

56. FLW ms., FLWA 2401.379, GG, 7.

57. Ibid., 7–8.

58. From Wright's text submitted with the drawings, Preface, 2, FLWA.

59. The orientation toward Mecca appears on most of his drawings, with the opera and the university mosque both oriented to Mecca.

60. FLW ms., FLWA 2401.379, EE, 10.

61. Ibid., JJ, 1–2.

62. Ibid., HH, 1.

63. The exact number of seats was never finalized. In one text Wright notes 1,600 seats, with an additional 7,500 seats possible. Ibid., 12. In another he wrote, "The opera is about 2,000 and the whole thing about 12,000." Talk delivered to the Taliesin Fellowship, transcript, 19–20, FLWA. A plan for the garden level shows 1,890 seats, with a grand total of 8,800 seats possible. FLW ms., FLWA 5733.029–030.

64. See doc. 5732.001, FLWA, reproduced in Drexler, ed., *Drawings of Wright,* 54. The lattic dome is also related to the dome of cast concrete and lattice he was designing for the same building.

65. FLW ms., FLWA 2401.379, 3.

66. Ibid., HH, 5–6.

67. Drexler, ed., *Drawings of Wright,* 160.

68. Wright's concept for this museum was related to the gallery he was designing for the Barnsdall Estate in Los Angeles, California (doc. 5428.006, FLWA, reproduced in ibid., 156). Wright modified the plan and enlarged it with circular courts along the front and skylights to highlight the grand sculptures on display.

69. Other parts of the Baghdad scheme also reappeared in later designs. A smaller version of the opera with the crescent arch reversed in direction (doc. 5911.006, FLWA, reproduced in ibid., 171) became the 1959 Grady Gamage Memorial Auditorium. For a discussion and comparison, see Helmer, "Gamage Auditorium and the Baghdad Project." Originally, the opera plan was related to the music building for Florida Southern College (1943); doc. 4211.001, FLWA, in Drexler, ed., *Drawings of Wright,* 144.

70. FLW ms., FLWA 2401.379, II, 1. Wright was critical of the work of Western architects in Baghdad in general, but may have written this statement with the knowledge that Gropius had been asked to design the university. Wright was not commissioned to work on the university (as was pointed out in the 1958 *Architectural Forum* article).

71. Wright was already designing a university in the United States, Florida Southern University, and he had just completed a museum for the Barnsdall Estate. While the university campus he proposed was very different, the museum was closely related to the Barnsdall Museum.

72. Wright used the term "curriculum" interchangeably with "ziggurat." See FLW ms., FLWA 2401.379, II, 2–3.

73. This was the first time Wright mentioned climate. Living in the southwestern United States, he was very familiar with a warm, arid climate and did not use it as the overwhelming design principle the way other Western architects did.

74. FLW ms., FLWA 2401.379, II, 2–4.

75. A section of Wright's typewritten text accompanying the drawings, marked "sent," has been struck through, indicating that this portion may not in fact have been sent (ibid.).

76. According to Fakri Bakr, "Wright was too arrogant, too grandiose. The time was not right for that kind of project." Unlike Wright, Gropius survived the political exigencies that befell Iraq. Although the coup occurred prior to completion of the project, TAC's contract had been arranged

with automatic payments; the architects thus continued to work and presented their first phase to General Kassem. Harkness, ed., *Gropius Archive: Work of the Architects Collaborative*, 189. The Gropius project for Baghdad was widely publicized in architectural journals. See, for example, "Planning the University of Baghdad," *Architectural Record,* February 1961, 108–22; and *Casabella,* no. 267 (September 1962).

77.   In the early decades of the twentieth century brick factories produced cast ornamental brick of various dimensions for the construction of houses, especially for the well-to-do.

78.   The author would like to give a special thanks to Mr. Amery for sharing his story and drawings, and to Mrs. Amery. Mr. Amery's recollections support the starting of the drawings for his house after the Baghdad trip, as the dates on the drawings themselves indicate. Interview with author, March 1997.

79.   Amery later included the open loggia wrapped around the courtyard in one of his own designs. Many of the projects Amery designed in Iran were directly inspired by Frank Lloyd Wright. He considered himself Wright's—and after Wright's death, Taliesin's—representative in Iran. He maintained close associations with Mrs. Wright and Taliesin for many years.

80.   The project was inspired by one of Wright's own last palatial designs, one for Mr. and Mrs. Arthur Miller in 1957, and lasted several years (it was completed in 1973). Over time it grew into a complex of buildings, the central piece of which was an extravagant palatial dwelling complete with circular bedroom suites, a cinema, and a swimming pool in the living room. The compound also included an eighteen-hole golf course and numerous auxiliary buildings, from birdhouses to solitary retreats. William Wesley Peters was the designer, Mrs. Wright the interior designer, with Tom Casey (currently dean of the Frank Lloyd Wright School) the project representative in Iran; Taliesin architects Frances and Stephen Nimton also spent several years in Iran working on the palace. See Effi Bantzeer, "Royalty's Exotic Residence," *Progressive Architecture,* June 1977, 82–85; *Arizona Living: Scottsdale Weekly,* 29 January 1971; W. W. Peters, "Taliesin in Tehran," *Art in America,* July–August 1969, 44–51.

81.   Manfredo Tafuri and Francesco Dal Co, *Modern Architecture,* vol. 2 (New York: Rizzoli, 1986), 328.

82.   Norris Kelly Smith, *Frank Lloyd Wright: A Study in Architectural Content* (New York: American Life Foundation, 1979), 172.

Anthony Alofsin is Martin Kermacy Centennial Professor of Architecture at the University of Texas at Austin. A professional designer and art historian, he has provided a new understanding of Wright's relationship to Europe, as seen in his *Frank Lloyd Wright: The Lost Years, 1910–1922* (1993). He also was Consulting Curator for "Frank Lloyd Wright, Architect," the major retrospective held at the Museum of Modern Art in 1994. His ongoing research investigates the nature of modernism, specifically as transferred from Europe to America, and its various expressions in Central Europe from 1867 to 1933.

Maristella Casciato teaches architecture in the Department of Civil Engineering at the University of Rome, Tor Vergata, and has taught at the Harvard Graduate School of Design. Much of her research has focused on Dutch modernist architects, and she is the author of numerous publications on Dudok and on Bijvoet and Duiker.

Jean-Louis Cohen is Professor at the Institute of Fine Arts, New York, and at the Ecole d'Architecture Paris-Villemin, as well as a prolific author. His works include *Paris: A City in the Making* (1989), *Twentieth-Century Architecture and Urbanism* (1990), *Le Corbusier and the Mystique of the USSR* (1992), *Scenes of the World to Come: European Architecture and the American Challenge, 1893–1960* (1995), and *Russian Modernism: The Collections of the Getty Research Institute for the History of Art and the Humanities* (1997). In 1998 he became Director of the Institut Français d'Architecture.

Keith Eggener earned his Ph.D. from Stanford University and teaches American art and architectural history at the University of Missouri, Columbia. His articles on nineteenth- and twentieth-century Latin and North American architecture and art have appeared in *Architectura, Winterthur Portfolio, American Art, Source,* and other publications. At present he is completing a book on Luis Barragán's Jardines del Pedregal in Mexico City and conducting research on architecture and melancholia.

Mina Marefat is an architect and architectural historian with Design Research, a private agency in Washington, D.C., dedicated to research in architecture and cultural heritage. As the former Architectural Education Director at the Aga Khan Trust and the former Senior Architectural Historian at the National Museum of American History, she designed many programs to promote public and professional understanding of architecture. She is a graduate of Tehran University and earned her Ph.D. from MIT with a dissertation focused on architecture in Tehran between the world wars.

Andrew Saint is Professor in the Department of Architecture, Cambridge University. Formerly, he was the chief historian with the London Division of English Heritage and for many years the architectural editor of the *Survey of London*. His books include *Richard Norman Shaw* (1976), *The Image of the Architect* (1983), and *Towards a Social Architecture* (1987). He is the coauthor of many other works and a Fellow of the Royal Insitute of British Architects.

Alberto Sartori is a practicing architect in Santiago and has taught at the Architecture School at the University of Chile, where he studied in the 1950s. He has also taught at universities in Italy, South Africa, and the United States and has traveled frequently to the U.S. to visit the works of Frank Lloyd Wright. In his work, which ranges from domestic projects to large sports arenas, he always remains true to his belief in the principles of organic architecture.

Margo Stipe is Registrar at the Frank Lloyd Wright Archives in Scottsdale, Arizona. She plays a major role in the production of the Frank Lloyd Wright Foundation's publications and exhibitions. She earned an M.A. in art history from the University of Michigan, has lived and worked in Japan, and is fluent in Japanese.

Mariëtte van Stralen is an independent scholar in the Netherlands. Her research focuses on the domestic architecture of the Dutch Modern Movement, and specifically on H. Th. Wijdeveld. Her publications include *The Country Houses of H. Th. Wijdeveld* (1994).

Bruno Zevi was born in Rome in 1918 and lived and studied there until he left Italy, in 1939, for political reasons. He continued his studies at the Architectural Association in London and at the Harvard Graduate School of Design, then returned to Italy in 1943 to fight in the antifascist underground. He subsequently was appointed Professor of Architectural History in Venice and later in Rome, where he taught until 1979. He was the foremost proponent of the architecture of Frank Lloyd Wright in the postwar period, and his publications include the seminal *Towards an Organic Architecture, Frank Lloyd Wright,* and numerous other monographs. He is editor of the journal *Architettura, cronache e storia.*

1.7, 1.9–1.12, 1.14, 2.1, 2.3, 2.4, 2.6, 2.8, 2.12, 2.14, 3.4, 3.6, 3.11, 3.16, 3.17, 4.7, 4.9, 4.10, 5.5, 5.6, 7.3, 7.11, 9.10, 9.11   Courtesy The Frank Lloyd Wright Archives, Scottsdale, AZ

1.15, 3.8, 3.13, 8.5, 8.11, 10.1, 10.2, 10.5–10.15   Copyright © 1998 The Frank Lloyd Wright Foundation, Scottsdale, AZ

1.5, 3.1–3.3, 3.5, 3.10, 3.12, 3.14, 3.15   Courtesy Nederlands Architectuurinstituut, Rotterdam, and Retina

2.5   Courtesy Jos Biviano

2.7   Courtesy The Frank Lloyd Wright Foundation, Scottsdale, Arizona, and Arata Endo

2.11, 2.13, 2.15   Copyright Shozo Uchii

2.16   Copyright Mitsui Norin

3.7   Courtesy Nederlands Fotoarchief, Copyright Bernard F. Eilers

4.1–4.6, 4.8   Courtesy Bruno Zevi

5.1, 5.4   Courtesy Ragghianti Archive, Archivio "seleArte," Florence

5.7, 5.8   Copyright Rizzoli/Electa, New York

5.9, 5.10   Courtesy Samonà Archive, Rome

5.11, 5.12   Courtesy Figini and Pollini Archive, Milan, and MART, Rovereto

6.1–6.6, 6.8–6.14   Courtesy Jean-Louis Cohen

7.2   Copyright Martin Charles

7.4, 7.5   Copyright Felicity Ashbee

7.6   Copyright Guild of Handicraft Trust

7.7   Copyright Greater London Record Office

7.8–7.10   Copyright EMAP Group

7.12   Copyright EMAP Group, Courtesy Library of the Architectural Press

7.13, 7.14   Copyright English Heritage

7.15   Copyright Richard MacCormac

7.16   Copyright Lucinda Lambton/Arcaid

8.3   Courtesy Hugo Gaggero

8.6, 8.7   Courtesy Sepp Michaeli

8.8   Courtesy Enrique Browne

9.2   Copyright 1998 Artists Rights Society (ARS), New York/ADAGP, Paris/FLC

9.8   Courtesy Chicago Historical Society

9.9   Copyright 1998 Center for Creative Photography, The University of Arizona Foundation

10.3   Courtesy Rifat Chadirji and Ellen and Nizar Jawdat

10.4   Courtesy Kamal Amin

Italic page numbers denote illustrations.

Aalto, Alvar, 39, 93, 236n35, 259n14;
    Aalborg (Denmark) museum, 189;
    Baghdad art museum, 188, 189, 206;
    on *Metron* cover, *81*; Revel (Estonia)
    museum, 189; Shiraz (Iran) museum,
    189
Abbasids, Baghdad, 191, 196, 212, 260n31
Abdul Ilah, Crown Prince, 23, 208
abstraction: in Dutch architecture, 48; in
    "Frank Lloyd Wright, Architect" exhi-
    bition, *14*; in Japanese architecture, 36–
    38; O'Gorman and, 175, 180; Wright's
    obsession with, 9
Aburto, Alvaro, 167, 170
Académie Européenne Méditerranée, 61
Addams, Jane, 123
Adler, Dankmar, 27, 137, 143; Charnley
    House, Chicago (Wright for Adler and
    Sullivan), 122, *122*; Chicago Auditorium,
    137, 200
Adler, Leo, 217n15
Agricultural and Industrial Exposition for
    the Compañía Maderera Malva pavilion
    (Smith Solar), 151
Ahmedabad, India, Sarabhai Calico Mills
    Store (Wright), *22*, 23
Albini, Franco, 92
Alegría, Ricardo, 152
Alexander, Christopher, 144
Alofsin, Anthony, 1–23, 31
Ambaz, Emilio, 159
American Academy, Rome, 66, 74
American Architect and Building News, 122
American architecture: archetypal, 31; Dutch
    architects and, 5, 45–46; Iofan on, 109;
    Prague Modern Gallery exhibition, 5,
    216n6; pre-Columbian, 9, 27, 31, 147,
    148, 177, 252n1; Wright back in favor
    in, 131; Wright marginal in, 143, 217–
    18n21; and Wright's Imperial Hotel, 30.

See also Latin America; Wright, Frank
    Lloyd—works
American City Planning Institute, 69
"American civilization," Prévost on, 117–18
Americanism: British, 123; European notion
    of, 20, 100; French, 20, 120; Italians and,
    79–83, 234nn19,20; Russian, 20, 101,
    109, 110–11, 120
American Luxfer Prism project (Wright),
    133
American Radiator Building, New York City,
    132
Amerikaansche reisherinneringen (Reminiscences
    of an American journey), Berlage, 45,
    226n2
Das amerikanische Haus (Vogel), 100, 101
Amersfoort, De Wachter (Wijdeveld), 57
Amery, Nezam, 193–94, 208–9, 261nn40,43,
    263n79; "Pearl Palace" (Tehran), 211,
    263n80; Tehran house (Wright), 186,
    209–11, *210*, 261n43
Amin, Kamal, 194, 261n48
Amin, Mohamad and Mrs. Mohamad, *195*
Amsterdam: National Park (Wijdeveld), 57,
    57; State Academy design (Duiker and
    Bijvoet), 52. *See also* Stedelijk Museum
Amsterdam School, 20, 46, 51, 52
Anahuacalli Museum (Rivera and O'Gorman),
    Mexico City, 178, *178*, 179–80
Ando, Tadao, 39
Anglo-American Society, 130–31
"Les Années 30" exhibition (Musée National
    des Monuments Français, 1997), Paris, 120
Ansderegg, Ernest E., 16
anti-Semitism, of Wright's Italian critics, 83
APAO. *See* Associazione per l'Architettura
    Organica
Aprile, Nello, Fosse Ardeatine Memorial
    (Rome), *68*
Arab architecture, Wright and, 192

Arabian Nights, and Wright's Baghdad plans,
    23, 184, 190–92, 196, 199–201, 208
Arana, Mariano, *Arquitectura renovadora en
    Montevideo, 1915–1940*, 149
archetypes: Wright and, 10, 31, 201. *See also*
    primitivism
Architects' Journal, 133, 139–40
Architectural Association (AA), London, 130,
    133, 136, *137*
Architectural Forum, *158*, 159, 183, 184,
    224n43
architectural press, 1; Boston, 5; Britain, 123,
    133, 134, 136, 139–40, 143; Dutch, 49,
    78, 228nn23,31; France, *112*, 113, *113*,
    117, 118–19, 120, 245–47; Germany,
    112; Italy, 19, 67, 75, 78, 79, 233–40;
    Mexican, 169, 170, 177–78, 257n59;
    Russia, 101, *106*, 107, *109*, *110*; U.S.,
    5, 11, 111, 122–23. See also *Architectural
    Forum*; *Metron*; publications; *Wendingen*
    journal
Architectural Press, London, 139–40, *140*
Architectural Record, 11, 111, 170
Architectural Review (Boston), 5
architecture: Arts and Crafts movement,
    20–21, 75, 122–27; colleges of, 60–63;
    Dávila definition, 153; delight in, 11;
    Hindu, 192; Japanese postwar, 35–43;
    Latin American, 148; Mexican regional,
    175, 180; "universal standards of design,"
    31, 164–65. *See also* American archi-
    tecture; Beaux-Arts tradition; housing;
    industrial architecture; influence; Inter-
    national Style; modernism; organic archi-
    tecture; planning; traditional architecture;
    Wright, Frank Lloyd—works
Architecture (Lurçat), 116
*L'architecture aux Etats-Unis: Preuve de la force
    d'expansion du génie français* (Architecture
    in the United States: Proof of the

Mendelsohn, Erich, 12, 62, 217n15; Acadé-
mie Européenne Méditerranée, 61; de-
fending Wright, 15; Einstein Tower
(Potsdam), 8; on *Metron* cover, *81*; U.S.
trip, 8, 217n13
Mesa project (Wright), 47
Messel, Alfred, 11
Metabolist movement, 38–39, 224n51
Metron, 19, 80–82, *81*, 95, 234–35, 238n55;
Argan's "Introduzione a Wright," 83,
237n40; and Masieri Memorial, 80,
240n68; on Pavilion of the Book of Art,
95; and Wright's exhibition, 85, 232n4
Mexicanness, 180
Mexican Society of Architects, 177
Mexico, 21, 166–83, 252–57; influence of
Wright, 181–83; modernist discourse,
21, 166–67, 170, 183, 256n55; pre-
Columbian architecture, 9, 27, 31, 147,
148, 177, 252n1; regionalism, 175,
254n22
Mexico City: Anahuacalli Museum (Rivera
and O'Gorman), 178, *178*, 179–80;
Barragán, 168; cathedrals, 148; Main
Library, Universidad Nacional Autónoma
de México (O'Gorman, Saavedra, and
Martínez), 170–72, *171*; National
Academy of San Carlos, 167; O'Gorman
Airport murals, 174; Plaza Melchor
Ocampo (Barragán with Cetto and
Creixell), 168, *169*; Diego Rivera house,
San Angel (O'Gorman), 167, *167*, 178;
"Sixty Years of Living Architecture"
exhibition, 18, *176*, 177; Wright's visit,
176, 177, *177*. *See also* Pedregal, El
Meyer, Hannes, 107
Michaeli, Sepp, 157; Casa Habitación
(Santiago), *156*, 157
Michelucci, Giovanni, 83, 237n39, 239n57;
Florence Railway Station, 66–67
Michoacán, Hotel San José Purúa (Cetto and
Rubio), *172*, 173
Middle East, 21–23, 184–213; *brise soleil*
proliferations, 212; Cairo, 194–95, *195*;
oil, 186, 260n39; postmodern designs,
212; traditional building, 184, 190–
92, 196, 201, 206, 209–11, 260n31;
Wright's trip, 193–95. *See also* Iran; Iraq;
Persians
Midway Gardens (Wright), Chicago:
architectural ambience of leisure, 199;
decorativism, 9; French attention to,
114–15, 116; Japanese architecture and,
35, *37*; Mendelsohn visit, 218n13;
Robertson illustration, 133; Scarpa work
and, 95; van 't Hoff visit, 47

Mies van der Rohe, Ludwig, 151; Berlin
exhibition of Wright (1910), 4; British
architects and, 143; Lissitzky on, 101; on
Metron cover, *81*; Taliesin, 15; Venetian
school and, 93; and Wasmuth folios, 3;
Wright's influence on, 12
Milan: APAO, 67; Brera Academy, 101–2;
Church of the Madonna dei Poveri
(Figini and Pollini), 97, *98*; International
Exhibition of Modern Architecture at
Fifth Triennale (1933), 78; Monument to
the Dead in the Concentration Camps in
Germany (BBPR), 69, *69*; rationalism,
234n25; Venetian School of Architecture
recruits from, 92; Wright's exhibition at
Triennale (1960), 99, *99*
Mile High Project (Wright), Chicago, *58*,
59, 64–65, 229n41
Millard house (Wright), Pasadena, California,
9, 116, 209, 245n53
Minoprio, Spencely, and Macfarlane,
Baghdad Master Plan, 187, *187*, 193,
194, 199, 258n12
Minou Island Resort (TAA), Iran, 211
Mitla, Oaxaca, church, 148
Mitsui Norin: "Frank Lloyd Wright Resi-
dential Style" homes, *42*, 43, 225n59;
"Heurtley" home, 43
Modern Architectural Design (Robertson), 133
Modern Architecture (Tafuri and Dal Co), 211
Modern Architecture (Wright), 79–80
"Modern Architecture: International Exhibition" (1932), Museum of Modern
Art, 15, 117
*Modern Architecture: Romanticism and Re-
integration* (Hitchcock), 116
Der moderne Zweckbau (Behne), 11–12
modernism, 8–11, 17–18, 137; Aalto
museums, 189; British architecture and,
130, 146; Czech, 5, 16–18; Dutch
architects and, 6, 20, 45–46, 51–52, 57,
217–18n21, 227n17, 228n32; German,
2–3, 6, 8, 11, 14; Italians and, 19, 74, 75,
78–79, 80; Japanese, 34, 39; Latin American architects and, 157–59; Metabolist
movement and, 39; Mexican discourse,
21, 166–67, 170, 183, 256n55; Persico
on Wright and, 66; postwar, 35; *sachlich*,
11, 16, 46; socially directed, 130; solitary,
23; Sullivan, 5; Swiss, 16; urbanist, 36;
Wright as protomodernist, 133; and
Wright's Baghdad plans, 184, 196, 208,
211–12; Wright's fit in, 14–15, 87;
Wright vs. Le Corbusier, 20, 21, 119,
219n49. *See also* avant-garde; objectivity;
postmodernism

modernization/westernization: Iraq, 190;
Japan, 25–26, 33, 34, 35, 43, 225n61
Möhring, Bruno, 4, 216–17n13
Mondrian, Piet, 49–50
Monona Terrace Civic Center (Wright),
Madison, 199
Monte degli Ulivi (Ricci), 87
Montes Rega, J. C., 149
Montuori, Eugenio, Rome Railway Station,
68
Monument to the Dead in the Concentra-
tion Camps in Germany (BBPR), Milan,
69, *69*
Nathan G. Moore House (Wright), Oak
Park, *124*
Morasutti, Bruno, 77, 240n73
Morris, William, 75, 125, 126–27, 133
Moscow, 120; "The Architecture of the
U.S.A." exhibition (1944), 111; Center
for Architects, 110, 111; Conference of
Architects, 107–9, *109*; Le Corbusier on,
110; Lurçat stay, 116
Moser, Sylva, 8
Moser, Werner M., 7, 8, 16; Rapperswil-
Jona primary school plan, 16, *17*; "Sixty
Years of Living Architecture" exhibition
mounting/catalog, 18, 218n37
Mullgardt, Louis Christian, 30
Mumford, Lewis, 52–53, 62, 111, 131; *Sticks
and Stones*, 107
Munich, "Sixty Years of Living Architec-
ture" exhibition, 18
Munich agreement, Hitler's repudiation of,
130
Murillo, Gerardo (Dr. Atl), 179
Museum of Modern Art: "Deconstructivist
Architecture" exhibition (1988), 75;
exclusively Wright's exhibition (1940),
218n33; "Frank Lloyd Wright, Archi-
tect" exhibition (1994), 18–19; "Modern
Architecture: International Exhibition"
(1932), 15, 117
Mussolini, Benito, 79

Nakagin Capsule building (Kurokawa),
Tokyo, 224n51
Naples: APAO, 67, 235n32; Olivetti factory
(Pozzuoli), 70, *71*; Persico, 233n13
Nara, Todai-ji temple, 31
National Academy of San Carlos, Mexico
City, 167
National Institute of Arts and Letters, New
York City, 89–90
nationalism: Japanese, 35; Mexican, 255n43
nature: O'Gorman and, 175; Wijdeveld and,
55–57, 59; Wright and, 9, 10, 55–57,

Designer:	Steve Renick
Compositor:	Integrated Composition Systems
Text:	11/13 Bembo
Display:	Frutiger Light
Printer/Binder:	Imago